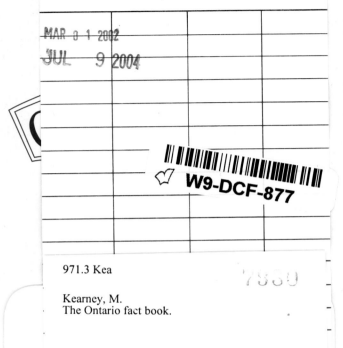

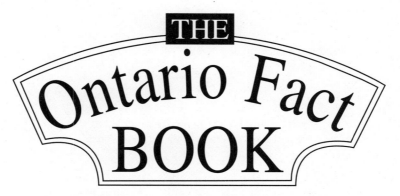

# THE Ontario Fact BOOK

### Everything You Ever Wanted To Know About Ontario

## Mark Kearney / Randy Ray

**Whitecap Books**
Vancouver/Toronto

Edited by Elizabeth McLean
Proofread by Lisa Collins and Kathy Evans
Cover design and illustrations by Rose Cowles
Interior design by Warren Clark
Map by Barry Levely, Cartography Unit, University of Waterloo

Printed and bound in Canada

**Canadian Cataloguing in Publication Data**

Kearney, Mark, 1955–
    The Ontario fact book

    Includes index.
    ISBN 1-55285-020-X

    1. Ontario.  I. Ray, Randy. 1952- II. Title.
FC3061.K42 2000      971.3     C00-910066-0
F1057.K42 2000

The publisher acknowledges the support of the Canada Council and the Cultural Services
Branch of the Government of British Columbia in making this publication possible. We
acknowledge the financial support of the Government of Canada through the Book Publishing
Industry Development Program for our publishing activities.

*For Janis, the Ray boys, and Catherine.*

# Contents

## W

## Y

## Z

# Acknowledgements

Writing a book such as this could not be done without the many people who helped us research and track down information on various topics. Those we must thank work in government offices, notably at the provincial ministries of Natural Resources, Tourism, and Education; at museums, parks, and tourist attractions; and in marketing, public relations, and other departments at industry associations, municipalities, the federal government, and many other organizations too numerous to mention.

We also owe a big thanks to Mark Zuehlke, who opened the door for us at Whitecap, and whose *Fact Books* on Alberta, British Columbia, and the Yukon provided us with interesting reading and a blueprint for how to write this book on Ontario.

We're especially grateful to Janis Ray and Catherine Blake for their support and advice on what should be included in this book, and also to Marcus Ray who helped track down photographs at the National Archives in Ottawa. Others who provided ideas and valuable suggestions include John Firth, Ed Janiszewski, Gary May, Brian McAndrew, and Gerry Killan.

We also want to acknowledge the staffs and excellent collections of the Ottawa Public Library, the London Public Library, the University of Western Ontario Library, and the National Archives in Ottawa. Without them, this book could not have been researched and written.

Our biggest thanks go to Elizabeth McLean, whose sharp eye, editing skills, and sense of humour made this a better book.

# Introduction

Having lived in Ontario all our lives, both of us have many favourite spots in this vast province—the scenic Trans-Canada Highway near Thunder Bay, a shady picnic site close to Stratford's Festival Theatre, a seat along the third base line at SkyDome, a cross-country ski trail near the shores of Georgian Bay, in the lead car on the old Flyer roller coaster at the CNE, and the expansive lawns at Parliament Hill on a sunny afternoon—to name a few.

But one of the places we enjoy the most is a dock, on a lake not far from Peterborough, at a cottage that has been in the Ray family since the early 1960s. It's on this dock, which juts into a tiny lake in the Kawarthas, where we've relaxed with family and friends, a glass of wine or a can of cold beer in our hands, and traded dozens of ideas and hashed over writing projects.

When we started preparing a list of subjects we wanted to cover in *The Ontario Fact Book*, the many hours spent on the dock provided us with plenty of inspiration. From our vantage point at the water's edge, we have enjoyed views of the sparkling lake, the rocky landscape, deep green forests, brilliant autumn colours, and crimson sunsets. At other times we have listened to the cry of loons and watched as people fish, glide past on water skis, or simply wind down at the beach after a hectic work week in the city. Like everyone else, we've also scurried for cover when mosquitoes and black flies made early summer evenings unbearable or when dark clouds overhead signalled an impending thunderstorm.

At the end of many delightful weekends, we've packed our bags and headed home on the various highways and byways that run through the villages, towns, and cities that dot this corner of the province.

All of Ontario contains such variety. It is as much a place of bustling cities, where commuters curse the traffic while they drive by busy factories churning out the manufactured goods that are its economic backbone, as it is small towns, rushing streams, rolling farmland, and breathtaking scenery. All are essential to the character of Ontario—the most populated province in Canada with some of the biggest and most ethnically diverse cities—where, even when you live in big cities such as Ottawa and Toronto, you're never too far away from large expanses of wilderness, water, and wildlife.

Perhaps it's the province's diversity that makes it so hard to pin down, to categorize, or to define. Perhaps it's because Ontario's history has formed such a major part of Canada's history that many of us who live here define ourselves as Canadians before we consider the province.

Naturally, no single book can capture all of Ontario. But it can try to encapsulate as much information about the province as possible. In these pages, you'll find facts about the people, cities, history, culture, economics, wildlife, and social life of Ontario. Each item is a strand in the fabric of Ontario, connected at times in unusual ways, but all vital to the province's character. It's our hope that this book will provide enjoyable and informative reading on a subject-by-subject basis and enhance your knowledge of Ontario, whether you're a resident or just passing through.

It should be noted that not every community in Ontario can be mentioned here. The decision to profile some communities and not others was arrived at with considerable thought and care. Communities were selected on the basis of their overall importance to the province, its development and history, and to some extent, their role in representing specific regions.

This book is also not a biography. Many people are mentioned throughout, but there are many more whose importance to Ontario in the past or present cannot be detailed here.

So, wherever you're reading this—on a living room couch, in a backyard, in a subway car, on an airplane, in the back seat of the family van, or on a dock at your favourite cottage—get ready to discover Ontario.

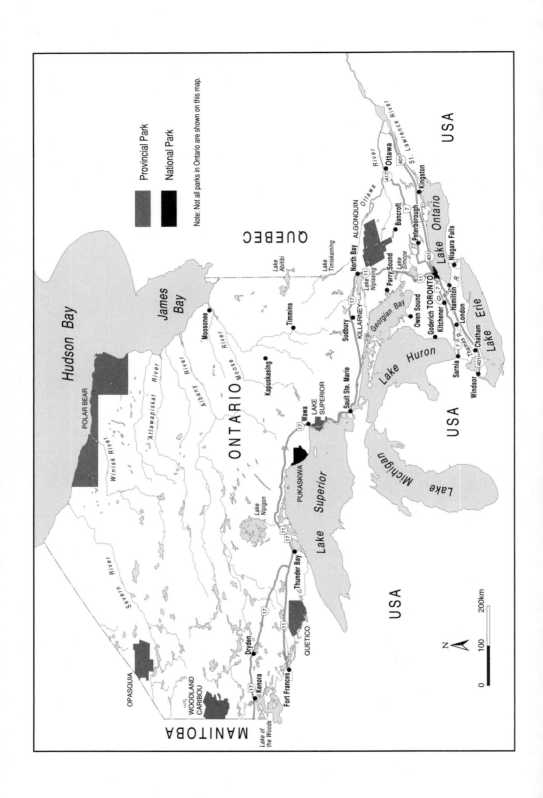

**Provincial Park**

**National Park**

Note: Not all parks in Ontario are shown on this map.

QUÉBEC

Hudson Bay

James Bay

ONTARIO

Moosonee

Timmins

Kapuskasing

Sault Ste. Marie

Wawa

LAKE SUPERIOR

PUKASKWA

Lake Superior

Thunder Bay

QUETICO

Fort Frances

Dryden

Kenora

WOODLAND CARIBOU

OPASQUIA

MANITOBA

Lake of the Woods

Severn River

Winisk River

Attawapiskat River

Albany River

Moose River

Lake Nipigon

POLAR BEAR

Lake Abitibi

Lake Timiskaming

North Bay

Lake Nipissing

Sudbury

KILLARNEY

Georgian Bay

Parry Sound

Owen Sound

Lake Huron

Lake Michigan

Goderich

Kitchener

Hamilton

Grand R.

London

Sarnia

Thames R.

Chatham

Windsor

Lake Erie

401

ALGONQUIN

Bancroft

Peterborough

Lake Simcoe

TORONTO

Niagara Falls

Lake Ontario

Kingston

401

417

Ottawa

Ottawa River

St. Lawrence River

USA

USA

USA

N

0    100    200km

# Ontario Facts at a Glance

- Ontario has a total area of 1,068,580 square kilometres or approximately 11 percent of Canada, making it the second-largest province in the country.
- There are more than 250,000 lakes in Ontario, and water covers about 20 percent of the province.
- The three main geographic regions are the Canadian Shield, the Great Lakes–St. Lawrence Lowlands, and the Hudson Bay Lowlands. The Canadian Shield runs across the middle two-thirds of the province and is covered with forest and thousands of lakes. The Great Lakes–St. Lawrence Lowlands contain some of the richest farmland in Canada along with most of Ontario's population, while the Hudson Bay Lowlands is flat marshland that encircles Hudson Bay and James Bay and has few inhabitants.
- At its widest point running diagonally from east to west, the province measures 1,690 kilometres and is 1,730 kilometres from north to south. Its boundaries were last established in 1912 when parts of the then Northwest Territories were added to the provinces of Ontario, Quebec, and Manitoba.
- The province's boundaries are: southernmost boundary 41° 41' south latitude, northernmost boundary 56° 51' north latitude, easternmost boundary 74° 20' west longitude, westernmost boundary 95° 09' west longitude. Ontario is bounded on the west by Manitoba and then traces an irregular line southward that borders on Minnesota, Lake Superior, Lake Huron, and Michigan; on the south by Lake Erie, New York State, Lake Ontario, and the St. Lawrence River; by Quebec on the east; and James Bay and Hudson Bay on the north.
- Ontario's climate is continental, typified by cold winters and warm, humid summers in the southern portion, and by cold winters and cool summers in the far north, which is classified as subarctic continental. On average, January is the coldest month and July the warmest.

- The highest point above sea level is 693 metres in the District of Timiskaming near Lady Evelyn Smoothwater Provincial Park. The lowest is the Hudson Bay shore, at sea level.
- Time zone for most of Ontario is Eastern Standard Time (noon Greenwich Mean Time = 7:00 a.m. EST), but a portion west of Thunder Bay is Central Standard Time (noon GMT = 6:00 a.m. CST). The province changes to Daylight Saving Time in the spring (noon GMT = 8:00 a.m. EST and 7:00 a.m. CST).
- Total population is 11.4 million. The biggest city is Toronto with a population of 2.4 million (4.6 million in the Greater Toronto Area).
- The capital city is Toronto. Canada's capital, Ottawa, is also located in Ontario.
- Ontario entered Confederation on July 1, 1867, as one of the four founding provinces, along with Quebec, New Brunswick, and Nova Scotia.

# Agawa Canyon

The bedrock below this scenic canyon north of Sault Ste. Marie was formed 2.5 billion years ago and is among the oldest rock in the world. Created through a series of faults, Agawa Canyon has been shaped and widened by several ice ages over hundreds of thousands of years.

Today, the canyon walls are 175 metres at their highest point, with waterfalls spaced along the canyon's 20-kilometre length. At its narrowest point, the walls are only about 15 metres wide. The canyon is now part of the Agawa Canyon Park and is accessible only by rail. A railway has served the Agawa area for almost 90 years, and members of the **Group of Seven** used it as a way to explore the region. Some of their most famous paintings are of this area.

Development of the park began in the 1950s, and by the 1970s thousands of visitors each year were taking the Agawa Canyon tour train, which is operated by the Algoma Central Railway and begins its journey in Sault Ste. Marie. More than 85,000 people now take the canyon train tour annually, to experience some of Ontario's most breathtaking scenery. The train descends some 150 metres for more than 19 kilometres to reach the canyon's floor.

Agawa Canyon Park shelters a wide range of wildlife within its borders, including **beavers,** otters, golden eagles, and broad-winged hawks. The plant life is remarkably varied because the park lies between the Great Lakes–St. Lawrence forest region and the boreal forest and contains flora from both these zones.

# Agriculture

With slightly more than half of Canada's most productive farmland inside its borders, Ontario is Canada's agricultural leader. Its farmers produce 25 percent of all Canadian farm products, ringing up cash receipts of $7 billion every year.

Approximately $5.3 billion worth of this annual production is exported to more than 50 countries.

The province's farm economy is concentrated mainly in the southern part of Ontario where more than 200 commodities are produced, including fruits, vegetables, dairy, poultry, **tobacco, maple syrup,** beans, grains, and oilseeds. In **northern Ontario,** more than 2,900 farms produce a variety of commodities, including hay, barley, mixed grains, oats, potatoes, strawberries, vegetables, and dairy products.

The province's top five agricultural commodities are dairy goods, cattle, soybeans, hogs, and floriculture and nursery products, which together earn total farm cash receipts of nearly $4 billion.

There are more than 67,000 farms in Ontario and each farmer produces on average enough food to feed 120 people. It was not always that way, though. In the early years, settlers grew corn, squash, and kidney beans, and later wheat, but often just enough to sustain their own families. In the late 1700s, **United Empire Loyalists** arrived and, on farms near the **St. Lawrence River,** Lake Ontario, and in the Niagara Region, began growing wheat, which became Ontario's most widely grown and marketable crop. Eventually grist mills were built to turn wheat into flour, which was sold to the United States and Britain.

In the late 1800s, animals and animal products, such as cheddar cheese, became more important than wheat. Farmers sought improved livestock strains, bringing Holstein dairy cattle from Britain. As a result, most turned to mixed farming, producing forage crops, corn, mixed grains, winter wheat, and barley to earn income and sustain dairy and beef cattle and hogs.

As plant and animal diseases, pests, and the severe climate challenged farmers, Ontario farms began to be operated on a more scientific basis. The Ontario Agricultural College was established in 1874 and later became part of the University of Guelph to give direction and support to scientific farming methods. Pest and disease control, genetic improvements to plants and animals, and innovative farm tools, such as improved threshing machines and windmills, greatly increased farm productivity in the 20th century.

As in other sectors of the Ontario economy, farming has faced many challenges over the years. Concerns over maintaining environmental integrity, while continuing to supply abundant quantities of high-quality, affordable food, have seen the farming community and the federal and provincial governments launch a number of initiatives to diminish the environmental impact of food production.

In Ontario, all agricultural pesticide users must be trained and certified in proper handling, storage, and application practices. Thorough training, along with the adoption of other practices, such as integrated pest management and the availability of newer, safer pesticide products, have contributed to a 40 percent reduction in agricultural pesticide use in the past 15 years. Many Ontario farm families have also completed Environmental Farm Plans, which help farmers to identify potential environmental hazards and develop action plans for addressing those risks. The widespread adoption of other farming practices, such as minimum or no tillage, nutrient management programs, and crop rotation, has also contributed to protecting the environment and sustaining Ontario's farmland.

Ontario's agri-food industry now contributes more than $25 billion to the provincial **economy** every year and employs more than 640,000 people. The province is Canada's leading producer of poultry, eggs, vegetables, lamb, fruit, corn, tobacco, and soybeans. Flowers and ornamental plant nurseries also constitute a thriving industry in Ontario, with annual sales of more than $577 million. In addition, more than 1,000 food and beverage processors are located in Ontario and about 60 percent of their head offices are found in the province. Annual food and beverage production totals $23.4 billion.

People working within the agricultural sector go far beyond the farm gate. Agriculture-related jobs are found in wholesaling, packaging, distilling, farm machinery, transportation equipment, chemicals, food services, and research.

Several regions of Ontario are known for their specialty farms. The Niagara Region has been famous for over a century for its peaches, grapes, cherries, and other fruits. Marshes in southern Ontario, in particular Holland, Thedford, Erieau, and Pelee, have been drained and now produce a variety of vegetables such as celery, peppers, and cucumbers. Apple orchards thrive along the southern shore of **Georgian Bay** and the northern shores of lakes Erie and Ontario. Tobacco, despite declining production in recent years, has been a lucrative crop in the Tillsonburg, Delhi, and Simcoe areas of southwestern Ontario. Canning tomatoes are grown in the extreme southwest of the province, while blueberries, both wild and cultivated, are harvested throughout Ontario. The dairy industry, which represents about 25 percent of Ontario farm production, is concentrated in the **London**-Woodstock region, on the Bruce Peninsula, and in eastern Ontario. It produces receipts of about $1.3 billion a year.

Agriculture means more to the province than food, however. Cloth, paper, and a variety of industrial products begin in farm fields as hemp, an experimental crop. Corn grown in Ontario is used to produce a huge variety of goods, including soap, toothpaste, paint, and sparkplugs, as well as ethanol, a fuel that is being used as a replacement for gasoline.

Three Canadians living in early Ontario have made major contributions to agriculture: in the early 1800s, Dundas County farmer John McIntosh discovered the McIntosh apple, which is grown throughout North America; in 1843, David Fife planted the first Red Fife wheat, for many years the most widely used variety of wheat in Canada because of its good yield and excellent milling and baking qualities; and in 1847, Daniel Massey started a small factory in Newcastle, which became Massey-Harris, Canada's first international builder of farm machines.

# Air Travel

Ontario has more than 600 airports, including 60 that receive scheduled flights, 20 that can service jet aircraft, 126 for seaplanes, and more than 129 heliports. These facilities service 40 percent of total national passenger traffic, making the airspace over Ontario the busiest in Canada.

The province's three most active airports are Lester B. Pearson International Airport in **Toronto**—one of the world's 25 largest facilities—Macdonald-Cartier International Airport in **Ottawa,** and **Thunder Bay** International Airport. Other busy airports are located at **Windsor, London,** and **Sudbury,** and on Toronto Island.

As Canada's busiest airport, Pearson is served by 56 carriers who handle 26.7 million passengers a year and 350,000 tonnes of freight, or 40 percent of Canada's yearly air cargo. Pearson is operated by the Greater Toronto Airports Authority and provides direct air service to 45 U.S. markets, 38 international destinations, and 27 centres in Canada. A number of additional airlines provide charter services on a seasonal basis.

Macdonald-Cartier International Airport is operated by the Ottawa International Airports Authority and is serviced by 11 airlines that serve more than three million passengers per year. Eighty-two nonstop flights a day service 14 Canadian centres; another 44 direct flights go to 10 American cities and there are between 6 and 10 direct flights per week to Europe. The airport handles about 5,200 tonnes of cargo annually.

As Ontario's third-busiest airport, Thunder Bay International Airport serves 500,000 passengers on 50,000 flights a year and handles 571 tonnes of freight annually. Nine airlines provide regularly scheduled and charter service to and from destinations within the region, across Canada, and to Minneapolis. It is operated by the Thunder Bay International Airports Authority.

The province has about 300 commercial air cargo and passenger carriers that vary from single-engine seaplane operators to national companies such as Air Canada and Canadian, which fly Boeing and other large aircraft. As in the rest of Canada, air transport has played and continues to play a vital role in the economies of Ontario's remote areas by making it possible to transport food, medical supplies, manufactured goods, and tourists in and out of areas that are difficult to reach by other modes of transportation.

The majority of Ontario's airports are tiny unlicensed facilities, often privately owned, with grass or gravel air strips, which service one or two airplanes owned by recreational pilots, business people, cottagers, and flying clubs.

# Algonquin Provincial Park

Algonquin Provincial Park was established in 1893 by the Ontario government to create a wildlife sanctuary and, by excluding **agriculture,** to protect the headwaters of the five major rivers that flow from the park.

Named after the Algonquian-speaking peoples who lived along the Ottawa River and its tributaries, Algonquin encompasses 7,600 square kilometres and lies across the southern edge of the **Canadian Shield** between **Georgian Bay** and the Ottawa River, about 200 kilometres north of **Toronto.**

For most of its history, human settlement has not been an important element of the area's development. Scattered family groups of **First Nations peoples** came to fish, hunt, and pick berries, but their numbers were never large. It was not until the 1800s that big changes came to the rugged Algonquin highlands. Pioneer loggers pushing up from the **Ottawa Valley** reached Algonquin in search of the great white pine trees whose prime wood was increasingly in demand by an expanding British economy.

Living in remote, primitive camps, they felled and squared the giant pines, and when spring came, drove them down swollen rivers to the Ottawa River and the outside world. The story of that colourful era and subsequent logging in the park is told at one of Algonquin's two **museums,** the Algonquin Logging Museum, located near the East Gate.

Once established as a provincial park, the area quickly became popular. Among those to discover its potential were adventurous hunters and anglers, Tom Thomson and the **Group of Seven,** and eventually, visitors from around the world who came to stay at hotels located within the park boundaries. It is estimated that between 250,000 and 300,000 people now visit annually.

Its rolling topography is dissected by more than 2,500 lakes that provide access by boat to the interior. The park is famous for the mournful cry of wolves and sightings of other species, including deer, **moose**, bear, and raccoons. Its varied and changing second-growth forest consists of pine, fir, birch, and poplar. Some 240 bird species have been recorded, including the grey jay, spruce grouse, brown thrasher, scarlet tanager, and common loon. **Fish** found in the park include trout and smallmouth bass, pike, whitefish, muskellunge, and walleye.

Algonquin's facilities include four campgrounds set at the ends of sometimes long and dusty roads, far from the Highway 60 corridor, which cuts across the southwest corner of the park. There's also a large visitor centre, a logging museum, an art gallery, and lodges. Adventurous spirits can explore 13 walking trails, three overnight backpacking trails, two bicycle trails, three ski trail networks covering about 80 kilometres, and more than 1,600 kilometres of lake and river canoe routes. Among the park's most popular activities are public wolf howling expeditions, which take place in August. Park naturalists locate a pack of wolves, then guide visitors through a night of listening to wolves answer human imitations of their howls.

The park's interpretive and educational facilities are enhanced by the Friends of Algonquin Park, a nonprofit organization with more than 3,000 members, established in 1983 under an agreement with the Ontario Ministry of Natural Resources.

(*See also* **Provincial Parks**)

# Amphibians

Of the more than 4,200 species of amphibians in the world, 24 make their home in Ontario. The province's amphibians can be classed according to the following categories: newts, salamanders, toads, and frogs. Newts and salamanders common to the province are the mudpuppy, spotted salamander, blue-spotted salamander, Jefferson salamander, Tremblay's salamander, silvery salamander, red-spotted newt, northern two-lined salamander, four-toed salamander, and eastern red-back salamander. The tiger salamander and small-mouth salamander have an extremely limited range in the south of the province. The small-mouth has also interbred with the blue-spotted salamander and may be indistinguishable to most observers.

Salamanders differ from newts in that they spend less time in the water, but all salamanders except the eastern red-back need water for breeding and egg laying. In most newts and salamanders, the female picks up sperm deposits from the male and keeps them in a special storage area near the base of her tail until she is ready to lay the eggs. They will hatch into larvae with external gills. The eastern red-back, however, lays its eggs in damp spots on land, such as in rotted wood stumps. It passes its entire larval stage within the egg. The number of eggs laid varies from species to species, with the eastern red-back laying as few as 6 and the mudpuppy as many as 150.

Three salamander species, the eastern red-back, the four-toed, and the northern two-lined have no lungs, breathing instead through their skins.

Most of the province's newts and salamanders live in south and central Ontario, but a few species, such as the mudpuppy and blue-spotted salamander, are found west of Lake Superior. Mudpuppies are the largest salamander species in Ontario, reaching about 30 centimetres in length. Other species of salamanders range from about 5 to 18 centimetres, while the red-spotted newt grows to about 7 to 10 centimetres.

Salamanders and newts are carnivorous, eating a wide range of insects, larvae, snails, **fish**, worms, and tadpoles. They migrate to ponds in early spring and remain active during wet cool weather in early fall. During the winter they live in deep or flowing water to avoid freezing.

Ontario's toads and frogs include the American toad, Fowler's toad, bullfrog, pickerel frog, spring peeper, grey treefrog, mink frog, striped chorus frog, green frog, wood frog, and the northern leopard frog. Both toad species, as well as the spring peeper, wood frog, chorus frog, and grey treefrog, hibernate on land, while the remaining frog species spend winter underwater or in bottom mud. The province's frogs and toads generally emerge from hibernation in late March and early April. In order to attract a mate and define their territory, males call or croak using their vocal pouches. Each species has a distinctive call.

All Ontario toads and frogs lay their eggs in the water. They are prolific breeders, and some species start laying eggs as early as March or April, while others wait for the warmth of late spring. A female bullfrog may lay as many as 8,000 eggs, while the American toad lays up to 5,000 eggs, under submerged rocks and plants. The tadpoles feed on algae and other vegetable matter. Tadpoles will also feed on their own dead and eat the tails of other smaller tadpoles.

Toads and frogs are carnivorous and will eat beetles, moths, earwigs, flies, spiders, caterpillars, **mosquitoes**, dragonflies, and crickets. These amphibians also shed their skin regularly as they grow, then eat it. Toads tend to have rough, dry skin, while frogs have smooth, moist skin and spend more time in or near water.

Toads are most active after dusk. Although they have poisonous glands behind their eyes that make them distasteful to predators, they pose no danger to humans. Of the two toad species, Fowler's is the rarest, ranging only along the shore of Lake Erie. The American toad is found in most of the province and is the most terrestrial of all the amphibians.

Frogs range in size from the 2- or 3-centimetre spring peeper to the 10- to 15-centimetre bullfrog. The northern leopard frog, spring peeper, and the wood frog live in virtually every region of the province, while the pickerel frog, Blanchard's cricket frog, and bullfrogs are found only in the southern portions of Ontario. The pickerel's skin secretions also make it one of the most poisonous amphibians in the province, although it isn't dangerous to people who handle it.

# Archaeology

More than 16,000 archaeological sites are registered in Ontario, with another 600 or 700 added each year. It's estimated that this number represents only 10 to 15 percent of all the archaeological sites in the province. The sites include First Nations hunting and fishing camps, spiritual places and ceremonial sites, battlefields, villages, pioneer dwellings, shipwrecks, and cemeteries.

The archaeological sites document human life stretching back some 11,000 years, when the province was inhabited solely by **First Nations peoples.** But the sites also include a record of Europeans and others who arrived and settled here in the past 350 years.

Since the retreat of the last ice sheets that covered the province more than 10,000 years ago, people have lived throughout the province. Ontario's network of lakes and rivers made travel in the province relatively efficient. The prehistory of Ontario has been divided by historians and archaeologists into the Paleo-Indian (approximately 10,000 to 11,000 years ago), the Archaic (about 10,000 to 3,000 years ago), and the Early (3,000 to 2,400 years ago), Middle (2,400 to 1,200 years ago), and Late/Terminal Woodland periods (1,200 to 300 years ago).

Among the artifacts unearthed from Paleo-Indian Period sites are dart heads and other stone projectiles, flakes, and tools characterized by the use of large spear points with a distinctive "fluting" or groove down their length. The people responsible for these artifacts were hunters of caribou, giant bison, and mastodons. Quarries on **Manitoulin Island** and around Lake Superior have yielded deposits of stone such as taconite and quartzite, which were used by these hunters to make their tools.

By the Archaic Period, tools made from copper, projectile points made hunting easier, and gouges or polished stone adzes had been brought by people who moved into southern Ontario from what is now the midwest United States. The people from this time were also hunters of big game, but supplemented their diet with berries, nuts, **fish,** and **birds.** Many of the archaeological sites representing this period are found on rivers and interior lakes, suggesting that the people who lived there used watercraft such as birchbark canoes. Although little evidence exists about the kind of houses they lived in, the burial grounds indicate that it was common practice to paint the dead with red ochre and place objects with them such as tools and ornaments.

Pottery made its first appearance during the Early and Middle Woodland periods. Among the artifacts unearthed have been beaker-shaped vessels, some smooth and others with impressions. Burial sites from this period include stone and copper goods, flaked triangular flint blades, and tubular pottery pipes. A variety of pottery styles have been found from this time. Later in the period, the pottery became more complex, with more intricate designs. For the most part, the people of ancient Ontario were still hunters and migrated throughout regions in search of food. Communities during this time became larger and more territorial, and there is evidence of long-distance trade and exchange networks as far away as Mexico.

During the Middle to Late/Terminal Woodland periods between A.D. 1000 and A.D. 1600, two significant linguistic and cultural groups emerged. The Algonquians lived mostly in the north and were migratory hunters and fishers. The Iroquoians in the south tended to be settled village dwellers and farmers who also fished and hunted. Iroquoian villages from this time could be as large as five hectares. Their tool and pottery designs were more sophisticated, although Algonquian-speaking peoples also used pottery at this time for cooking. Corn was an important staple of the southern diet. The discovery of several kinds of pipes in archaeological sites from this period indicates that smoking **tobacco** had become a common habit among the Iroquois. Agricultural crops, particularly among the Iroquois, became increasingly varied up to the time the Europeans arrived in the late 16th and early 17th centuries.

Archaeologists also have an interest in the past 300 years, referring to it as the Historic Period. Sites from the early part of this period (pre-1800) include First Nations dwellings as well as European military forts, traders' cabins, and early pioneer sites. Sites from later in the period (post-1800) include pioneer cabins and homesteads of primarily European settlers, who moved here in great numbers during this time.

Underwater archaeology is another important facet of Ontario's heritage. The many shipwrecks in the **Great Lakes** over the years have proved popular with divers and souvenir hunters, but efforts have been made to prevent the removal of artifacts so that sites can be studied and interpreted more effectively. The Ontario Heritage Act specifies that anyone undertaking archaeological fieldwork must hold a valid licence issued by the province.

# Art Gallery of Ontario

As the eighth largest museum in North America, the Art Gallery of Ontario (AGO) in **Toronto** is one of Canada's oldest and most respected cultural institutions. Founded in 1900 as the Art Museum of Toronto, the gallery has a permanent collection of 20,000 works in all media, ranging from 15th-century European paintings to an array of international contemporary works of art. More than half its collection is made up of Canadian works.

The AGO's Henry Moore Sculpture Centre, which opened in 1974, holds the world's largest collection of works by the noted English sculptor, many of which were gifts from Moore himself. The Moore collection contains 142 sculptures, 76 drawings, and 710 prints. The AGO also has the third-largest collection in the world of works by Inuit artists, focusing primarily on works produced in Canada since 1948.

For the first 11 years of its life, the museum did not have a permanent home. In 1911, however, Harriette Dixon Boulton Smith bequeathed The Grange, a

15-room Georgian mansion in downtown Toronto, and the museum was officially opened in 1913. Three new galleries were opened on the site in 1918, and the institution's name was changed the following year to the Art Gallery of Toronto. It was here in 1920 that the **Group of Seven** had their first exhibition.

The gallery expanded again in 1925 and 1933, and in 1966 it became the Art Gallery of Ontario, with a mandate to serve everyone in the province. With more activities and a growing collection, it underwent a three-stage expansion beginning in 1968 and ending in January 1993. These additions increased exhibition space by nearly 60 percent and allowed for permanent Inuit and contemporary galleries, as well as a print and drawing study centre.

The AGO's collection of Canadian works represents a who's who of this country's art world, including Tom Thomson, Lawren Harris, Emily Carr, Paul-Émile Borduas, and Paterson Ewen. But the AGO is more than just Canadian art. The gallery contains European art from the Italian Renaissance to the French Impressionists, and has one of the best collections of Florentine Baroque bronzes in the world. The AGO began to purchase American contemporary paintings in the early 1960s and contemporary European art two decades later, including works by Andy Warhol, Pablo Picasso, and Marc Chagall. The AGO also houses the largest collection of artists' films in Canada, as well as a wide selection of photographs, prints, and drawings.

Its Edward P. Taylor Research Library and Archives is a major resource for studying art history. With 100,000 volumes on the history of western art, 40,000 sales and auction catalogues, and 55,000 files on Canadian contemporary artists, the library attracts historians, curators, journalists, and students.

# Bay Street

Bay Street, and more specifically its intersection with King Street, is the geographic centre of Toronto's financial district and symbolizes the city's role as the business and finance capital of Canada.

At the intersection of the two streets stand the towers of four of Canada's five major banks. Radiating from that point are dozens of offices that headquarter Canada's brokerage firms, insurance companies, trust companies, law firms, international banks, and the **Toronto Stock Exchange,** located at 130 King Street West, a short walk from Bay Street. The power brokers who sit at the helm of these institutions and organizations negotiate contracts, mergers, and other business transactions worth hundreds of billions of dollars to the Canadian **economy** annually.

Originally, the business and financial community was concentrated on King Street East, near the St. Lawrence Market, but when **Yonge Street** was completed in the late 19th century, the financiers moved west to more modern offices. By the turn of the century, city hall (now a courthouse) had moved to Queen and Bay Streets. The proximity of the municipal government and banks attracted other financial institutions.

By 1910 the city's first skyscrapers went up, and in the 1960s and 1970s, many old downtown buildings fell to the wrecker's ball, replaced by the steel and glass towers that shape the skyline of **Toronto** today.

## Beavers

It may be Canada's national symbol but as far as many private landowners in Ontario are concerned, the beaver is nothing more than a sharp-toothed pest that backs up waterways, plugs culverts, and damages or destroys healthy trees.

Beavers are found in greatest abundance in forested northern regions of the province. They reside in ponds, meandering streams, and small lakes with muddy bottoms.

Canada's largest rodent, beavers are valued for their lush pelts, which are made into coats, hats, and other garments, and for their castor gland, which produces an oil the beaver uses as a territorial scent marker but which people use in medicines and perfume. On average, trappers in Ontario reap more than $2 million every year from the sale of beaver pelts.

It is not illegal to shoot or trap beavers in Ontario. Trappers can capture and kill beavers during predetermined seasons every spring and fall, and if beavers cause problems on private property, landowners can shoot, trap, or move them to other areas at any time of year.

Beavers were abundant in Ontario until the 1800s but by 1900, after long years of unrestricted commercial exploitation, few colonies remained, as was the case in many parts of North America. However, in the 1920s, as a result of government protection, a resurgence began and populations began to recover and stabilize through the 1970s and early 1980s. Today, Ontario's beaver population is estimated to be between 600,000 and 900,000, higher than at any point in the 20th century.

The beaver has been much maligned over the years, usually by critics who contend that the economic losses attributed to its dam-building activities surpass the value of its pelts. But the furry rodent does have its share of allies: some say dam building helps refurbish poor soil, while tree-cutting thins vegetation and allows flowers and new trees to revitalize the area.

Although the beaver is despised by many, its name has been immortalized in more than a thousand place names across Canada. In Ontario, these include the communities of Beaverdale, Beaverstone Bay, Beaverton, the Beavers Corner Indian Reserve, Beaver Island Lake, Beavertone River, and Beavertrap Creek.

# Birds

Ontario is home to more than 450 species of birds, with close to 300 of them nesting in the province. The rest travel through during migration.

Because of Ontario's large size, stretching from the warm **Carolinian Zone** in the southwest to the cold, harsh tundra of the north, an amazing range of species is found within its borders. Ontario contains five distinct habitats: the tundra, the Hudson Bay Lowlands, the boreal forest, the Great Lakes–St. Lawrence forest, and the deciduous forest, which contains the Carolinian Zone.

The high human population density in the Great Lakes–St. Lawrence forest and the Carolinian Zone has had a significant impact on bird populations in these areas. Deforestation and **agriculture** have led to a decline in forest birds, but have also led to an increase and diversification of open-country birds. As well, several bird species have adapted to both urban and rural settings and are seen frequently. These include the blue jay, northern cardinal, house sparrow, American crow, and black-capped chickadee.

The Carolinian Zone has one of the richest concentrations of bird populations in North America. Not only is it situated in an area frequented by migrating birds, but it also has a climate warm enough to allow species to overwinter. Among the species found here are the Carolina wren, red-bellied woodpecker, white-eyed vireo, northern mockingbird, and the rare prothonotary warbler. The region's **Point Pelee National Park** is one of the most popular spots for bird-watchers, who congregate in spring to view the bird species migrating north. The Aylmer Wildlife Management Area southeast of **London** is a stopping-point for thousands of migrating tundra swans each spring, while Hawk Cliff on Lake Erie is the best place in Ontario for viewing migrating hawks in the fall.

Birds common to the Great Lakes–St. Lawrence forest are the turkey vulture, several types of warblers, purple martin, common raven, dark-eyed junco, hermit thrush, bobolink, and northern cardinal. The boreal forest covers much of **northern Ontario** and is the breeding site for such species as purple finches, crossbills, and evening grosbeaks. The tundra area hosts a relatively smaller bird population, including the king eider, willow ptarmigan, and snowy owl, while the Hudson Bay Lowlands are home to the black-backed woodpecker, sharp-tailed sparrow, grey jay, yellow warbler, tree swallow, northern shrike, and pine grosbeak.

Ontario also contains enormous stretches of shoreline, more than 3,800 kilometres along the **Great Lakes** and another 1,000 kilometres of sea coast along **James Bay** and Hudson Bay. The thousands of small lakes and other wetlands within the province make it a haven for birds. Among the species found in these areas are sandpipers, gulls, herons, ducks, cormorants, and terns. In marshy regions, Canada geese, moorhens, marsh wrens, and red-winged blackbirds are common. Northern wetland areas are home to the common **loon,** which is Ontario's official bird, as well as the osprey, belted kingfisher, common snipe, and alder flycatcher.

Thirteen birds are considered endangered in Ontario, although a few of them have healthier populations outside the province. They are the bald eagle, golden eagle, Eskimo curlew, white pelican, peregrine falcon, loggerhead shrike, northern bobwhite, king rail, piping plover, kirtland's warbler, prothonotary warbler, Henslow's sparrow, and the Acadian flycatcher.

**Black Flies**. *See* **Invertebrates**

# Bruce Peninsula National Park

The idea for a national park in the Bruce Peninsula region first surfaced in the early 1960s, but provincial wildlife officials, hunters, and some politicians, who objected to the cost, successfully opposed the idea. Although the government continued to develop a provincial park at the tip of the peninsula, it wasn't until July 1987 that a national park was finally established there.

Bruce Peninsula National Park, located at the northern end of the **Niagara Escarpment,** is noted for its limestone cliffs along the **Georgian Bay** shoreline. Erosion over millions of years has created caves along several trails in the park.

The park contains an unusually rich variety of wildflowers, including 43 species of orchids. These plants grow along with specific fungi and are almost impossible to transplant. The peninsula is also home to half the world's dwarf lake iris, most of Canada's Indian plantain, and 20 species of ferns, including the rare northern holly fern. Some old-growth forests are found here.

**Mammals** in the park include white-tailed deer, black bear, porcupine, raccoon, and fox. The eastern massasauga rattlesnake, an endangered species rarely seen, is also found here. As part of an international program, park officials have established a permanent one-hectare forest monitoring plot to help detect species loss over the next several years. The park is at the core of the Niagara Escarpment's Biosphere Reserve, which received that designation in 1990 by the United Nations Educational, Scientific and Cultural Organization (UNESCO).

Visitors to the park can hike several trails with varying degrees of difficulty, and **camping** is available at Cyprus Lake. Other activities include canoeing, kayaking, cross-country skiing, and snowshoeing. The park provides educational programs in the summer as well as student outreach programs on environmental and biological concerns during the rest of the year.

# Bruce Trail

Of the hundreds of hiking trails in the province, the Bruce Trail is arguably the most famous and popular. It was the brainchild of Raymond Lowes, a **Hamilton** hiker who wanted a public trail to draw attention to the natural beauty of the **Niagara Escarpment.** The trail, named for James Bruce, Governor General of Canada from 1847 to 1854, officially opened in June 1967. At a thousand kilometres of main and side pathways, it's the longest and oldest continuous volunteer-maintained trail in Ontario.

The trail follows the escarpment, a stretch of cliff, woodland, valley, and waterfall running from the village of Queenston near **Niagara Falls** to Tobermory and through the **Bruce Peninsula National Park** to the tip of the Bruce Peninsula. About one-third of the trail crosses private land. More than 40 percent is on Crown land, conservation areas, and land owned by the Bruce Trail Association.

The scenery along the trail is spectacular, and anyone walking there will come across many species of flowers and such animals as white-tailed deer, black bears, coyotes, and foxes. The path is marked by white blazes on trees, fence posts, stiles, and rocks. On the portions of the trail that are on private property, landowners have given permission for people to pass through. Fourteen outdoor education centres and eight interpretive centres on or near the trail provide a living classroom for hikers to explore, and **camping** is available in designated areas.

The Bruce Trail Association, which has about 8,000 members and 800 volunteers in nine clubs, oversees the care and maintenance of the trail. As many as 1.3 million people visit the Bruce Trail each year.

# Camping

Algonquin, Bon Echo, Pinery, Killbear, Rideau River, René Brunelle: For anyone who has spent time in Ontario's outdoors, these names evoke great memories of nature and family vacations in a tent or trailer.

When it comes to camping, there's certainly no shortage of places to set up a campsite. Ontario's provincially run parks system is among the largest in the world with 272 parks covering more than seven million hectares, some less than an hour from such major cities as **Toronto** and **Ottawa,** and others hundreds of kilometres from the nearest community. In addition, there are more than 400 privately owned campgrounds with 70,000 campsites operated by members of the Ontario Private Campground Association, plus sites at some of the national parks located in Ontario and at more than 70 of the province's conservation areas.

Tenting and trailering opportunities range from backcountry camping in unspoiled wilderness areas far from flush toilets and swimming pools, to hydro-serviced campgrounds for trailers and recreational vehicles, where facilities may include showers, coffee shops, sandy beaches, laundromats, amusement parks, and outdoor theatres. Most parks, whether government or privately operated, offer easy access to beaches, picnicking, bird watching, fishing, hiking, boating, and a wide range of other outdoor activities.

Ontario's full-service provincially operated campgrounds are generally open from the second weekend in May until Labour Day weekend in September. Eleven provincial parks operate year round and offer winter camping, day use, and other services.

(*See also* **Provincial Parks**)

# Canada's Sports Hall of Fame

Since June 1955, Canada's Sports Hall of Fame has recognized and preserved the record of athletic achievement in our country while promoting awareness of our sports heritage.

Located on the grounds of the **Canadian National Exhibition** in **Toronto,** the Sports Hall of Fame honours over 400 Canadian athletes and builders of sport, of whom more than 200 are Ontarians. More than 50 professional and amateur sports are represented by inductees into the hall, as well as representatives from sports broadcasting and journalism. There are no specific criteria for earning membership in the hall; instead, a national selection committee determines new inductees each year.

The hall features three exhibit galleries, a theatre, library, and archives, and houses more than 40,000 photographs of historical significance and a wealth of biographical data for researchers, students, and members of the media. Among its 3,000 artifacts are Ned Hanlan's rowing shell, Kurt Browning's "first ever quad" skates, Olympic gold medals, athletic equipment, trophies, and uniforms that detail Canadian achievements in a variety of sports.

The hall's Heritage Gallery contains some of the hall's most prized artifacts, including several trophies, one of which stands more than 1.8 metres high. In the gallery's theatre, visitors can view such videos as *Great Moments in Canadian Sport* and *The Terry Fox Story.*

The Sports Hall of Fame, which is funded primarily through private donations, underwent a $1.4 million renovation in 1985 that saw the addition of interactive videos and quizzes to test visitors' knowledge of Canada's sports history. More than 275,000 people visit the hall annually.

## Canadian Baseball Hall of Fame and Museum

In June 1998, the Canadian Baseball Hall of Fame and Museum officially opened in St. Marys, north of **London,** as a tribute to the men and women whose exploits in the sport made them famous and helped develop the game in Canada and elsewhere.

The hall is located in a century-old stone house, but plans for a new structure to be opened in 2001 are underway. A baseball diamond in an amphitheatre setting sits nearby on a 12.3-hectare site, and a grandstand that will seat 2,000 spectators should be completed by late 2000. Construction on two other diamonds began in 1999.

St. Marys had successfully bid to become the new site for the hall of fame in 1994. Prior to opening in St. Marys, the hall had been housed at **Ontario Place** in **Toronto** and before that as part of **Canada's Sports Hall of Fame** on the CNE grounds.

The new hall and museum, which will cost approximately $3.2 million when all phases are completed, is designed to foster an appreciation for Canada's role in baseball, to display artifacts of the sport, and to provide information on such inductees as former pitching star and Chatham native Ferguson Jenkins.

St. Marys was the home of Dr. Adam Ford, who published an account in 1886 of a baseball game he saw played in 1838 in nearby Beachville. That game, which has been validated by historians, took place before Abner Doubleday is supposed to have "invented" baseball in Cooperstown, New York, about a year later. Ford's account described the rules, the way the game was played at the time, and the players who participated.

## Canadian Football Hall of Fame

In 1962, the city of **Hamilton** asked the Canadian Football League (CFL) for the privilege of housing memorabilia in what was to be a newly established Canadian Football Hall of Fame. No structure was prepared at the time, but the city's parks board made an old residence temporarily available near what is now Ivor Wynne Stadium, where the **Hamilton Tiger-Cats** play their home games. The city soon decided a new structure should be built. Several proposals were made before Hamilton and the CFL agreed in 1968 to use land beside city hall and the Hamilton Public Library.

Completed in 1972, the hall was officially opened during Grey Cup week-end. Although many visited the hall in its first year, it lost money in the new location. In 1979, in an attempt to boost attendance, the hall's directors decided to begin inducting Canadian professional and amateur football players. A $500,000 renovation began in late 1998, which was completed in June 1999. In addition to the more than 30,000 different football-related items ranging from 1900 to the present, the newly revitalized hall now features interactive displays, video clips, a 100-seat theatre, and a virtual field goal kick exhibit.

The hall is designed to give visitors a strong sense of the richness of Canadian football's long history. Among the artifacts are the jerseys of former CFL greats Terry Evanshen and Peter Dalla Riva, several player trophies, busts of the football players and builders of the game who have been inducted into the hall, as well as photos and biographical information on the more than 185 hall of fame members. An induction weekend is held each fall to formally accept the newest members to the hall.

(*See also* **Hamilton Tiger-Cats**; **Toronto Argonauts**)

# Canadian National Exhibition

Going to the "Ex," as the Canadian National Exhibition (CNE) is affectionately known, has been a late-summer tradition for Ontarians for more than a hundred years. The CNE was founded in 1879 to foster the development of **agriculture,** industry, and the arts. Though originally known as the **Toronto** Industrial Exhibition, the name was officially changed in 1912 to better represent the national nature of the fair.

*An entrance to the Canadian National Exhibition grounds as it appeared in 1917.* (C.M. Johnston, Public Archives PA-56191)

Agricultural advances have been an important part of the Ex for many years, and today visitors can still see produce displays, horticultural exhibits, the annual horse show, and displays of farm animals. Throughout its long history the CNE has featured exhibits of the latest technological advances. Among the "modern" marvels that CNE visitors have experienced were the first electric streetcar in North America in 1883, the phonograph in 1888, radio in 1922, television in 1939, and Virtual Reality in 1992.

In addition, the CNE has been a showcase of fine art. Between 1905 and the 1970s, international and Canadian artworks were displayed in the CNE Art Gallery, built specifically for this purpose. The building was torn down in the early 1970s, however, and art is no longer a feature of the CNE. Sports have also formed an integral part of the CNE, with Marilyn Bell's swim across Lake Ontario in 1954 arguably the most memorable event. Few sports competitions are held there today.

The Ex has featured a variety of entertainment in its history. Historical pageants in the early years often involved casts of hundreds. Stars such as Tommy Dorsey, Guy Lombardo, and Benny Goodman attracted large crowds during the Swing Era of the 1940s, while a range of rock stars such as the Beach Boys, the Guess Who, and Neil Young performed at the CNE stadium through the 1960s, '70s, and '80s. The stadium was also the home of the **Toronto Argonauts** and the **Toronto Blue Jays** before the **SkyDome** was built. Some of the current popular features at the CNE are the Canadian International Air Show, the garden show, sports demonstrations, a casino, and KidsWorld, an interactive area for children and parents.

The Ex has several architecturally interesting buildings on its grounds and its well-known entranceway, the Princes' Gates, was built in 1927. The CNE's midway has long been a favourite for young people, and throughout its history has featured side shows, games, and the latest gut-churning rides, including a former roller coaster known as the Flyer, which has not been replaced. The Ex is one of the world's largest annual exhibitions, with attendance reaching more than 1.5 million.

(*See also* **Fall Fairs**)

# Canadian Shield

The Canadian Shield is the main continental block of the earth's crust underlying North America. It is composed of Precambrian rocks that have been relatively stable for billions of years. In geological terms, the Shield is known as a craton, the geological centre from which the continent first evolved.

Stretching from Labrador to Alberta and from the Arctic Ocean to the southern United States, the Canadian Shield is the largest craton in the world, covering an area of more than 5.5 million square kilometres. About two-thirds of Ontario lies under the Shield, containing some of the oldest rocks in the world, dating back more than 3 billion years. More than half of the Shield is composed of granite, a very hard and almost weatherproof rock commonly used as a building material.

In Ontario, the Canadian Shield is divided into three geological areas called "provinces," each containing rocks of similar age and type. These provinces—Superior, Southern, and Grenville—were formed at different periods. As each developed, it attached itself to older rocks, forming the bedrock that is visible throughout northern and central Ontario.

Superior Province was the first to develop, between 2.5 and 3 billion years ago. Covering most of **northern Ontario,** it is divided into 12 subprovinces based on rock type. Geologists believe this first piece of Ontario appeared in the Red Lake area where the first section of crust grew in several stages: First, volcanoes spread lava from east to west, creating several chains of volcanic islands or volcanic arcs; over time, these islands collected on the edges of the young Ontario. Gradually, the volcanic islands eroded and powerful currents swept the sediments into basins along Ontario's edges, a process that occurred at least three times.

The final stage occurred when pieces of crust—including the island arcs and the sedimentary basins—collided with a force strong enough to create a mountain range as tall as the Rockies in western Canada. The impact of the colliding plates forced huge volumes of molten rock to rise up, forming enormous granite bodies beneath northern Ontario. This action also baked and compressed the volcanic and sedimentary rocks, creating new metamorphic rocks.

Some of the world's most famous mining camps are found in Superior Province, including the rich Hemlo gold camp near Marathon and the giant Kidd Creek copper, zinc, and silver deposit at Timmins. Since 1909, the Timmins district has produced 60 million ounces of gold, the Kirkland Lake district more than 38 million ounces, and the Red Lake area more than 16 million ounces of the yellow metal. Superior Province is also the home of much of Ontario's iron ore, which is mined in the Steep Rock, Atikokan, Algoma, Michipicoten, and North Spirit Lake areas.

Southern Province evolved between 570 million and 2.4 billion years ago but only a section lies within Ontario, with the majority in the states of Michigan, Minnesota, and Wisconsin. This section, located around Lake Huron and the north shore of Lake Superior, had its start when sediments eroded from the Superior Province were laid down between 2.2 and 2.4 billion years ago. Three supergroups of rocks were formed near the two lakes, followed by a major mountain-building event, the Penokean Orogeny, triggered when the young Ontario collided with another piece of crust located just off its southern edge, resulting in a huge mountain range north of Lake Huron. About 1.1 billion years ago, the earth's crust cracked, volcanoes erupted, and when lava and sediment collected in the resulting fault valley or rift, a fourth supergroup of igneous rocks was formed.

Southern Province is home to what is known as the Sudbury Structure, consisting of the Sudbury Igneous Complex and the Sudbury Basin. The basin is a huge oval-shaped bowl that measures 27 by 60 kilometres and extends some 30 kilometres beneath the surface. It is nestled in the Sudbury Igneous Complex, a thick bowl of igneous rock.

Geologists believe the Sudbury Structure was formed either by a violent volcano or, more likely, by a meteorite impact about 1.85 billion years ago when the area was under the sea. Whatever its origin, it is the site of Sudbury's world-famous nickel-copper deposits. In addition, sediments containing grains of uranium eroded from Superior Province, forming Elliot Lake's uranium and iron deposits. About 1.1 billion years ago, further mineral deposits were formed when the young North American continent nearly split apart along a line centred through Lake Superior. They include copper in the volcanic rocks along the north shore of Lake Superior, and silver-bearing veins and deposits of amethyst near Thunder Bay.

Grenville Province is the youngest part of the Canadian Shield, 570 million to one billion years old, stretching southeast from the area around Sudbury to the **St. Lawrence River** and including **Algonquin Park.** It is best described as a patchwork of many different pieces of crust, which were thrust together like a deck of cards in a series of mountain-building episodes. Today, this mountain range and others that once existed in Superior and Southern provinces have been eroded by wind, rain, and ice. As in the other two provinces, rocks once deeply buried in Grenville Province are now exposed. This activity left behind many valuable minerals. The first gold discovery was made in Grenville Province in 1866, north of Madoc in Hastings County. Iron, copper, zinc, molybdenum, and uranium have all been mined in Grenville Province, as well as a variety of industrial minerals, such as graphite, nepheline syenite, talc, marble, and dolomite.

(*See also* **Mining Industry**)

# Canals

With 20 percent of Ontario covered by **water,** five canals make it possible for commercial and personal watercraft to bypass rapids, falls, and dams that impede travel on the province's network of lakes and rivers. Three of these artificial waterways are national historic sites operated by Parks Canada.

The Welland Canal was built to circumvent **Niagara Falls** and provide a navigable connection between Lake Ontario and Lake Erie. It was the first major navigation project in what today is the **Great Lakes–St. Lawrence Seaway,** and provides a deep waterway system that enables lakers and ocean vessels to travel into the heart of North America.

The first Welland Canal opened in 1829; three other versions have since been built, including the present eight-lock canal, which was officially opened on August 6, 1932. On average it takes a ship about 11 hours to travel the 42-kilometre canal, which helps navigate an elevation difference of 99.5 metres between the two lakes. The current canal cost the Canadian government $249 million and is capable of handling vessels up to 222 metres long.

The Iroquois Canal, which is also part of the seaway system, consists of a single lock spanning just 0.3 nautical miles between Morrisburg and Prescott. It enables vessels to bypass the Iroquois Dam and allows ships to adjust to the water level of Lake Ontario.

The province's historic canals are the Trent-Severn Waterway, the Sault Canal, and the Rideau Canal. The Trent-Severn is an inland series of lakes, rivers, and artificial canals that winds through 386 kilometres of central Ontario from the north shore of Lake Ontario at Trenton to Port Severn on the eastern shore of **Georgian Bay.** Draining in a southerly direction into Lake Ontario, the waterway comprises 43 locks, including the massive **Peterborough Lift Lock,** two marine railways, and about 53 kilometres of canal channels. The rest of the waterway follows an improved lake and river route.

Construction began in 1833 and was completed in 1920. In its early years, the system was used as a fast and cheap way to move goods and people out of the interior to Lake Ontario. The waterway also harnessed water power for industries. Today, it is primarily a recreational waterway, taking travellers through the **Canadian Shield** and drumlins, rolling farmland, limestone banks, and wetlands. It continues to produce hydroelectric power, which is a significant part of Ontario's power production.

The Sault Canal is located at Sault Ste. Marie where it overcomes a drop of six metres and bypasses the St. Marys River rapids to connect Lake Superior and Lake Huron. The 2.4-kilometre canal opened in 1895, completing an all-Canadian waterway from the Atlantic Ocean to the head of Lake Superior. The fact that Canada could not count on easy access for wheat and mineral shipments through the American-operated St. Marys Falls Canal at Sault Ste. Marie, Michigan, was a key reason for its construction. When completed, the Sault Canal was the first in the world to use electrically operated gates and valves.

In 1979, the canal was retired from the St. Lawrence Seaway system and in 1987, due to a structural failure, it was closed to navigation. In July 1998, the lock was re-opened for recreational use, while large seagoing ships now use the American canal.

The 202-kilometre Rideau Canal, which connects **Ottawa** and **Kingston,** was built between 1826 and 1832 under the direction of Colonel John By, as a safe military transportation route from Montreal to Upper Canada. Although it was never used for military purposes, the waterway served as an artery for immigration, commerce, local transportation, and recreation.

Today the canal is used mainly for recreation. There are 47 locks and 24 lock stations, all with picnic areas, some with museums, and most with camping areas for boaters. Every February, a stretch of the canal that flows through Ottawa becomes a skating rink and forms an integral part of Ottawa's annual Winterlude Festival.

# Carolinian Zone

Because of its latitude and the moderating effects of the **Great Lakes,** a portion of southwestern Ontario is able to support an ecosystem similar to that of the Carolinas. A narrow band of Carolinian forest extends along an area north of Lake Erie to western Lake Ontario. The zone's habitats encompass sand dunes, marshes, tall grass prairie, and deciduous forests.

Although it is a relatively small area of land in relation to the province's size, the Carolinian Zone contains more types of flora and fauna than anywhere else in Canada. More than 2,000 species of plants flourish here, some 400 types of **birds,** and 50 kinds of **invertebrates** not found elsewhere in Canada. Exotic species include opossums, cucumber trees, wild turkeys, eastern prickly pear cactus, sassafras, black gum trees, the rare eastern spiny soft-shell turtle, and the Lake Erie water snake. The red mulberry is considered to be the rarest tree in Canada, with only about 100 plants left in the Carolinian Zone.

The zone's diversity is remarkable, considering that about 87 percent of it lies on either clay or sandy soil with little topographic variety and few, if any, small inland lakes and river valleys still in their natural state.

The warm **climate** and good soil have also made the Carolinian Zone ideal for farming and urban growth. European settlers seeking rich farmland and longer growing seasons than those found in other parts of the country cleared much of the land over the past 200 years. The forests provided a ready supply of timber for export. Today only about 3 percent of the original forest cover is still in place, and species such as the eastern cougar and eastern elk no longer exist here. Some 90 percent of the wetlands have been lost, which has increased the threat to endangered species.

To slow the destruction, Carolinian Canada was set up in 1984 as a cooperative project between the government and nonprofit conservation groups, such as the World Wildlife Fund, the Ontario Heritage Foundation, and the Federation of Ontario Naturalists. More than 6,000 hectares are currently protected by private landowners, while another 5,900 hectares are owned by conservation organizations.

Nevertheless, the Carolinian Zone is considered to be one of the five most threatened natural regions in the country, and many groups and individuals continue to work to protect this habitat and its remaining species.

# Casa Loma

One of the finest houses ever built in Ontario, Casa Loma was the dream of Sir Henry Pellatt, a wealthy Torontonian who wanted a building that would combine the best elements of overseas castles. He chose a site on the Spadina escarpment of **Toronto** and construction on the main building began in 1911. It took more than three years, 300 workers, and $3.5 million to complete, and was approximately 180,000 square feet.

A European-style chateau, Casa Loma had 98 rooms, many with teak floors and oak panelling, woodwork carved in England, and enormous bronze doors made in New York. Several formal and informal gardens complemented the home. Among the features of the house were a conservatory, the first electric elevator in Toronto, 59 telephones, 22 fireplaces, a library with shelf space for 10,000 books, and an enormous wine cellar. A 244-metre tunnel connects to the horse stables, which had mahogany stalls and Spanish tile floors. The Great Hall, with its lofty oak-beamed ceiling and marble floors, is one of the most impressive features of the house.

The Pellatts lived in the house only from 1913 to 1923, as the expense of maintaining the home was enormous. Pellatt left the home to the city of Toronto, but it remained unused for more than 10 years. The Kiwanis Club leased Casa Loma from the city in 1937, refurbished the building, and since then has run it as a not-for-profit business. Casa Loma continues to be one of the top tourist attractions in Toronto, with about 375,000 visitors annually, and also serves as a location for numerous special functions. Proceeds from the operation of Casa Loma go to charitable works and community projects.

In recent years, the city has been restoring the exterior of the house to ensure that its structure is stabilized. The estimated cost of restoration is $16 million.

# Casinos

Legalized casino gambling arrived in Ontario on May 17, 1994, when the provincial government's Ontario Casino Corporation opened the province's first gambling establishment in temporary quarters in **Windsor.**

Although gambling opponents might not agree, gambling has been a financial godsend for the province, creating thousands of jobs and generating more than $2.4 billion worth of new economic activity in Ontario. According to the

Ontario government, casinos can take credit for reduced unemployment, higher housing sales, lower hotel vacancy rates, and increased **tourism** activity in areas where casinos are located. In 1997–98, the province's three commercial casinos attracted more than 20 million visitors.

In July 1998, Casino Windsor moved from its interim facility into a $505 million permanent home on the city's waterfront. The 100,000-square-foot gaming area features more than 130 table games and 3,000 slot machines, and the casino is attached to a 23-storey hotel overlooking the Detroit River. Employing 5,000 people, the casino is the city's third-largest employer, and has generated a total of 13,000 direct and indirect jobs in Ontario.

The 65,000-square-foot Casino Rama opened in 1996 on land owned by the Chippewas of Rama First Nation, 90 minutes north of **Toronto.** It offers 65,000 square feet of gaming, with more than 2,200 slot machines and 110 table games. The only Ontario casino hosted by a First Nations community, it is also the only facility not located in a border city. Casino Rama is the largest employer in Central Ontario, providing year-round employment for 2,500 people and reducing the area's unemployment rate from 80 percent to less than 10 percent. In 1997–98, the average daily attendance was 11,200, up from 10,400 the previous year.

Casino Niagara opened in 1996 in temporary quarters in the heart of **Niagara Falls'** tourist district. Work was scheduled to begin in 2000 on a new facility which will be connected to a hotel. With 100,000 square feet of gaming area in a 240,000-square-foot complex, the interim building houses Canada's largest casino. It is designed with a 1920s colonial theme and has 2,670 slot machines and 144 table games. Casino Niagara employs 3,600 people and has created 9,000 direct and indirect jobs in Ontario, 6,000 of them in the Niagara Region. Since opening, it has brought $1.3 billion annually in new economic activity to the province, through casino activities and an increased number of tourists. Average daily visits in 1997–98 totalled 25,500.

All commercial casinos are open 24 hours a day, 365 days a year. The province also oversees charity casinos in the communities of Sault Ste. Marie, Brantford, Point Edward, and **Thunder Bay.** In addition, slot machines are found at some Ontario horse racing tracks.

Profits from gambling are funnelled into Ontario's consolidated revenue fund and used for road building and the delivery of health care and education programs. Among the direct beneficiaries of casino cash is St. Catharines General

Hospital, which in 1997–98 received money from the Casino Niagara for the purchase of a magnetic resonance imaging scanner to serve the Niagara Region. An Ontario Casino Corporation official notes that beefed-up policing in the area of each casino has helped reduce general crime rates: in the Orillia area, for example, criminal code violations decreased by 30 percent in 1998 compared to 1997, while in Windsor violations during the same period dropped by 14 percent and instances of fraud were down by 28 percent.

This has not been enough to silence those who oppose gambling, however. They argue that the proliferation of casinos has also led to an increase in gambling, an assertion that is supported by various studies.

In 1998, an Addiction Research Foundation report on the social effects of opening Casino Niagara said that the number of people surveyed who reported two or more problems associated with gambling (such as financial problems, marriage breakdowns, or alcohol abuse) had increased to 4.4 percent in 1997 from 2.5 percent in 1996. The report states that "gambling-related problems have increased in Niagara Falls."

In a study done four years after the opening of Casino Windsor, researchers said a "conservative estimate" indicated the number of adults with gambling-related problems increased from 4,600 in 1994 to 6,000 in 1998. The study noted, however, that there has been no significant change in the percentage of problem or pathological gambling in the Windsor area.

# Central Experimental Farm

As the only operating farm within the boundaries of a national capital city, the Central Experimental Farm in **Ottawa** is much more than a plot of greenspace surrounded by urban sprawl.

Dozens of crops are planted, grown, and harvested every year on the 425-hectare farm, which is 15 minutes southwest of the **Parliament Buildings.** The head office of the federal department of agriculture is located here, as well as a busy research centre.

The farm was founded in 1886 as one of a series of cross-Canada experimental sites to conduct research on **agriculture** and foods, and that remains one of its most important functions. At the Eastern Cereal and Oilseed Research Centre more than 80 scientists develop new varieties of corn, wheat, barley, oats, and soybeans, research genetically modified crops, and develop land-use systems for sustainable agricultural production in Canada.

Every spring more than 300 hectares of land serve as outdoor laboratories where crops are grown for research and testing purposes. The development of early maturing corn and soybeans and Marquis wheat are among the research accomplishments of the farm. The farm's insect collection, with more than 15 million specimens used for research purposes, is ranked among the top five collections in the world.

The museum and the livestock barns, which house a dairy herd, beef cattle, sheep, swine, horses, and small animals, make the Central Experimental Farm one of the city's popular attractions, with an annual visitor count of 150,000 people. There's also a 28-hectare arboretum with 2,400 species and varieties of trees and shrubs, a 7.4-hectare wildlife garden, an ornamental garden, and jogging and bicycling paths.

In 1998, the entire farm property was designated a National Historic Site by the Department of Canadian Heritage.

# Chemical Valley

The discovery of **oil** near Oil Springs in 1858 led to the development of many wells and refineries throughout Lambton County in southwestern Ontario. Such activity throughout the 1870s caught the interest of Standard Oil Company and ultimately led to the development of Chemical Valley. This area south of Sarnia has been home to many refineries and well-known chemical companies for several decades, such as Polysar (which was purchased by the German company Bayer AG in the 1990s), Du Pont, Imperial Oil, and Shell Canada.

Dominion of Canada Oils Refinery Company built the first refinery in Sarnia in 1871. Imperial Oil, which had been bought by Standard Oil, set up in Sarnia in 1898 and built a pipeline to its refinery from Lambton County's oil fields. Imperial Oil thrived in Sarnia in the early 20th century, growing tremendously in the years leading up to World War I.

The key event in Chemical Valley's development occurred in 1942 when Polymer Corporation was set up by the Canadian government to produce synthetic rubber for use in World War II. Sarnia was chosen as a site for this project because of its location on the St. Clair River, which separates Ontario from Michigan; its rail and road transportation links; and the existence of the Imperial Oil refinery and its reliable pipeline. Rubber was crucial to the Allied effort during World War II, and production of a synthetic kind was necessary because supplies of natural rubber from southeast Asia had been cut off.

In what many experts consider one of the greatest industrial miracles of the 20th century, the Polymer plant was built and began producing synthetic rubber within 14 months. Polymer, which changed its name to Polysar in 1973, has become known internationally for its production of rubber products and petrochemicals.

Dow Chemical built a styrene plant here in 1942 because the product was essential in the process of synthetic rubber. It marked the first time the American company had ventured beyond the U.S. border, and after the war the plant continued to produce a variety of chemicals and plastics. Another early factory established here was Cabot Canada, which arrived in 1950, and began producing carbon black, a substance used in printing inks and cosmetics.

A major development in Chemical Valley's history was the construction of the interprovincial pipeline, which today runs from Edmonton and the oil fields of Alberta to Montreal. The pipeline, built in 1950, originally ran from Edmonton to Lake Superior, but in 1953 it was extended more than 1,000 kilometres to Sarnia, ensuring a year-round supply of oil for Chemical Valley. The pipeline was extended to Montreal in the mid-1970s.

For more than 50 years, the lights and flare stacks of Chemical Valley (once described in local promotional literature as "a fairyland by night") have twinkled in the evening as a reminder of its importance to Sarnia and Lambton's prosperity. During the 1970s, more than $1 billion was invested in new and expanded plants and another $1 billion was spent in the early part of the 1980s. Although there has been little new investment in the Chemical Valley since the early 1980s, there were signs in late 1999 that the trend might be reversed.

Chemical Valley industries employ thousands of workers and have created many spin-off jobs over the years. The existence of high-tech laboratories and research and development facilities in the area has also been due to the chemical industry presence.

One environmental consequence of all these industries located in one area, however, was the discovery in the mid-1980s of a chemical "blob" in the St. Clair River. Thousands of litres of perchloroethylene, a dry-cleaning solvent, had leaked into the river and attracted several other chemicals already there to create a mass of tarlike consistency at the bottom of the river. It cost $1 million to clean up. To ensure such a thing would not happen again, officials from

Chemical Valley helped found the Awareness and Preparedness for Emergencies at Local Level (APELL) program, which is designed both to improve public awareness about hazards and to prevent future problems. One project launched by Dow in 1990 to cut pollution in the St. Clair River has reduced spills and river discharges by more than 90 percent.

With such a large concentration of industries in the Sarnia-Lambton area, air quality remains a concern. However, continuous monitoring has shown that emissions from local industries have been dropping steadily since 1993.

# Climate

Ontario is often considered to have two distinct regions, but many different patterns of weather. Although the province's weather is variable in all seasons, weather experts say that no area east of the Rocky Mountains has a greater chance of getting the weather that's predicted than Ontario.

The province's two regions are **northern Ontario,** which is **Canadian Shield** country, and southern Ontario, the area south of Lake Nipissing. Northern Ontario occupies 90 percent of the province but contains only 10 percent of the population.

The region northwest of Lake Superior experiences low winter and high summer precipitation, with a range of 35° to 40° Celsius between the average temperatures of the warmest and coldest months. Some moderation of temperatures occurs in the Hudson Bay and **James Bay** area and around Lake Superior. Annual hours of sunshine are about the same as in the south—1,800 to 2,000 hours—but somewhat less than in the Prairies.

As you travel south, temperatures, rainfall, and snow all increase but the spread in average temperature decreases. Southern Ontario has a modified continental climate and experiences much less severe weather than the north. In fact, its climate is one of the mildest in Canada—a factor that has contributed to the area's industrialization and concentrated population. The region's climate owes much to the moderating presence of the **Great Lakes,** as well as its southerly location. Middle Island in Lake Erie, the province's southernmost spot, is at the same latitude as northern California.

In addition to the Great Lakes, regional and local climates are shaped by latitude, air mass, storm movement, altitude, and topography. The Ontario countryside south of the Canadian Shield consists of level terrain and gently rolling hills that permit the unobstructed movement of air masses and storms through-out the year. Although differences in relief are not great, topography does have a significant impact on local climate, especially in areas downwind of the Great Lakes. The southern uplands regions with large areas above 425 metres in ele-vation—the Ontario Highlands immediately east of Lake Huron and the slopes of the Canadian Shield in **Algonquin Park,** east of **Georgian Bay**—are notably cooler and, because of greater snowfall, are also wetter than the surrounding lowlands. In the north, uplands around Lake Superior have elevations of 600 metres to the west of the lake and 450 metres to the east, causing cooler temperatures in this region.

Among the most prominent landforms in southern Ontario is the **Niagara Escarpment.** It begins at a height of 100 metres near Queenston and continues along the south shore of Lake Ontario through Hamilton and northward to Georgian Bay, where the ski slopes of Collingwood reach elevations of 300 metres or more. It then extends through the Bruce Peninsula and reap-pears on **Manitoulin Island.** While not a massive barrier, the escarpment does have significant local effects on climate. Most obvious is its capacity to wring snow out of lake storms. Less dramatic, but more welcome, is its year-round ability to dissipate clouds and precipitation, take the punch out of winds, and warm the air masses that sink east of the escarpment on its downwind side.

The physical feature that has the most profound effect on Ontario's climate is probably the Appalachian Mountain system, which lies outside the province along the eastern rim of the Great Lakes Basin and directs storms moving along the Atlantic coast away from Ontario. On occasion, however, tropical storms push over the Appalachians and redevelop in Ontario, bringing heavy precipitation.

Located near the centre of North America, Ontario could be expected to experience dramatic changes in temperature from winter to summer or from day to night—especially considering that more than 1,700 kilometres separate its southernmost tip from its northern border. But that is not the case. The climate is a hybrid of continental and maritime regimes, with a less extreme temperature range than the Prairies and less precipitation than the Maritimes.

Ontario's climate features a steady progression of settled and stormy weather throughout the year with systems generally not lasting more than a day or two. The settled weather is associated with high-pressure systems, which bring exten-sive masses of air from the tropics, the arctic, and the Pacific and Atlantic Oceans. Shallow, cold, and dry arctic air is predominant in the north during the winter, but southern Ontario also receives its share of cold, sunny days under arctic air, which is present about 22 percent of the time in winter in most of the province.

Atlantic air is associated with cloudy skies, while Pacific air usually brings cool, moist, cloudy weather, or at times, sunny and mild weather. Tropical air enters the south regularly in summer but rarely in winter at ground level where people notice it. This is the air mass that brings oppressively high temperatures and humidity, high concentrations of pollution, and the afternoon **thunderstorms** that are a common feature during Ontario's summers. Tropical air occurs about 30 percent of the time over the lower Great Lakes in summer but less than 10 percent of the time north of Lake Superior.

Storms develop along the fronts that separate these contrasting and competing air masses. They favour a northeasterly path through southern Ontario on their way out to the Gulf of St. Lawrence and the North Atlantic. Storms are more vigorous in winter, bringing strong winds and a potpourri of precipitation types—rain, freezing rain, ice pellets, snow, or a mixture. When such storms depart the province, they leave behind strong winds, low temperatures, and blowing snow. In spring and summer, cold fronts may trigger occasional tornadoes and violent thunderstorms that supply much of the summer rainfall.

Ontario's climate features four distinct seasons with a variety of precipitation types and sources. Warm summers are common, with frequent uncomfortable periods of humid, hazy weather. Warm, sunny days and crisp, cool nights are typical of autumn. Winters last three to five months and spring is normally the shortest season of the year, lasting from a few weeks to a couple of months, depending on the area.

Generally, temperature severity increases as you move east and north in Ontario. Winter temperatures are highest along the Great Lakes, and even in northern Ontario the warming effect of Lake Superior keeps average temperatures 3° to 5° Celsius above those at stations inland. North of Lake Superior, winters are extremely cold, averaging −20° Celsius in January from Lake of the Woods to James Bay. The urban effect that exists in most Canadian cities keeps most core urban areas 2° to 3° warmer in midwinter than the surrounding rural areas. Sometimes, these differences exceed 10° Celsius.

The temperature differences across the province are much less pronounced in summer than in winter. The **Windsor**-Leamington area in the extreme southwest is the warmest, with afternoon temperatures averaging more than

27ºCelsius; towards **James Bay** summer afternoon temperatures exceed 20ºCelsius but the season is short. In **cottage country** areas, including, Georgian Bay, Haliburton, Muskoka, and the Kawarthas, average summer temperatures are in the 18º to 20º Celsius range, with frequent hot spells.

On average, the last killing frost in southern Ontario occurs about the first week of May, and the first frost of fall arrives during the first half of October, leaving a frost-free season of 160 days. Around the Great Lakes, frost-free periods are up to two months longer than inland areas. In the north, frost-free days number between 50 and 120 per year.

Precipitation in southern Ontario is fairly uniformly distributed throughout the year. More rain falls during the growing season than at any other time of year, and February is the driest month. Northern Ontario also receives its maximum precipitation in summer. The amount of precipitation is affected by a region's location relative to the Great Lakes, prevailing winds, elevation, and slope of the land. The south is about one-third wetter than the north, with totals ranging from 500 millimetres in the Patricia area of northwestern Ontario to 1,000 millimetres or more on the western flanks of the highlands of Lake Superior, Georgian Bay, and Lake Huron. Another area of heavy precipitation is along the **St. Lawrence River.**

The driest parts of the south are the fruit belt areas of Essex County and the Niagara Peninsula, the eastern half of Algonquin Park, and the Simcoe-**Toronto** corridor. The wettest station on record is Chatsworth with 1,077 millimetres, and the driest is Big Trout Lake with 581 millimetres.

Ontario's snowfall patterns are highly variable, especially in the southern part of the province, where a single storm can bring as much or more snow to a locality in one or two days than it would receive in an entire winter in another year. The number of snow days (days with measurable snowfall) exceeds 75 a year on average in the **snowbelts.** There are 75 to 100 snow days each year from Lake Superior to the shore of Hudson Bay, more than 40 snow days on the north shore of Lake Ontario, and 50 snow days in the **Ottawa Valley.** By contrast, Point Pelee in the extreme southwest has fewer than 20 snow days a year.

Below is a list of Ontario weather records:

- The highest recorded temperature in Ontario was 42.2º Celsius, in Atikokan and Fort Frances on July 11 and 12 and July 13, 1936, respectively.

- The lowest temperature is –58.3º Celsius, recorded at Iroquois Falls on January 23, 1936.

- Ontario's annual precipitation record was set at Stratford in 1884 when it received 1,620 millimetres of moisture.

- The most snowfall in one year occurred at Steep Hill Falls in the winter of 1938–39 when 766 centimetres fell.

- In 1978, Mount Forest experienced 99 days of fog.

- In 1980, the record for the highest number of wet days was set when Burk's Falls experienced 232 days of rain.

- During the winter of 1962–63, Winisk Airport experienced 52 days of blowing snow.

- The record for the most sunshine in a year is 2,454 hours at **Thunder Bay,** in 1976.

- The greatest wind speed ever recorded in Ontario was at Caribou Island, when winds blew at 114 kilometres per hour on November 22, 1946.

- **Pelee Island** has recorded the greatest number of frost-free days in Ontario—228 days in 1948.

# CN Tower

This 553.33-metre tower soaring over downtown **Toronto** is the world's tallest free-standing structure. Canadian National (CN) built it to be a transmission tower and to demonstrate the strength of Canadian industry.

The CN Tower, which opened to the public on June 26, 1976, took 40 months to build, cost $63 million, and was designed to overcome communications problems for existing transmission towers that weren't high enough to broadcast over the city's tall buildings. The tower has microwave receptors at 338 metres and at its peak. It continues to be a centre of telecommunications for Toronto, serving 16 television and FM radio stations.

Approximately two million people visit the tower each year. The lookout level at 346 metres high can be reached by a 58-second elevator ride, and from there another elevator travels an extra 33 storeys up to Sky Pod, the world's highest observation gallery. The tower's revolving restaurant, just above the lookout

*The 553.33-metre tower has soared over downtown Toronto since 1976. It cost $63 million to build.* (Mark Kearney)

level, provides a 360-degree view of the city. One rotation takes 72 minutes. On a clear day, visitors can see all the way to **Niagara Falls,** approximately 30 kilometres away directly across Lake Ontario.

In June 1998, the CN Tower officially opened a $26 million entertainment expansion on various levels, featuring new multimedia displays, motion simulator rides, films, a themed arcade, and shopping and food areas.

The American Society of Civil Engineers has classified the tower as one of the Seven Wonders of the Modern World.

# Conservation Authorities

As long ago as the 1880s, farmers began calling on the provincial government to take action on deforestation and soil conservation programs, but little was done for almost 50 years. Further deforestation and drought in the 1920s and 1930s started to get the provincial government's attention, while a drought in 1936 aggravated soil erosion problems.

In the early 1940s, the Ontario Conservation and Reforestation Association, the Ontario Federation of Anglers and Hunters, the Ontario Department of Lands and Forests, and rural landowners began laying the groundwork for conservation. Their work resulted in the establishment of the Conservation Authorities Act of 1946.

The authorities initially dealt with soil erosion problems, but flood control became important as well, particularly after **Hurricane Hazel** devastated parts of **Toronto** in 1954. The authorities began acquiring land, and by the late 1990s the 38 conservation authorities in Ontario owned more than 138,000 hectares.

There are almost 400 conservation areas in the province. About 250 offer a range of recreational activities and facilities. The conservation areas see an estimated total of five million visitors a year.

Conservation authorities help develop programs for students on forestry, wildlife, and water management, as well as **environmental protection** and planning programs. In addition to preserving many natural heritage sites, they also provide planning, assistance, and advice to municipalities, developers, and landowners on such issues as erosion and flood control. Conservation authorities can impose development restrictions on private lands if they fall within certain areas—for example, those designated as flood plain.

# Cottage Country

The term "going to the cottage" has been an Ontario tradition for more than 100 years. For many Ontarians, hopping into a packed car and braving heavy traffic to reach a place on or near a lake or river is a big part of their family heritage.

While locations such as Muskoka, Haliburton, and **Georgian Bay** are most commonly associated with cottage life, cottage country can be just about any part of the province that's frequented by Ontarians fleeing urban areas on weekends or for prolonged vacations. There are approximately 500,000 cottages in Ontario, which range from luxurious year-round waterfront properties on huge lakes, to hobby farms, trailers, woodland retreats, and tiny cabins on small streams and remote islands. The average value of a cottage in Ontario in 1997 was $158,000.

Once they arrive at the water, cottagers sink as much as $1.25 billion a year into the economies of cottage country communities by buying boat fuel, fishing lures, building materials, food, bait, beer, wine, and charcoal. Cottagers own more than 500,000 pleasure boats of all shapes and sizes, making them the single largest group of boaters in Ontario.

Muskoka, straight up Highways 400 and 11 about two and a half hours north of **Toronto,** is considered the elite of Ontario's cottage regions. Every summer the population of Muskoka increases about 400 percent, due in large part to the arrival of cottagers. Million-dollar-plus cottages in this area have been owned by such stars as hockey player Eric Lindros and entertainers Goldie Hawn and Martin Short. These and more modest retreats are spread along the shores of its three big lakes—Muskoka, Rosseau, and Joseph.

Other popular areas are the lakes in and around the community of Haliburton; on the shores and islands of Georgian Bay; in **Algonquin Park** and surrounding area; in the Kawartha Lakes district in and around Peterborough, Lindsay, and Bancroft; the Rideau Lakes and along the Rideau River south of **Ottawa**; the **1000 Islands** and areas north of **Kingston**; near Lake Simcoe; along the shores of Lakes Huron, Ontario, and Erie; and in north and north-eastern Ontario, around Temagami and Lake of the Woods.

# Diefenbunker

The Diefenbunker, located 25 kilometres west of **Ottawa** near the village of Carp, was the most famous of a series of bunkers built in Canada during the Cold War years to ensure that governments could continue to function in the event of nuclear attack.

Today, the 34-hectare site is owned by a nonprofit group that sponsors public tours and has opened a Cold War museum at the site. When it was built between 1959 and 1961, the four-storey, 100,000-square-foot subterranean office building was designed to house top government officials and support staff if a nuclear bomb were dropped on or near Ottawa.

High-level members of the team which would have run the country from the bunker would have included the governor general, prime minister, minister of external affairs, minister of national defence, and one additional minister appointed by the PM. Deputy ministers, directors general, assistant deputy ministers, radio broadcasters, and technicians from various telecommunications agencies such as Bell Canada would also have been housed in the facility.

The bunker could accommodate about 500 occupants for 30 days until the primary fallout from an attack had dissipated. It was also intended to serve as a communications hub, which, as it turned out, was its main function throughout its 33 years of service. Initially the government firmly maintained that the massive new structure, officially known as the Central Emergency Government Headquarters, was an army signals establishment, and this was one reason the facility was built. When information about the bunker's real purpose leaked out, the media dubbed it the Diefenbunker after John Diefenbaker, the prime minister at the time.

Its layout included a hospital, bedrooms and offices for the Governor General and prime minister, a Bank of Canada vault, a decontamination unit, a huge kitchen and cafeteria, and a CBC radio studio to broadcast advice to the nation if Canada or the U.S. were ever threatened by nuclear radiation.

The Diefenbunker was decommissioned in 1994 when Canadian Forces Station Carp closed. In the same year, it was declared a National Historic Site and the most important surviving Cold War site in Canada.

# Drumlins and Moraines

The topography of Ontario was formed in large part during the end of the last ice age more than 10,000 years ago. Glacial ice eroded bedrock and moved soil and rock, shaping the landscape in a variety of ways. Among Ontario's most common landforms resulting from this process are drumlins and moraines.

Drumlins form under glaciers. They are smooth, oval hills shaped like an inverted spoon that are aligned parallel to the glacier's direction of movement. They can be single hills but are usually found in groups. On average, drumlins range from 15 to 40 metres high and can be more than two kilometres long. More than 4,000 drumlins have been counted in the region north of Lake Ontario between Lake Simcoe and Trenton. There are hundreds of others in the area south of Georgian Bay, west of Lake Ontario, and in eastern Ontario south of **Ottawa.**

Moraines are ridges created by an accumulation of sediment deposited against a glacier and by **water** melting from it. Moraines have a knobby surface different from the terrain below them and are a mix of clay, silt, pebbles, and sand. They can be classified by their form, origin, and position on the landscape. The large Oak Ridges moraine north of **Toronto,** for example, is known as an interlobate moraine because it was formed by two separate glaciers that deposited sediment between them. Most moraines in southern Ontario crudely parallel the edges of the **Great Lakes,** reflecting the positions of glaciers that once occupied the lake basins.

# Dundurn Castle

As one of the oldest architectural gems in Ontario, Dundurn Castle was originally the home of Allan Napier MacNab. A **War of 1812** hero, MacNab later became a lawyer and in 1832 acquired property in **Hamilton** on which to build his mansion. MacNab, who modelled his new house on the ancestral family home in Perthshire, Scotland, was also the prime minister of the United Province of Canada from 1854 to 1856.

The house was completed in 1835 at a cost of $175,000. It had 72 rooms, oak panelling, grand chandeliers, and such "modern" amenities as running water and gas lighting. Dundurn Castle was the site of several extravagant parties and important meetings in its early history. The Prince of Wales visited the home in 1860.

When MacNab died in 1862, the mansion was sold to pay off his debts. The provincial government owned the estate until 1871, using the house as the Upper Canada Institute for the Deaf and Dumb. Dundurn Castle had several owners over the next two decades as it hosted meetings and occasional theatrical productions. The city of Hamilton bought the castle in 1899 and in 1900 opened the grounds and a museum there to the public. The castle experienced financial problems in the 1930s and closed for three years, but a private donation allowed it to be re-opened in 1937.

In the 1950s, Dundurn Castle was receiving 25,000 visitors annually. By the late 1950s, however, the building needed major renovations. Government and private funding was secured by 1965, and within two years the interior had been restored to its 1850s design. More renovations were done in the early 1990s. The castle has been used as a set for several movies, contains a military museum, and continues to draw about 50,000 visitors annually, making it one of the premier attractions in the Hamilton area.

# Economy

Ontario has a diversified economy with strength across a range of sectors, including secondary **manufacturing** and business and financial services. With a gross domestic product (GDP) of $386 billion, Ontario has Canada's largest economy, ahead of Quebec with $196 billion and British Columbia with $114 billion.

Real provincial GDP growth in 2000 is estimated to be 2.8 percent, down slightly from 1999 when annual growth was pegged at 3 percent. According to several private sector forecasts, Ontario's economic growth over the next three years is expected to outpace that of Canada as a whole and the rest of the G7 countries.

Ontario's housing sector is usually a good economic indicator. As the century drew to a close, the housing market was booming, with the construction of new dwellings 22 percent higher than in 1998 and the value of new construction forecast to reach $18.5 billion. Consequently, real residential investment spending rose by 10.8 percent in 1999 and was forecast to increase by 5.7 percent in 2000.

The manufacturing sector accounts for about one-quarter of the total provincial output. Ontario's top three manufacturing industries, based on shipments of product, are: transportation equipment, led by the $80-billion-a-year auto industry; food industries; and electrical and electronic products. Other key manufacturing industries are chemicals and chemical products; primary metals, such as steel manufacturing; petroleum products; and mining. The forest industry contributes some $14 billion annually to the provincial economy, while **agriculture** rings up cash receipts of $7 billion every year, including $5.3 billion worth of farm products exported to more than 50 countries. The industrial sector is supported by a strong and growing service sector, including financial, insurance, and real estate services, **tourism,** and wholesale and retail trade. Among the fastest-growing sectors is the high-technology industry, which is expanding in several pockets of the province, including **Toronto, Kitchener-Waterloo,** and most significantly in **Ottawa,** where more than 900 technology companies export their products and services around the world.

Ontario's communications networks are efficient, affordable, and among the most advanced in the world. Ontario firms are world leaders in communications technologies, including telecommunications, broadcasting, satellite and space technologies, short- and long-distance telephone, fibre optics, and terminal equipment such as private business exchanges and customer premises equipment.

The province's economy has benefitted from energy prices that are lower than in most developed nations. Plentiful domestic energy resources and an efficient energy industry are major factors. Almost all of the energy consumed in Ontario is generated in Canada. Electricity is generated from a mix of hydro-electric, fossil fuel, and nuclear sources.

Like the rest of Canada, Ontario has a well-developed financial system with a variety of institutions providing a complete range of financial services. Toronto is an international financial centre and the centre of Canada's capital and money markets. Thirty-eight of Canada's 52 banks operate from Ontario, most in the **Bay Street** area. Forty-eight of the 53 foreign banks that operate in Canada have their Canadian head offices in Toronto, which is also the site of the **Toronto Stock Exchange.**

Ontario's level of taxation compares favourably with other major industrialized countries. Combined federal and Ontario personal income tax rates range from about 24 percent to about 50 percent, with the top marginal rate applying to taxable incomes over $65,000. Ontario's provincial taxation rate is 45 percent of federal taxes payable, the third-lowest rate of all Canadian provinces and territories, a factor that persuades new and expanding companies to locate in Ontario.

Ontario's unit labour cost performance compares favourably with the U.S. and has improved compared to Germany and Japan. Since 1992, Ontario's manufacturing unit labour costs, measured in national currency, have decreased by about 0.4 percent, while labour costs in the U.S. have increased by 13.4 percent. This pattern of steadily improving cost competitiveness is expected to continue.

Wages in Ontario are competitive with those in U.S. jurisdictions. In the manufacturing sector, for instance, average wages in 1998 were lower in Ontario than in neighbouring U.S. states. When total compensation rates are compared, Ontario provides even more of a cost advantage, largely because of its publicly funded health care system. The Ontario government says total compensation rates were more than $5 (CDN) an hour less than in Illinois and about $13 (CDN) less than in Michigan.

A big advantage for the province's economy is its location at the heart of North America's consumer and industrial markets and at the hub of a world-class transportation infrastructure, which includes air, rail, and road links as well as the **Great Lakes–St. Lawrence Seaway** system. Ontario is integrated into the $11 trillion (US) North American market, and its goods and services have access to more than 380 million people. As barriers to international trade have disappeared in recent years, Ontario businesses have gained unprecedented access to new markets abroad. More than 135 million people live within a one-day drive of southern Ontario. When these consumers are in spending mode, the province's economy prospers; when they put their wallets away, orders for Ontario goods and services shrink, and the economy suffers.

The province's leading exports are automobiles and auto parts, machines, electrical products, metals, and pulp and paper. In 1997, Ontario exports totalled more than $154 billion (CDN), while imports were worth more than $175 billion (CDN). The U.S. is Ontario's largest export market, accounting for more than 90 percent of the province's total exports. Ontario supplies 55 percent of all Canadian exports to the U.S. and 50 percent of Canada's total exports. The province's major international markets outside the U.S. include the United Kingdom, Germany, South Korea, and Japan.

As is the case in all Canadian provinces, the 7 percent federal Goods and Services Tax (GST), is levied against the consumer like a European value-added tax. Some goods and services are exempt from the GST, such as exports, basic groceries, prescription drugs, medical devices, and agricultural and fishery products. The Ontario retail sales tax of 8 percent applies to most goods and to select services. Significant exemptions include food, children's clothing, and energy, as well as exemptions for research and development, machinery, and other equipment.

In 1999 the province's unemployment rate sat at 6.6 percent, its lowest rate since 1990. In Newfoundland, the 1999 unemployment rate was 17.5 percent, while British Columbia's was 8.6 percent. The Conference Board of Canada forecast a 2-percent increase in jobs in Ontario in 2000. In contrast, its job increase forecast for Newfoundland was 1.2 percent in 2000, and for B.C., 1.3 percent in 2000.

# Education

Ontario has been concerned with formal education for some 200 years. Several grammar schools or small classical academies for a limited number of male students had been set up in each district in the early 1800s, and elementary schools were added by an act of the legislature in 1816. But by the 1830s, only about 10 percent of children were receiving instruction in basic reading, writing, and arithmetic skills, generally the wealthier segment of the population.

In 1841, the province instituted a government-financed public school system. A key figure during this time was Egerton Ryerson, a Methodist minister and president of Victoria College, who acted as chief superintendent of education from 1844 to 1876. He believed that schools should teach Christian moral values but not be connected to any specific religious denomination. Several acts were drafted in the 1840s and 1850s to establish such features as school boards and taxes to support education.

As the province grew and prospered in the latter half of the 1890s, the ideal of mass education came closer to reality as the majority of children were attending elementary school. Separate schools for Catholics had been guaranteed by

*The University of Toronto is Ontario's largest university.* (Mark Kearney)

the Confederation of Canada in 1867, but the provincial governments of the day supported them reluctantly. Full funding for Catholic separate schools to the end of high school was not implemented until 1984, when Premier Bill Davis extended it beyond the elementary level.

In the late 1960s and early 1970s, the provincial education system went through a series of radical changes on the heels of the Hall-Dennis Commission, which implemented new educational theories on classroom structure and teaching styles and practices. Province-wide exams, for example, were dropped during this period. A new system of county school boards, which better reflected the population base, was also in place by 1968.

**Post-secondary education** underwent changes during the 1960s as well, particularly with the establishment of about 20 community colleges that specialized in vocational and technical training. The province's three biggest universities for much of the 20th century, Queen's in **Kingston,** the University of Toronto, and the University of Western Ontario in **London,** experienced great growth in the 1960s and 1970s, but by then had been joined by two French language universities and more than a dozen English ones, including such smaller universities as Brock in St. Catharines, Lakehead in **Thunder Bay,** Trent in Peterborough, and Laurentian in **Sudbury.**

Ontario's publicly financed school system today includes non-denominational public and Roman Catholic separate schools. At a local level, school boards, made up of elected representatives from the area, are responsible for running both elementary and secondary schools and overseeing teaching and support staff. Schools are funded by property taxes from residents, who can direct their money toward either the public or separate systems.

Total funding for education in Ontario is more than $14 billion annually. There are approximately 4,700 publicly funded schools in the province; close to 1,600 are Roman Catholic separate schools. More than 2 million students attend school in Ontario with about 1.37 million enrolled in the elementary level and 696,000 in secondary schools. Approximately 100,000 students study in French in both public and Roman Catholic separate schools.

These figures do not include students enrolled in Ontario's schools for the blind or deaf or those in various care and treatment and correctional facilities. There are also approximately 590 private schools in Ontario, which are operated independently and receive no government funding, serving the needs of about 86,700 students.

Elementary schools provide junior kindergarten and kindergarten programs (for children aged four and five) and programs for grades 1 through 8. Secondary schools currently offer programs from grades 9 through 12, as well as Ontario Academic Courses (OACs), which are considered the equivalent of Grade 13. For many years, Ontario was the only province to offer Grade 13 (more recently referred to as OAC), but as of September 1999, beginning with grade 9 students, the government began phasing in a new four-year high school program to bring it in line with the rest of Canada.

In 1997, the government re-introduced the concept of province-wide testing of students. It has also taken such measures as reducing the number of school boards in Ontario, increasing the emphasis on the core subjects of English, science, and math, and making it mandatory for high school students to do 40 hours of community work before they can graduate.

In Ontario, all permanent residents between the ages of six and sixteen must attend school or study through distance education. More than 78 percent of Ontario's students graduate from high school, compared to about 30 percent in the mid-1950s.

## Endangered and Extinct Species

In Ontario and elsewhere, five **fish,** bird and mammal species are considered extinct: the deepwater cisco, longjaw cisco, blue pike, passenger pigeon, and eastern elk. Extirpated species—meaning they still exist but not in Ontario—are paddlefish and gravel chub, the greater prairie chicken, and two plants, the Illinois tick-trefoil plant and spring blue-eyed mary.

Another 36 species are considered endangered and are close to disappearing. Others are designated as threatened, indicating that they are at risk of becoming endangered if conservation measures are not taken, and others are designated as vulnerable, with population levels that need to be monitored closely.

Fifteen plants have been declared endangered: the cucumber tree, drooping **trillium,** eastern prickly pear cactus, Gattinger's agalinis, heart-leaved plantain, hoary mountain-mint, large whorled pogonia, small whorled pogonia, pink milkwort, Skinner's agalinis, slender bush clover, small white lady's slipper, Engelmann's quillwort, white prairie gentian, and the wood poppy. Thirteen **birds** are considered endangered: the bald eagle, golden eagle, Eskimo curlew, white pelican, peregrine falcon, loggerhead shrike, northern bobwhite, king rail, piping plover, kirtland's warbler, prothonotary warbler, Henslow's sparrow, and the Acadian flycatcher.

Ontario's three endangered **reptiles** are the blue racer, Lake Erie water snake, and the timber rattlesnake. Endangered insects are the frosted elfin and the karner blue butterfly. Blanchard's cricket frog is the lone endangered species of amphibian, and the only endangered mammal is the eastern cougar. The only endangered species of fish is the aurora trout.

Species considered vulnerable or threatened include the smallmouth salamander, prairie warbler, grey fox, American chestnut tree, and bigmouth buffalo, a fish.

Threats to species include habitat loss due to urbanization, clearing of **forests**, and draining of wetlands; agricultural runoff; accumulation of pesticides; and natural factors such as predators and changing water levels. In Ontario, protected areas fall into three broad categories: national parks, **provincial parks** (including recreational and historic parks and nature preserves), and conservation reserves.

In Ontario, species that are endangered, vulnerable, or threatened may be listed either provincially or nationally, or both. Protection is offered under the Endangered Species Act, the Fish and Wildlife Conservation Act, and the federal Migratory Birds Conservation Act, under which violators can be fined up to $100,000.

Provincially listed endangered species consist of species protected under the Endangered Species Act. Provincially listed threatened or vulnerable species consist of those species listed by the Ontario Ministry of Natural Resources. The ministry's Committee on the Status of Species at Risk in Ontario (COSSARO) evaluates candidates for listing and makes recommendations for placing species in the appropriate category.

# Environmental Protection

As Canada's most populated and industrialized province, Ontario faces stiff challenges in caring for the quality of its environment. Industries across the province pour 68 million kilograms of pollution each year into air, **water,** and landfill sites, making Ontario the second-biggest polluter in North America based on a comparison of industrial emissions in Canada and the United States.

The Ministry of Environment, the primary Ontario government agency charged with environmental protection and promoting conservation and stewardship of the province's resources, has seen its budget cut from $365 million in 1995 to $223 million in 1998–99. This reduction in spending forced a 36 percent reduction in staff, weakened sewage treatment programs, and cut back the testing of water and air for pollutants. Despite these hurdles, the ministry has forged ahead, aided by the Ontario Ministry of Natural Resources, the federal government, municipalities, environmental groups, industries, and health organizations, all of which play a role in pollution prevention.

The environment ministry focusses on finding solutions to the problems that present the greatest threat to human health and the environment. One of the most serious and best-documented threats is caused by the burning of fossil fuels such as oil, coal, and gas.

Ontario's Smog Plan, which calls for a 45 percent reduction in smog-causing emissions by 2015, reflects input from health organizations, environmental groups, representatives of the scientific and academic communities, government agencies, and industrial manufacturers and associations. All of these organizations were among the 44 signatories to the original Smog Plan Accord, signed in 1997, with several more partners added later. Drive Clean, a vehicle emissions testing program, is another important program for combatting the sources of smog. When fully implemented in 2001, it is expected to reduce smog-causing emissions from vehicles by as much as 22 percent.

The government is also working on further reductions in smog-causing pollutants, as well as in acid gases and the pollutants that cause climate change, through the strict environmental protection measures being introduced into Ontario's electricity market. The government is investing more than $6 million in environmental monitoring, analysis, and data collection mechanisms to better evaluate emerging environmental trends, track compliance with environmental laws, and assess the effectiveness of these actions.

To assist in meeting environmental protection and conservation goals, in 1998 the Ontario legislature approved Bill 82, An Act to Strengthen Environmental Protection and Enforcement. This aggressive act provides greater powers to deter and punish polluters who transgress the law and threaten the environment. It closes loopholes that for years have enabled polluters to violate the law and avoid millions of dollars worth of penalties. The environment ministry's Investigations and Enforcement Branch (IEB) is responsible for all aspects of environmental enforcement.

The most significant Ontario legislation to protect water quality is the Municipal/Industrial Strategy for Abatement (MISA) regulations, introduced in 1986 to control the quality of effluent from nine industrial sectors. The treatment and disposal of waste is controlled through regulations that require manifesting of hazardous waste and permit disposal of waste only in designated landfills.

Partnerships are vital in Ontario's efforts to protect the province's water quality and health. The environment ministry formed the Ontario Great Lakes Renewal Foundation in 1998 to explore new ways to generate significant investments in **Great Lakes** renewal, starting with a donation of $5 million to spur similar contributions from individuals and corporations. In 1999, environmental improvement projects were launched in the Bay of Quinte, Severn Sound, Lake Nipigon, and **Thunder Bay.**

As in other provinces, protection and conservation of Ontario's water is a challenge. In 1999, the province passed a regulation under the Ontario Water Resources Act that prohibits large-scale transfer or diversion of water out of three designated basins, the Great Lakes–St. Lawrence Basin, the Nelson Basin in the extreme west, and the Hudson Bay Basin.

The Ministry of Natural Resources (MNR) has responsibility for ensuring the protection and sustainable development of the province's natural resources. The mandate of the MNR includes ensuring the long-term health of natural resources by protecting and conserving valuable soil, **fish,** forest, and wildlife resources, and protecting human life, natural resources, and property from forest fires, floods, and erosion. It also works to protect natural areas and biological features of provincial significance such as **provincial parks,** wetlands, and areas of natural and scientific interest, including the Mer Bleu Bog in Ottawa and Stone Road Alvar on **Pelee Island**.

In a bid to conserve and protect Ontario's natural resources, all forest policies and associated management practices must conform to the Policy Framework for Sustainable Forests. This policy ensures Ontario's crown **forests** are managed in the broad public interest. Key legislation to protect forests includes the Crown Forest Sustainability Act, which regulates forest planning, licensing, and trust funds for reforestation. In 1999, the MNR was reviewing its land-use plans through the Lands for Life program. The program contains a number of objectives, including completion of a system of protected natural heritage areas representing the full range of the province's natural features and ecosystems.

Municipalities also share responsibility for protecting the environment. Control of noise pollution, recycling programs (including the Blue Box program, which was launched in Kitchener), stormwater control, and sewage treatment and disposal are some of the responsibilities carried out by cities, towns, and regions in the province.

A significant challenge is ensuring the viability of the Blue Box program and finding additional ways to reach Ontario's goal of diverting and re-using 50 percent of the waste sent for disposal. In 1999, the province's per capita waste diversion rate was about 35 percent.

Federal government legislation developed by departments such as Environment, Fisheries and Oceans, and Transportation help to protect the environment in Ontario. Examples include regulations that phase out ozone-depleting substances, require permission to import or export hazardous waste, control the transportation of dangerous goods, and reduce the sulphur content in fuels.

# Ethnicity

The largest proportion of Ontario residents have roots in the British Isles and other European countries. According to the 1996 census, the province's predominant ethnic origin is British: 2,250,700 or about 21 percent of Ontario residents have roots in England (926,655), Ireland (224,965), Scotland (290,760), and Wales (11,930). Another 772,275 people are of mixed British origin, such as English and Irish, and 24,115 people are British but their specific origin could not be classified.

Eighteen percent of Ontarians—or about 1,895,000 people—are of European descent, led by Italians, who number 482,830, accounting for more than half of all Canadians with Italian roots. About 301,630 people in the province are of French descent, followed by Germans at 234,585, Portuguese at 181,465, Dutch at 168,215, and Polish at 164,080. The largest groups of non-British and non-Europeans are Chinese, numbering 365,415, and East Indians at 242,250.

First Peoples total 69,385, of whom 65,480 are First Nations, 3,415 Métis, and 490 Inuit. Only 6,855 Ontario residents are of American descent. The rest of the province's residents claim a wide variety of ethnic origins, with some, such as Jamaicans, Lebanese, and Sri Lankans, numbering in the thousands, and others, such as Algerians, Cubans, and Moroccans, each totalling less than 1,000.

In all, Ontario is home to more than 160 cultural groups, including Portuguese, Indo-Iranian, Greek, Polish, Spanish, Dutch, Ukrainian, and Somali, most of whom have come to the province for economic reasons, to escape political persecution, or to join family members already living here.

(*See also* **Languages**; **Population**)

# Fall Colours

In most parts of the province, Ontario's scenery is at its most spectacular in September and October. The transition between summer and winter is extraordinary as the green leaves of deciduous trees such as oaks, maples, and sumacs turn to striking shades of gold, orange, burgundy, and red.

The process by which leaves change colour actually begins in the summer. Deciduous trees rely on sunlight for energy to manufacture the food they need. As the amount of daylight begins to shorten in July, the trees prepare for winter by reducing the moisture and nutrient supply that keeps their leaves green and storing it in more permanent parts of the plant. The green chlorophyll slowly breaks down and leaves begin to turn yellow as summer ends.

With autumn's cool nights and often clear sunny days, some trees also produce anthocyanin, a red chemical that mixes with the yellow of the leaves to create other colours. On the sugar maple, for example, red, orange, and yellow leaves can be found on a single tree.

Among the best places to see Ontario's fall colours is the Muskoka–Parry Sound region in central Ontario, where maples, oaks, aspen, and tamaracks grow beside evergreens such as pine, spruce, and balsam. The Kawartha Lakes–Haliburton area can also produce spectacular scenery at this time because it lies in a transition zone between the southern broadleaf and northern coniferous forests. The **Ottawa Valley,** with its rolling hills, lakes, and forests is renowned for dramatic, colour-filled vistas.

Even large cities such as **Toronto, Ottawa, Hamilton,** and **London** are at their most attractive in the fall. Tourist agencies provide cruises, airplane tours, and information on driving routes for people interested in enjoying the changing landscape at this time. The popular train ride through the **Agawa Canyon** north of Sault Ste. Marie attracts people from around the world in autumn to savour the scenery.

## Fall Fairs

From September to mid-October, every week includes festivities at fall fairs throughout Ontario. Some 150 such fairs in the province at this time commemorate the harvest season and offer an array of home-baked food, handmade crafts, parades, livestock and other competitions, and a range of midway rides.

Agricultural fairs have been a tradition in Ontario since 1792, when the first one was held in Niagara-on-the-Lake. A celebration of **agriculture,** the fairs provide an opportunity for people to learn about food production, animals, and farming techniques such as sheep shearing and goat milking. In addition to the fairs held in autumn, about another 80 take place during spring and summer. The Ontario Association of Agricultural Societies is the unifying body for all these fairs.

Fairs range from small events that may only last half a day to large ones such as the **Canadian National Exhibition** in **Toronto,** the Central Canada Exhibition in **Ottawa,** the Western Fair in **London,** and the **Royal Agricultural Winter Fair,** also in Toronto, which run for 10 days or more. The oldest continuously held fall fair is held in Williamstown in eastern Ontario, where it has been a fixture in that community since 1853.

A 1994 economic impact study done on the fairs indicated that Ontario agricultural societies, which rely heavily on volunteers to run their events, directly contribute more than $38 million annually to the **economy.**

# Fathom Five National Marine Park

Canada has more coastline than any other country in the world and shares responsibility for the world's greatest freshwater lake system. Aquatic and marine resources constitute a special part of Canada and contribute to the country's identity.

That is why Fathom Five National Marine Park was established in 1987. Located north of Tobermory on the Bruce Peninsula, it represents the Georgian Bay Marine Region. As the first of three national marine conservation areas established in Canada, it provides Parks Canada with an opportunity to inform the public about the unique qualities of such areas and the difference between these parks areas and terrestrial parks.

*Flowerpot Island is a unique limestone formation that is popular with visitors to Fathom Five National Marine Park.* (© 2000 Ontario Tourism)

Fathom Five is well known for its 19 islands and clean, clear **water** where 23 shipwrecks and geological formations, such as cliffs, caves, and overhangs, can be seen by scuba divers and from glass-bottom tour boats. During boat tours, passengers can view shipwrecks through special windows in the bottom of the vessels. The park's most notable island is Flowerpot Island, where visitors can see unique limestone formations known as flowerpots, explore caves, camp, picnic, swim, walk a loop trail, and view wildlife, ferns, and more than 20 species of orchids.

# Federal Penitentiaries

With 14 prisons, Ontario has more federal penitentiaries than any other province in Canada. Quebec has the second-largest number, with 12. In 1999, approximately 3,400 inmates were being housed in Ontario's federal prisons to serve sentences of two years or more under the auspices of Correctional Services Canada.

The largest concentration of federal "pens" in Ontario is in the **Kingston** area, which has 10 facilities. Those located inside the city are: Kingston Penitentiary (maximum security), built in 1835 and the oldest federal institution in Canada; the Prison for Women (maximum security), which is scheduled to close by 2001; Isabel McNeil House (minimum security); The Regional Treatment Centre (maximum security); Collins Bay Institution (medium security); and Frontenac Institution (minimum security). Joyceville Institution (medium security), Pittsburgh Institution (minimum security), Millhaven Institution (maximum security), and Bath Institution (medium security) are located outside Kingston.

Other federal prisons are Warkworth Institution northwest of Belleville (medium security), the largest federal correctional institution in Canada, housing some 600 inmates; Grand Valley Institution in Kitchener (medium/minimum security); and Fenbrook Institution (medium security) and Beaver Creek Institution (minimum security), both north of Gravenhurst.

*The Kingston Penitentiary as it appeared in the late 1800s. It was built in 1835 and is the oldest federal institution in Canada.* (Correctional Service of Canada Museum, Kingston, Ontario)

There are also 47 provincially run institutions, 42 for adults and 5 for youth. These facilities, which are operated by the Ontario Ministry of Correctional Services, are for adult offenders 18 years of age and over who are sentenced to terms of imprisonment of under two years and/or terms of probation up to three years, and 16- and 17-year-old offenders under the Young Offenders Act. On any given day, about 8,950 adults and young offenders in Ontario are in custody in provincial institutions, between one-third and half awaiting trial, and the remainder serving short sentences.

# Festivals

Flowers, fruit, theatre, **fall colours**, art, winter sports, ethnic cultures, wine, antiques, minerals, fireworks, music, comedy, food. At some point during the year, all are the themes of the more than 2,500 festivals, carnivals, and derbies celebrated in Ontario communities. Four of the province's largest festivals are described below.

The Canadian Tulip Festival in **Ottawa** grew out of a gift of 100,000 tulips, given to the city in 1945 in appreciation of the safe haven received by Holland's exiled royal family during World War II, and the role played by Canadian troops in liberating the Netherlands. It is now the largest tulip festival in the world as, every May, the colourful blooms of more than three million tulips light up the landscape in the National Capital Region.

The tulips were presented to the city by Princess Juliana (later Queen Juliana) of the Netherlands, who took refuge at Government House in Ottawa with her family during the war. She gave birth to a daughter in an Ottawa hospital room, which was made an official part of the Netherlands by an Act of Parliament. This ensured that her baby, Princess Margriet, would be an eligible heir to the Dutch throne.

The first festival was held in 1953 when the Ottawa Board of Trade, with the assistance of world-renowned photographer Malak, coordinated the event with the tulips' annual bloom. Each year its theme is tied to friendship. The festival attracts about 300,000 visitors annually.

Each summer, Toronto's Caribbean community and revellers from across Canada, the U.S., and countries around the world take part in Caribana, a two-week celebration of music, food, costumes, dance, arts, and crafts. The festival has its roots in the Caribbean Carnival and the traditions of Trinidad and

Tobago, and is now one of North America's largest cultural festivals.

Caribana began as a gift from the city's Caribbean community to honour Canada's Centennial in 1967. Since then, it has been an annual affair and an essential part of summer in **Toronto.** The cultures of Trinidad and Tobago, Guyana, St. Vincent, Brazil, Cuba, Jamaica, Grenada, Barbados, Guadeloupe, Martinique, Antigua, St. Lucia, Dominica, Haiti, Nevis, and St. Kitts are represented.

Caribana attracts hundreds of thousands of Torontonians and visitors. Some 4,000 people take part in the annual parade, a highlight of the festival that also includes a band competition. Another key element of Caribana is the King and Queen of the Bands program, featuring spectacular costumes. The festival has an estimated economic impact in Toronto of more than $200 million each year.

The annual **Kitchener-Waterloo** Oktoberfest, a Bavarian festival that attracts 700,000 participants, is second in size only to a similar festival in Munich, Germany. Kitchener-Waterloo's Oktoberfest has been an annual event since 1969. Several other Ontario cities also host smaller Oktoberfests.

The Kitchener-Waterloo Oktoberfest begins the Thursday before Thanksgiving with the Miss Oktoberfest Pageant, which attracts contestants from around North America. Canada's largest Thanksgiving parade is held on Friday. Throughout the nine-day festival there are more than 40 cultural and sporting events, arts and crafts displays, entertainment for children, and some 22 Festhallen—clubs and halls set up throughout the city to offer food, music, and of course, beer.

Oktoberfest began here to celebrate the region's strong German roots. Throughout its history, the festival has grown consistently, and today contributes more than $18 million to the local **economy.** It also raises money for local charities.

Every year more than 600,000 people descend on Ottawa for the city's annual Winterlude festival. For some it's a great excuse to visit the nation's capital, for others it's a chance to skate and slide, and for just about everyone, it's a way to escape the drudgery of Canada's winter.

Winterlude was founded in 1979 by the National Capital Commission as a means of celebrating Canada's unique northern climate and culture. And despite the occasional shortage of funds and a February thaw or two, the festival celebrated its 22nd anniversary in 2000.

During three consecutive weeks in February (with many special activities on weekends), visitors can skate through the heart of Ottawa on a 7.8-kilometre stretch of the Rideau Canal (*see* **Canals**), Canada's longest skating rink. The canal is also the site of bed races, horsedrawn sleigh rides, figure-skating shows, and snow-sculpting competitions.

A host of other events and attractions takes place at other sites in and around the nation's capital, including international ice- and snow-carving competitions and exhibits, a snow playground, an international cross-country ski event, fireworks, and live entertainment. Winterlude generates more than $40 million for the economy of the Ottawa-Hull area every winter.

Thousands of smaller festivals also take place in Ontario, including Canada's Ice Cream Festival in Woodstock; the Haliburton Winterfest; County Celtic Weekend in Perth; and the Minden Sled Dog Derby.

(*See also* **Fall Fairs**; **Shaw Festival**; **Stratford Festival**)

# Film Industry

Motion pictures have had a presence in Ontario since July 21, 1896, when what is believed by many experts to be the first public exhibition of films in Canada took place in a park in **Ottawa.** The showing of silent movies soon spread to other cities, and by the early 1900s theatres began to be built so that patrons could watch their favourite films in comfort. However, the majority of films that people watched were not Canadian, with most coming from the U.S. and others from Britain and France.

Although many Ontarians, such as **Toronto**-born Mary Pickford, would become important figures in the motion picture business of the early years, they generally moved south of the border to pursue their film careers there. Americans were responsible for making most of the films about Ontario and the rest of Canada in the early years of the 20th century. They also played key roles in two of the earliest film companies established in Ontario, the Conness Till Film Company of Toronto, which was incorporated in 1914, and the All-Red Feature Company of **Windsor,** which was formed the same year. Three years before, Ontario had established a Board of Censors to regulate movies.

The first "Hollywood of the North" was the small town of Trenton, east of Toronto, where studios were built in 1916. Several private films were shot in the town until the early 1920s when the Ontario government, which had established its Motion Picture Bureau in 1917, purchased the studios and continued to produce films there until 1934. With the establishment of the National Film Board in Ottawa in 1939, filmmaking in Ontario and Canada took on a different slant, with an emphasis on quality documentaries and animated shorts.

Throughout the 1950s and 1960s, Canadian filmmakers continued to produce movies, but the industry remained largely undeveloped as television grew rapidly. In 1963, however, the government created the Ontario Arts Council, which had a mandate to finance experimental films. In 1972, the provincial Ministry of Industry and Tourism set up a task force to study the Canadian film industry. The task force report concluded that there should be a quota set for theatres to show Canadian films, but little was done about it.

On the positive side, the Toronto Film Festival began in 1976 and drew movie enthusiasts and creators from abroad. Today, the festival is one of the largest and most important festivals in the world. In the meantime, however, the Ontario Censor Board continued to make headlines by banning such popular films as *Pretty Baby* and censoring parts of other films, such as *The Tin Drum*. The board's action created a public and professional backlash and eventually, in 1983 the Supreme Court of Ontario ruled that the board violated the Charter of Rights and Freedoms. The decision was upheld by the Ontario Court of Appeal.

Toronto and other parts of Ontario saw increased business from American filmmakers and others in the late 1970s after the federal government created a tax shelter plan. In the early 1980s, the film industry was contributing more than $40 million annually to the province. With few exceptions, however, many of the films were critically panned, but an industry of technicians and other behind-the-scenes workers did develop in the province.

The Ontario Film Development Corporation was established in 1986. As an agency of the government, it provides a range of programs and services to stimulate the growth of Ontario's film, television, and digital media industry. Growth in the industry throughout the 1990s has been tremendous. In 1999, film and television production in the province contributed more than $914 million to the Ontario economy, a 17.5 percent increase over the previous year. The increase was mainly due to productions from outside Canada, primarily the U.S. The province has a reputation for its highly skilled production and performing personnel.

The film industry in Ontario is centred around the Toronto area, which is also home to many of Canada's national television networks.

# First Nations Peoples

Archaeological evidence suggests that the first human beings arrived in Ontario about 11,000 years ago, during the end of the last ice age. Between 40,000 and 12,000 years ago, their ancestors had crossed from Siberia to Alaska over a then-existing land bridge on the Bering Sea and had then travelled further south into the North American continent. As the ice retreated, these people moved north through Ontario and established a hunting culture there.

By 5000 B.C., Native culture was divided into the Shield Archaic and the Laurentian Archaic, similar to the way in which northern and southern Ontario are divided today. Pottery was introduced about 1000 B.C. during what has been called the Woodland Period (*see* **Archaeology**). This culture would last until about A.D. 1600 when Europeans began to arrive in Ontario. During the Woodland Period, Native peoples in the north and south further developed their language, culture, and tribal system.

The two greatest linguistic and cultural groups who emerged between A.D. 1000 and 1600 were the Algonquians and the Iroquoians. The Algonquians lived mainly in the north, had a migratory lifestyle, and depended primarily on hunting and fishing. The Iroquoians, who lived in what is now southern Ontario, tended to be settled village dwellers and farmers who supplemented their daily diet by fishing and hunting.

The Algonquian-speaking tribes included the Algonquins, who lived along the Ottawa River and became involved in the French **fur trade**; the Nipissings, around the lake of the same name; the Ottawas, who were situated on **Manitoulin Island**; the Cree, who lived from **James Bay** to the prairies; and the Ojibways (also known as the Chippewas), who were located along the shores of Lake Superior. The social framework for most of these tribes was the band, a small local unit with specific territorial ranges. Chiefs were the most important members of the band, while the shamans acted as spiritual interpreters and guides.

The Iroquoians, who lived around the lower **Great Lakes** area, relied on such crops as corn, beans, squash, and pumpkins for their sustenance. A reliable and steady food source allowed them to form a stable way of life. They settled in villages, living in large wood-framed longhouses, which sometimes had fortifications around them to protect the residents from outside attack. The Iroquoians developed expertise in diplomacy and politics. Their social system often relied on tribal discussions, and chiefs, who were male, were usually chosen by women of the tribe. The women cultivated the crops while the men concentrated more on hunting and fishing.

Among the tribes making up the Iroquoian-speaking peoples were the Petun, Neutral, Huron, and the Five Nations Iroquois (or Hodenosaunee, as they called themselves), which consisted of the Mohawk, Oneidas, Onondagas, Cayugas, and Senecas. This confederacy of nations was originally centred in what is now New York State and allowed its members to hunt, farm, and live in peace among themselves. The Five Nations tribes were not equally represented on their council, but all decisions required consensus. When they began trading with the English, Dutch, and even at times the French, they were able to obtain guns and other supplies that allowed them to defeat rival tribes. Disputes and wars were common among the First Nations prior to the arrival of Europeans, and in many cases the conquered were absorbed by the victorious tribe.

First Nations peoples were crucial to the development of the North American fur trade, because they had explored large tracts of the wilderness. Their knowledge of the land and waterways, of how to survive harsh winters and grow crops made it easier for Europeans to move throughout Ontario and develop permanent settlements. They taught the newcomers how to travel by canoe and introduced them to snowshoes and toboggans, which enabled year-round exploration.

First Nations culture began to change as their dealings with the French and British increased. Although Native peoples had long made their own tools, pottery, and clothing, they began to trade for European tools and weapons, becoming more reliant on goods they could acquire than those they could make for themselves. They clashed with the Europeans on religious and social habits, leading to mistrust on both sides.

Europeans brought with them a range of diseases that First Nations tribes had never been exposed to: smallpox, scarlet fever, colds, influenza, and typhoid, among others. Thousands of First Nations people were killed by these diseases, particularly in the first half of the 17th century. In addition, the southern Iroquois tribes, who allied themselves with the British and Dutch, increased their conflicts with the Hurons to the north, who had favoured the French. In 1648, the Iroquois waged war against the Hurons and wiped out almost all of their villages within a year.

In the early 1700s, a southern tribe known as the Tuscarora moved north from South Carolina and, in the 1720s, they were admitted to the Iroquois confederacy as the sixth nation. Although the Iroquois began to adopt a more neutral role in the conflicts between French and English, that changed when the American Revolution broke out in 1775. Most of the Six Nations wished to remain neutral but decided that each tribe could decide its own position. The Mohawks, led by Joseph Brant, sided with the British, and attacks by Americans on Onondaga, Cayuga, and Seneca villages led those nations to form a stronger alliance with Britain as well.

When the war ended in 1783, Brant made an agreement with the British to receive land in southwestern Ontario where some of his people could relocate. The British acquired land along the Grand River near present-day Brantford for the Six Nations to live, and, while the reserve is still there today and plays a prominent role in First Nations life, it is much smaller than the area originally promised. First Nations peoples also played key roles in defending Canada in the **War of 1812** with the hope of receiving their own homeland in return, but that promise was never realized.

The British and French regulated the fur trade that First Nations tribes had come to rely on, setting the stage for a change in Native culture and society that would reverberate to the present. Though promised a variety of land tracts over the decades, especially in gratitude of the help they provided in wartime, in many cases treaties and proclamations left First Nations with steadily decreasing territory in Ontario and across Canada.

Throughout the 19th century, more European settlers arrived in Ontario and First Nations tribes continued to live on ever shrinking lands. Administrators of the new government believed that Native peoples should become self-sufficient citizens in the province, but within the framework of the European way of life. By the late 1820s, the view of First Nations peoples as allies had shifted toward developing a paternal reserve policy that would help "civilize" them. Several model villages were established in southern Ontario as a way of encouraging First Nations tribes, particularly the Algonquians—who were primarily hunters—to become increasingly reliant on agriculture as well as to convert to Christianity. Some villages succeeded while others did not.

Residential schools for Native peoples were introduced in Ontario as early as the 1840s. The schools removed children from their families and tried to forcefully wean them away from the habits, language, and culture of their ancestors. Although government officials may have believed this was the best way to educate Native children, those who experienced the schools have revealed details of sexual abuse and torture by those in charge. Generations of First Nations families were harmed by this system, and increased opposition to having children separated for long periods from their parents eventually led governments to close these schools and rethink their policies in the mid-1970s.

In 1850, the legislature approved a land act that attempted to protect Native peoples in Ontario: An Act for the Protection of the Indians of Upper Canada from Imposition, and the Property Occupied and Enjoyed by Them from Trespass and Injury. The act, among other things, made it an offence for private individuals to make land deals with Native peoples and provided for damages from such public works as railroad construction. The reality, however, was that European settlers' interests usually took precedence over those of the First Nations. Increasingly lands were sold off by First Nations, often under intense pressure, and in some cases they weren't even consulted when land ownership transfer was discussed between various governments. The result was that First Nations peoples were already marginalized in Ontario society by the time of Confederation in 1867.

Government continued to control the way that lands would be used by the First Nations and imposed a political system on the governance of the various bands. In 1895, for example, the federal government made elections mandatory and set the terms of office for the 42 Native bands in Ontario. The government also controlled which First Nations people were allowed to vote in general elections, and some restrictions stayed on the books past the midpoint of the 20th century.

Throughout the 20th century there has been a steady stream of court cases and land claims involving Native groups in Ontario, with varying results. There have also been continuing problems with discrimination, a relative lack of job opportunities, and a need for better educational programs. Despite decades of oppression, however, Ontario's First Nations have survived and in recent decades have experienced a revival of interest in their traditions, spirituality, and culture.

First Nations art, which had always been a vital part of the lives of both Algonquian and Iroquoian peoples, enjoyed something of a resurgence beginning in the 1960s and '70s. Led by such artists as Norval Morisseau, masks, paintings, pottery, stone carvings, and other art forms became an important element of the province's artistic landscape. Writing, theatre, music, dance, and

*Traditional works made by First Nations people.* (© 2000 Ontario Tourism)

traditional storytelling are other creative outlets that have been increasingly explored by many of Ontario's First Nations artists.

In the area of commerce, many successful businesses have been established on the province's reserves, including some lucrative **casinos,** and in the cities and towns where many Native people live today.

# Fish

Fish are an abundant and valuable resource in Ontario, providing a source of income for sport and commercial anglers. There are 124 native species in the province, representing 26 families of fish. Another 37 species have been introduced from outside the province, only 14 of which are now reproducing naturally, including rainbow trout, brown trout, chinook salmon, and coho salmon. Some species arrived by accident, including the sea lamprey, ruffe, and round goby, the latter two in ships' ballast water from Europe.

More than 1.6 million anglers fish Ontario's waters—the highest number of any province in Canada—and every year they pull more than 120 million fish out of the province's 400,000 lakes, rivers, and streams. Of those, 39 million are kept and, presumably, end up as tasty meals, or prized trophies. Sport fishing contributes more than $3 billion annually to the Ontario **economy** and supports thousands of jobs, largely due to the province's wide variety of places to catch fish—from clear, cold lakes of only a few hectares, to rushing streams, frothing rivers, and of course, the **Great Lakes.**

On the commercial side, Ontario's fisheries support more than 450 fishing operations and 4,000 direct jobs. Every year more than 17 million kilograms of fish are commercially harvested, with a landed value of between $42 million and $50 million. The value of processed commercial fish exports is $190 million, of which 85 percent is exported, 75 percent going to the United States and 25 percent to Japan and Europe. The commercial fishery operates year round if lakes remain free of ice during the winter months. In northern locations where ice cover is sufficient, a large commercial ice fishery supplies fresh fish to various markets.

The most popular sport fish in Ontario are walleye (eight million are caught each year), smallmouth bass, lake trout, brook trout, northern pike, rainbow trout (also known as steelhead), coho and chinook salmon, brown trout, large-mouth bass, muskellunge, yellow perch, bluegill (also known as sunfish), and black crappie. Among the largest fish ever caught in the province are a 76.4-kilogram lake sturgeon, a 29.5-kilogram muskellunge, and a 20.6-kilogram chinook salmon.

Walleye are found throughout the Great Lakes and Ontario's inland lakes. Lake trout live throughout the province, with the exception of extreme southern districts, and are very popular among resident anglers in the Algoma and Algonquin areas. Brook trout are widespread in the province's lakes and streams but most abundant in the Algonquin, Algoma, and Nipigon regions. Smallmouth bass live throughout the Great Lakes and inland waters of south-central and northern Ontario. Bluegill are found throughout southern Ontario and are particularly abundant in the Kawartha and Rideau lakes, while brown trout are found in the Great Lakes and their tributaries. Coho and chinook salmon live in the Great Lakes, with higher numbers in western Lake Ontario, Lake Huron, and Lake Superior.

Largemouth bass are found throughout southern Ontario, especially in the Kawartha lakes and Rideau lakes. Prime areas for muskellunge are **Georgian Bay** and the North Channel, Lake Nipissing, French River, Lake of the Woods, Eagle Lake, and the Ottawa River. Northern pike are widespread throughout the province. Rainbow trout live in the rivers and along the shoreline of Lake Superior, Georgian Bay between Owen Sound and Port Severn, Lake Huron, and Lake Ontario. Yellow perch are most populous in Lake Erie, Lake Simcoe, the **St. Lawrence River,** Lake St. Clair, and Georgian Bay. Black crappie are found in southern Ontario and extreme northwestern Ontario, Lake Simcoe, Rice Lake, the Rideau lakes, southeastern Georgian Bay, and Lake of the Woods.

Most of the commercial fish value on Lake Erie is provided by yellow perch, walleye, and smelt. On lakes Huron, Ontario, Superior, Nipigon, and Lake of the Woods, the main commercial species are lake whitefish, chub, lake trout, crappie, eel, and walleye.

Fishing licences are required by all those between 18 and 64 years of age, with the exception of disabled residents of Ontario. Fishing season opening and closing dates vary depending on the species and the area, as a way of protecting fish at vulnerable times of the year, such as spawning season.

In Ontario and elsewhere, three species of fish are extinct: the deepwater cisco, longjaw cisco, and blue pike. The aurora trout is considered to be endangered, while the bigmouth buffalo has been classed as vulnerable.

To protect the province's fish, the Ontario and federal governments have enacted a variety of measures designed to ward off harmful **water** and air pollution. An important Ontario Ministry of Environment program is the Municipal/Industrial Strategy for Abatement (MISA) regulations, which aim to control the quality of effluent from nine industrial sectors. Water quality is also monitored by the Ontario Great Lakes Renewal Foundation, set up by the environment ministry in 1998. In addition, part of the Ministry of Natural Resources' mandate is to protect and conserve valuable fish resources.

(*See also* **Endangered and Extinct Species**; **Environmental Protection**)

# Forest Industry

More than three-quarters of Ontario's land surface—approximately 79 million hectares—is covered by **forests**. That accounts for 17 percent of Canada's and 1 percent of the world's forests.

These forested areas support the forest products industry, which plays an important role in Ontario's **economy,** generating approximately 180,000 direct and indirect jobs. It also provides the lifeblood of many communities, particularly in **northern Ontario,** where more than 40 cities and towns are highly dependent on forest-based employment. Ontario's forest products industry generates sales of about $14 billion annually, including exports valued at more than $7 billion. Paper, paperboard, and newsprint account for 55 percent of all exports, wood pulp accounts for 12 percent, and softwood lumber makes up 11 percent. Ninety-five percent of all exports are used in the United States.

Newsprint, fine papers, and pulp are produced from the province's slow-growing northern conifers—spruce, pine, and fir—and are among the strongest made anywhere. Ontario also produces various hardwood lumbers and veneers, which are used to make floors, furniture, and many other products. The province's bird's-eye maple is prized worldwide for its beautiful grain.

About 91 percent of the forest in Ontario is on Crown land, owned by the public and held in trust by the provincial government. This land is the source of about 85 percent of the timber used by the forest products industry. Of the remainder, 6.6 million hectares are privately owned, and the federal government owns 340,000 hectares. Approximately 200,000 hectares of forest are harvested annually in Ontario, about one-quarter of one percent of the province's total forest area. In an effort to properly manage the forests and ensure an ongoing supply of timber, more than 100 million seedlings are planted every year and millions more seedlings regenerate naturally.

Under Ontario's Crown Forest Sustainability Act, companies are required to manage for the long-term health of the resource. Among other requirements, forest practices must maintain ecological processes, emulate natural disturbances and natural patterns of vegetation, and minimize effects on soil, **water**, **fish** and wildlife habitat, as well as recreation and heritage values. Companies are also required to fully regenerate all harvested areas. Members of the Ontario Forest Industries Association must comply with its Guiding Principles and Code of Forest Practices. The code was created in 1992 by a task force that included industry as well as representatives from the academic, environmental, labour, and Native communities, and updated in 1998. The code reflects different aspects of sustainable forest management, including policy and planning, regeneration and tending, **environmental protection**, and accountability to the public.

Although the forest products industry is essentially healthy, the sector has and continues to face serious challenges. These include the Asian market collapse, which reduced exports and resulted in excess capacity, falling commodity prices, and reductions in the amount of land available for harvest.

# Forests

Ontario is divided into four forest regions: the boreal, boreal-barrens, Great Lakes–St. Lawrence, and deciduous forest zones. The largest is the boreal forest, which covers most of northern Ontario, extending as far south as Wawa, Gogama, and Kirkland Lake. It contains both coniferous and deciduous trees, including tamarack, balsam, black spruce, fir, jack pine, white birch, and poplar. At its northern reaches, the boreal forest becomes subarctic tundra and is described as the boreal-barrens forest. Together, these forests account for 76 percent of Ontario's woodland and support most of its forest products industry.

South of the boreal forest is the Great Lakes–St. Lawrence forest, covering the central part of Ontario. Here, coniferous trees, such as eastern white pine, red pine, eastern hemlock, and white cedar, mix with deciduous broad-leaved species, such as yellow birch, sugar and red maple, basswood, and red oak. Some species common to the boreal forest, including black spruce, jack pine, and white birch, are also found in this area.

Ontario's deciduous forest is mainly in the southwestern part of the province but also encompasses a finger extending from **Toronto** to the Belleville area and about 100 kilometres north of Lake Ontario. It is the northern extension of the large deciduous forest of the northeastern United States. Many trees in this region are at the northern limit of their range, including black walnut, sycamore, and white oak.

A significant area of the deciduous forest is the **Carolinian Zone,** a narrow band that extends along an area north of Lake Erie to western Lake Ontario. This relatively small area contains more types of flora and fauna than anywhere else in Canada, including rare cucumber trees and black gum trees.

# Fort Henry

When the United States declared war on Great Britain in June of 1812, **Kingston** was strategically important and needed the protection of a fort. As a result, the original Fort Henry was built in 1813 atop Point Henry to guard the naval dockyard at Point Frederick, the town of Kingston, and the outlet to the **St. Lawrence River.**

The fort was approximately 30 metres wide by 36 metres long, and consisted of earth and rubble walls faced with stone, surrounded by a dry ditch

*Members of the Fort Henry Guard demonstrate precision drill manoeuvres. (© 2000 Ontario Tourism)*

9 metres wide and 4.5 metres deep. By 1815, after the war had ended, two stone blockhouses had been erected within the fort, along with stone barracks for the officers and other ranks. The fort was further protected by 18 guns of various sizes.

The first Fort Henry was torn down and replaced between 1832 and 1837 to strengthen the defence against the end of the Rideau Canal—which had been completed in 1832—most vulnerable to attack by the Americans. As the principal fortress of Upper Canada, it was garrisoned by the British Army until 1870 when Queen Victoria's troops were pulled out of Canada. For the next two decades, the fort was used as the residence of units of the Canadian militia, before being abandoned as a defensive structure.

During World War I, the fort was superficially repaired and used as an internment camp for political prisoners. Following the war, it sat empty and fell into a state of disrepair. Between 1936 and 1938, Fort Henry was restored as the result of a joint federal-provincial makework project, which cost more than $1 million. Officially opened on August 1, 1938 by Prime Minister MacKenzie King, the fort was established as a museum and historic site "in the name of all the British Soldiers who served there."

During World War II, Fort Henry became Camp #31, a prisoner-of-war camp for enemy merchant seamen, soldiers, sailors, and airmen. Following the war, the fort was re-opened in 1948 as a tourist attraction. Since then, millions of visitors have passed through its gates to view the internationally famous Fort

Henry Guard, which has manned the fort since 1948. Today, Fort Henry continues its role as a museum and historic site to residents of Kingston and visitors from around the world. Every summer, members of the Guard demonstrate precision drill manoeuvres.

# Fort York

What is now known as "Historic Fort York" was founded in 1793 by then Lieutenant-Governor John Graves Simcoe. Simcoe wanted a fort built overlooking **Toronto** harbour to better defend the colony of Upper Canada from possible American invasion. The fort was generally referred to as "the Garrison" in its early years, and in its first year consisted of two log barracks buildings. The following year another 28 log buildings were erected on the site.

Fort York did not develop as grandly as Simcoe had hoped, partly because British concerns for defence were focussed more at **Kingston,** further east along Lake Ontario. The harbour in York (now Toronto) did not have as much strategic value to Upper Canada in the 1790s. In fact, the fort was not granted official British army post status until 1798.

By the start of the 19th century, some of the original log buildings in the fort had rotted, while others had been torn down. Other structures, including a new blockhouse, had been erected. The construction of the fort and the military presence it created in the area played a significant role in the development of the town of York as a need was created for services and trades.

Fort York finally came into prominence with the advent of the **War of 1812,** and officials ordered a strengthening of its fortifications. In the spring of 1813, however, American troops sailed across Lake Ontario to York and met little resistance before British troops withdrew. The Americans occupied the fort for a few days, burned some of the buildings within its walls, then left because Fort York was of little military value to them. The Americans attacked the fort again in July 1813, met no resistance, and quickly left. The British then began reconstructing the fort in earnest, and when American ships returned again in 1814, its defences held.

The war ended in December 1814, but construction at Fort York continued out of concern that Americans might attack Upper Canada in the future. In the ensuing years of peace, approximately 200 to 300 troops were garrisoned at the fort. Through the 1820s and 1830s, the fort was often the centre of Toronto's cultural life, but the buildings began to deteriorate. In 1840, officials in Upper Canada decided to build a new fort to the west of Fort York. The "Old Fort" became an auxiliary headquarters, and after the 1870s when most British troops had withdrawn from Canada and Canadian troops took over, Fort York served as married quarters, storage facilities, and a training ground.

Historical markers were put up at Fort York as early as 1899, and school trips by students have been commonplace since the 1890s. In 1893, the Canadian Pacific Railroad wanted to tear the fort down so that tracks could be laid nearby, but military officials refused. The fight to preserve the fort as a historical site began in the early 1900s, and by 1909 city council had been convinced not to demolish any War of 1812 buildings housed there. Today the fort contains Canada's largest collection of War of 1812 buildings. Part of the fort was destroyed in 1916 for a streetcar line, however, and all post-1816 structures were torn down before Fort York became a museum in 1934.

More restorations took place after World War II, and the fort came under an attack of a different kind in the late 1950s when city officials wanted to move it to another site so that the Gardiner Expressway could be constructed along Toronto's waterfront. A public campaign to preserve Fort York was successful, and the expressway was built further to the south. In 1985, the site was designated as the Fort York Heritage Conservation District, and in 1987 was declared to be of national significance by the Historic Sites and Monuments Board of Canada.

Historic Fort York sits at the foot of Bathurst Street in Toronto. With the reclamation of land near Lake Ontario that has taken place over the years, it no longer sits on the harbour but is now about 100 metres to the north. Some 90,000 people visit the fort annually.

# Francophone Ontarians

It's not surprising in a province that used to be part of the colony of New France that the presence of French-speaking people in Ontario dates back more than 350 years. French Jesuit missionaries established a village at **Ste.-Marie-among-the-Hurons** in 1639 on the Wye River in an attempt to convert the **First Nations peoples** there to Christianity.

Although that settlement was short-lived, and many Hurons died either of disease brought by the Europeans or by attacks from neighbouring Iroquois, the

French explored much of what is Ontario today and established a range of set-tlements and forts. Some of the earliest settlements were built in and around what is now **Windsor.** French explorers, known as *coureurs de bois,* with the help of First Nations guides, travelled many of Ontario's rivers and developed the **fur trade,** which was critical to the development of the province. The French pushed westward through Ontario and established a presence on the north shore of Lake Superior.

In Europe and North America, the French and English skirmished and waged war several times throughout the 18th century, but with the end of the Seven Years War in 1763, the British gained control over most of the new land. As thousands of **United Empire Loyalists** moved into Upper Canada (which would become Ontario) in the 19th century, the province took on an even more British tone. By the time Upper and Lower Canada were united as the Province of Canada in 1841, it was clear that francophones were a minority in Ontario. However, a separate school system for Catholics, which accommodated many French-speaking families, was guaranteed in 1867 at the time of Confederation.

After 1850, francophones began immigrating to regions around Ottawa, eastern Ontario, and Essex and Kent counties. By the end of the 19th century and into the 20th century, they had also established settlements in **northern Ontario** around Timiskaming, Cochrane, and Hearst.

By the 1890s, there was some opposition by politicians and the English majority about the use of French in public schools, but Ontario premier Oliver Mowat believed that francophones should have that right. Many governments that followed did not share this belief and made it clear that English was to be the language of instruction, with few exceptions, throughout the province.

In 1912, a regulation was passed that French-language instruction should not continue beyond the third year of elementary school, and for more than a decade afterward governments and school jurisdictions wrestled with the issue. By 1927, Franco-Ontarians had won the right to French-language elementary schools in areas where numbers warranted, but it wasn't until the provincial gov-ernment passed amendments to the Education Act in 1968 that these schools were officially recognized. A year later, the first French-language public sec-ondary school opened in Ottawa.

Through the 1970s, '80s, and '90s, the government introduced a number of policies and services to benefit francophone Ontarians in the areas of education, justice, municipal government, and public service.

Today, there are 12 French-language school boards with some 100,000 students studying in French. There are also four French-language post-secondary institutions: Collège de technologie agricole et alimentaire d'Alfred, La Cité collégiale, Collège Boréal, and Collège des Grand Lacs. Other universities and colleges offer programs or courses taught entirely or partially in French.

In the second half of the 20th century, Ontario's francophone community has been increased by French-speaking peoples from Europe, Asia, Africa, and the West Indies. There are approximately 542,000 francophone Ontarians, which represents about 5 percent of the province's **population** and is Canada's largest French-speaking population outside Quebec.

Francophone Ontarians play an important role in the province's economy. They own more than 8,000 Ontario businesses, companies, and corporations, as well as 140 co-operatives, including 66 *caisses populaires* (similar to credit unions) with assets that exceed $1 billion.

The long presence of francophones has also enriched Ontario's cultural life. There are some 20 art galleries, 30 cultural centres, six professional theatre companies, five publishing houses, several magazines and newspapers, and many festivals directed at Franco-Ontarians.

# Fur Trade

The new fashion of beaver hats that swept Europe in the 17th century provided the stimulus for the fur trade in Canada. The fur trade would be the dominant economic force in what is now Ontario from the 1650s until the early 1800s. The demand for beaver pelts led to the establishment of such economic enterprises as the Hudson's Bay Company and North West Company, and the creation of trading posts throughout the region. **First Nations peoples** played a key role in the development of the fur trade, not only by selling furs to the Europeans, but also by showing them the best routes and teaching them skills that would allow the newcomers to thrive in the harsh and often difficult land.

Because of the fur trade, European explorers learned much about the province's geography, its waterways, and terrain. In the initial years of the trade, the Ottawa and French rivers were the main transportation routes, but by the late 17th century more northerly outposts such as lakes Huron and Superior became increasingly important.

The French traders, or *coureurs de bois,* who canoed and portaged through

*Fur traders pose in 1896 in a freight canoe at the Hudson's Bay Company trading post at Bear Island on Lake Temagami.* (G.M. Kelley, Public Archives PA-123355)

present-day Ontario and Michigan explored the interior of North America and brought back furs for the European market. The French-controlled fur trade was strongly bureaucratic in the early days, with strict regulations on its commerce. Dissatisfaction with the bureaucracy ultimately led to the creation of the English-backed Hudson's Bay Company in 1670. The trading posts established by the Hudson's Bay Company on rivers flowing into Hudson Bay and **James Bay** pushed the trade even further northward. The French also tried to establish a presence in the area, but eventually acknowledged the English claim with the Treaty of Utrecht in 1713.

Members of the Five Nations Iroquois became heavily involved in the fur trade, initially sending their furs to Europeans on the Hudson River in New York. Forts were established in the southern part of the province to further the trade by both English and French, although eventually the Five Nations tribes allied themselves with English fur traders.

An estimated 200 Europeans had been involved in the fur trade at the end of the 17th century, but by the 1750s that number had increased to about 1,000. In the 18th century, the fur trade expanded westward, and the **War of 1812** marked the beginning of the end for the enterprise in Ontario. In 1821, the

North West Company became part of the Hudson's Bay Company, and the centre of the trade moved away from the **Great Lakes** region to Manitoba. By this time the fur trade was only a minor economic pursuit in Ontario.

As more settlers moved into the province and began clearing land for settlements, the fur trade gradually disappeared. New pursuits, such as the timber trade, particularly in the **Ottawa Valley,** and more importantly, **agriculture,** became the new economic engines for Ontario in the 1800s. However, it had played a key role in allowing Great Britain to establish sovereignty over the northern portion of North America.

## Georgian Bay

Known to many people as "the sixth Great Lake," Georgian Bay has been and remains an important waterway in Ontario. Almost completely separated from Lake Huron by **Manitoulin Island** and the Bruce Peninsula, Georgian Bay is nearly as large as Lake Ontario and is home to thousands of small islands. The west shore of the bay consists of limestone that is part of the **Niagara Escarpment,** while the northeastern shore is an irregular coastline formed from the rock of the **Canadian Shield,** and the southern end of the bay is home to several sandy beaches.

Three of the rivers that flow into Georgian Bay—the Severn, the French, and the Nottawasaga—have played key roles in the history of the province. The French was an important waterway during the early days of the **fur trade,** the Severn had long been a vital transportation link for **First Nations peoples,** and the Nottawasaga played a prominent role in the **War of 1812** and during the settlement of the area that followed.

William Fitzwilliam Owen, a royal navy captain who first charted the Great

Lakes in 1815, called the bay Lake Manitoulin. When it was later determined to be an appendage of Lake Huron it was renamed Georgian Bay after King George IV.

Georgian Bay was an important body of **water** to the Hurons for centuries. With the arrival of French fur traders in the 17th and 18th centuries, Georgian Bay became an important route for westward and northern expansion by Europeans. By the mid-1800s, several small communities had developed along the southwestern shore of Georgian Bay. A railway was built from **Toronto** in the 1850s, and such towns as Owen Sound and Collingwood began to grow.

Despite its often rough waters, Georgian Bay possesses some excellent natural harbours, which encouraged settlement. Towns, helped by such industries as shipbuilding, fishing, and sawmills, began to spring up and further the area's prosperity. As these industries became less important in the 20th century, the **economy** suffered some setbacks. The natural beauty of Georgian Bay, however, has made it a haven for tourists for more than a century. Cottages have sprung up along the shores of the bay and its scenery was captured by the artists who formed the **Group of Seven.** Today, Georgian Bay remains a popular spot for visitors who enjoy its beaches, boating, cottages, and scenic attractions.

# Georgian Bay Islands National Park

Because **Georgian Bay** has long been such a popular spot for tourists, many wealthy people had bought islands in the bay as sites for private cottages. By the 1920s, few islands were left and local residents approached the federal government about making Beausoleil Island, the largest island available in the Thirty Thousand Islands area of the bay, a national park.

In 1929, the government announced that it was setting aside Beausoleil and 28 other islands. Today, the park contains 59 islands, but the total area is only 14 square kilometres. The park is home to a variety of wild **mammals, birds,** and about 35 types of **reptiles** and **amphibians,** more than anywhere else in Canada. Among the species found here are the eastern massasauga rattlesnake, the only snake in Ontario with poisonous venom, the eastern hognose snake, the blue-spotted salamander, the five-lined skink, and the yellow spotted turtle. The landscape in the park is varied, with glacier rock to the north, forests that cover more than 40 percent of Beausoleil Island, beaches, and a variety of wetlands.

Beausoleil Island was used by **First Nations peoples** for hundreds of years, and in 1836 it was set aside as an Ojibwa Reserve. For 20 years, the 200 members of the Ojibwa band fished and trapped, selling furs and timber, while enjoying life on an island that was somewhat removed from European culture. However, the soil was not ideal for farming and, after several crop failures and the government's encouragement to leave, the Ojibwa decided to move their reserve to nearby Christian Island in 1856.

In the years since the departure of the Ojibwa and the establishment of a national park, homesteaders squatted on Beausoleil and eked out a living fishing, trapping, quarrying gravel, and cutting timber for railway ties and ships. By the time the park was created, only three families were living on the island.

Georgian Bay Islands National Park has evolved over its 70-year history. In its earliest days, supplies were taken to the park by rowboat from Penetanguishene. People using the park were allowed to cut firewood and hunt such animals as wolves and porcupines. There was also extensive spraying of **mosquitoes** and weeds. Today, a more natural approach has been adopted, and none of those activities is allowed.

The park is open throughout the year, although full service is only available from mid-May to September. Visitors can reach the park by water taxi from Honey Harbour and once in the park can take guided walks, cross-country ski, camp, hike, and enjoy a range of water-based recreation, including canoeing, kayaking, and sailing.

# Golden Horseshoe

The name of the Golden Horseshoe is given to the prosperous and largely urban area that runs from approximately Oshawa to St. Catharines and **Niagara Falls,** around the western shore of Lake Ontario.

This is the most densely populated portion of Ontario and Canada, with 20 percent of the nation's population living here. It includes such large cities as **Toronto** and **Hamilton.** The Golden Horseshoe is home to a high proportion of **manufacturing** firms, financial organizations, and post-secondary institutions, as well as many national and international industries and other businesses. The area also contains unusual landforms, including the **Niagara Escarpment,** which runs along its southern and western sides, and the Oak Ridges Moraine, a series of rolling hills of gravel to the north of Toronto.

The term "Golden Horseshoe" to describe the area was apparently first coined in January 1954 by Herbert Rogge, president of Westinghouse, in a speech to the Hamilton Chamber of Commerce. However, the region has been an important focal point of Ontario from the 1750s onward. Much of the early European settlement of the province occurred here, and it saw several battles during the **War of 1812.**

Because it contained rich farmland and fine natural harbours, the region blossomed throughout the 19th and 20th centuries. In the mid-19th century, flour mills, breweries, and shipyards were among the leading industries in the Golden Horseshoe, but as the population grew and transportation links improved, factories that produced steel, textiles, and farm machinery began to gain prominence.

In the 20th century, the rise of the automobile ushered in new growth around the Golden Horseshoe. Automobile plants in Oakville and Oshawa and steel centres in Hamilton thrived as cars became increasingly popular in Ontario. New roads and **highways** were built in the area, notably Queen Elizabeth Way, which opened in 1939 as the first expressway in Canada and ran from St. Catharines to Toronto. After World War II, **Highway 401** was built on the northern side of the horseshoe to provide a bypass of Toronto.

Cars and highways led to a proliferation of suburbs in the Golden Horseshoe. The additional development of industrial parks and shopping malls created increased congestion and pollution in the region and a decline in prime farmland and natural areas. The Golden Horseshoe keeps growing at a fast rate, and new housing continues to proliferate, particularly in the areas just north, east, and west of Toronto.

# Great Lakes

Forming much of the southern border of Ontario, the Great Lakes are the largest body of fresh **water** in the world, with a total area of about 246,050 square kilometres. Lakes Ontario, Erie, Huron, Superior, and Michigan flank forests, farms, and some of North America's largest cities and have played a critical role in the development of the province and North America as a whole. Of the five Great Lakes, only Lake Michigan does not touch some part of Ontario, lying as it does completely within the confines of the U.S.

It has been estimated that the Great Lakes hold enough water to cover all the land in Canada to a depth of three metres, and that they drain an area almost as large as France and Great Britain combined. The lakes flow from a height of 183 metres above sea level at Lake Superior into the **St. Lawrence River** at 6 metres above sea level, and finally out to the Atlantic Ocean. Lake Superior is the largest of the Great Lakes with an area of 82,400 square kilometres, followed in size by Huron, Michigan, Erie, and Ontario. A series of locks at Sault Ste. Marie, across the Niagara Peninsula and along the St. Lawrence connect all five lakes and allow ocean-going vessels to travel as far inland as Duluth, Minnesota, at the western edge of Lake Superior.

The Great Lakes are the result of the Laurentide ice sheet, the last of the many glaciations that eventually covered about half the North American continent approximately 18,000 years ago. The ice sheet retreated and advanced depending on changes in climate, moving earth and rock and moulding the landscape of Ontario. As the glacier began to thaw and retreat for the final time more than 10,000 years ago, it created a variety of landforms, such as **drumlins and moraines.** The Great Lakes were formed from the meltwaters left by the glacier's retreat over thousands of years, as water filled the hollows the ice sheet had carved from the land.

When the Europeans first saw the Great Lakes, the population along their shores was estimated to be more than 100,000. Today, some 35 million people live near the lakes on both sides of the Canada–U.S. border. **First Nations peoples** had been living near the Great Lakes for thousands of years before the French explorers arrived in the 17th century. The French initially believed the lakes might provide a passage to the Orient and its untold wealth, but they soon learned there were riches of a different kind, particularly furs, in this new land. French explorer René-Robert Cavelier, the Sieur de La Salle, was searching for a new passage to China and believed it was important for the French to seize control of the Great Lakes by building a series of forts along their shores to oversee what would be their vast empire in North America. He failed to achieve his goals, but explored most of the Great Lakes area and later founded the new French province of Louisiana in the United States. Despite the success of voyageurs who explored the Great Lakes and the rivers that flowed into them during the birth of the **fur trade,** it was the British and the Americans who would eventually battle over control of this area.

During the **War of 1812,** the Great Lakes saw several clashes because control of the waterways was crucial to both sides. No clear winner emerged from the war and with the Treaty of Ghent, which officially ended the hostilities in 1814, the boundaries between the U.S. and Upper Canada began to take shape through the Great Lakes. Once the boundaries were established, more people settled along the lakes' shores, transforming the way both Canada and the U.S. would develop. Industries, cities, towns, temporary settlements, and recreational facilities sprang up along the Great Lakes throughout the 19th and 20th centuries.

The ships that have sailed on the Great Lakes have played a vital role in the growth and prosperity of North America. However, powerful storms on the lakes have proven dangerous to professional sailors and recreational boaters alike. The most deadly storm, in November 1913, destroyed 19 ships, damaged 52 others, and caused the deaths of 248 sailors.

It's estimated that more than 10,000 vessels have been destroyed in the lakes, and that close to $800 million worth of salvageable wrecks lie below the surface. Among the most famous wrecks are the *Carl D. Bradley,* which sank during a storm on Lake Michigan in 1958 and killed 32 crew members, and the *Edmund Fitzgerald,* which sank in Lake Superior in 1975, killing the entire crew of 29.

Increased settlement and industrial growth along the Great Lakes' shores has also led to more pollution. Steel mills in **Hamilton,** Sarnia's **Chemical Valley,** the highly industrial corridor of **Windsor**-Detroit, and the high population and number of manufacturers in the **Toronto** area have all put strains on the Great Lakes waterway. According to a 1964 report from the Ontario Water Resources Commission, about 220 tonnes of chemicals were being added daily into Hamilton Bay on Lake Ontario alone. Sewage, industrial waste, and runoff from farms, particularly phosphates, increased algae growth and has made swimming and other recreational activities in some of the Great Lakes unpleasant at best and dangerous at worst. Lake Erie, especially, suffered for many years and was considered by some to be a dying lake by the 1960s. During that decade, however, citizens and government leaders began to actively search for solutions to make the Great Lakes healthier.

Since Canada and the U.S. signed the Great Lakes Water Quality Agreement in 1972, the lakes have returned to better health, as evidenced by the return of many species of **fish, birds,** and other wildlife. Nevertheless, scores of chemicals continue to be dumped into the Great Lakes, and a number of beaches, including those along the Toronto waterfront, have had to be closed to the public during the summer because of the health risk they pose. As well, there have been aberrations in species of wildlife that use the lake, such as cleft palates, club feet, and crossed bills, as well as bird eggs so thin that few young are hatched. Pollution has disrupted the sexual development of several types of fish, and studies have shown that some contaminated fish are not safe to eat. Nevertheless, thanks to filtration systems, the Great Lakes are still the essential water supply for many communities in Ontario, although increasing numbers of people drink bottled water.

## Great Lakes–St. Lawrence Seaway System

The Great Lakes–St. Lawrence Seaway System as we know it today opened to navigation in 1959, but a seaway in some form has existed since the late 1600s, and in Ontario since the 1800s.

In 1680, Dollier de Casson, Superior of the Sulphican Seminary in Montreal, began building a shallow canal to link Quebec's Lac St. Louis and Montreal, a project that was finally completed in 1824. In 1833, Ontario became involved with the opening of the first Welland Canal, a 40-kilometre-long waterway between lakes Erie and Ontario with 40 locks, which enabled ships to bypass **Niagara Falls** and rapids on the Niagara River. In 1932, a fourth version of the Welland Canal was completed, which uses just eight locks to raise or lower vessels a total of 99.36 metres.

This was the first step toward completion of the modern seaway, which is often described as a system within a system, both of which touch Ontario. The entire waterway is known as the Great Lakes–St. Lawrence Seaway System. It covers a distance of 3,700 kilometres (2,700 nautical miles) from **Thunder Bay** to the Atlantic Ocean and consists of the five **Great Lakes,** the Seaway, and the **St. Lawrence River** from the Atlantic Ocean to the Port of Montreal. On average, a large ship takes 8.5 sailing days to make it from one end to the other.

The St. Lawrence Seaway is one leg of the system, and extends from Montreal to Lake Erie. It includes 13 Canadian locks, with nine in Ontario. Of these, eight are in the Welland Canal and the ninth is at the 0.3-kilometre-long Iroquois Canal, between Morrisburg and Prescott.

Utilizing a series of locks, **canals,** and channels, this marine highway system has opened the interior of North America for nine months of the year to deep-draft 300-metre-long ocean-going vessels known as "supercarriers," making the seaway one of the world's most successful international trade routes.

The approximate cost of this monumental engineering and construction feat was $470 million, of which Canada paid $336.5 million and the U.S. about $133.8 million. The electrical power portion of the project cost about $600 million and was shared equally by the two nations. But the opening of the modern-day seaway was not without controversy. It took years of bickering and negotiations between Canada and the United States to get the job done.

Although the seaway was seen as a viable project in the late 1800s, work was stalled for more than half a century, owing to strong opposition from competing railroads, private utilities, the coal mining industry, and east and Gulf coast ports.

The St. Lawrence Seaway can accommodate 300-metre ocean-going vessels, or "super-carriers." On average, a ship takes 8.5 sailing days to make it from one end of the seaway to the other. (The St. Lawrence Seaway Management Corporation)

Americans were also concerned that Canada would control and own the seaway, and along with it, access into the heart of America.

However, in the early 1950s, huge new iron ore fields were discovered in Canada's Labrador wilderness and the St. Lawrence waterway was soon seen as the most logical way to carry ore from Labrador to American and Canadian steel mills. From a security perspective, a submarine-free access from ore field to mill was cited as being in the best interests of national defence.

It was not until Canada threatened to build the seaway entirely within Canadian territory that the two countries agreed to embark on the project jointly. Construction began in 1954 on the Montreal–to–Lake Ontario section, and the system opened to commercial traffic on April 20, 1959.

Tonnage to pass through the Montreal–Lake Ontario and the Welland Canal sections of the new seaway in its first year totalled 30.5 million tonnes. It topped 60 million in 1966, 64 million in 1971, and 68 million in 1973. The annual tonnage record of 74.3 million was set in 1979. In 1998, 51.1 million tonnes of cargo passed through, with 4,366 vessel transits. Since 1959, total cargo has been more than 2.1 billion tonnes, valued at $258 billion Canadian.

The large lakers that ply the system bring iron ore from the Quebec-Labrador mining centres to the steel mills located in the Great Lakes region and carry grain to ports along the lower St. Lawrence River, where it is transferred to ocean vessels. Other major commodities shipped through the system include corn, barley, coal, salt, stone, scrap iron, newsprint, and a variety of manufactured products. Sixty percent of traffic moves to and from overseas ports, especially Europe, the Middle East, and Africa. The seaway is responsible for 75,000 direct and indirect jobs in Canada and 49,000 in the United States. The primary Ontario ports on the system are at **Toronto, Hamilton, Windsor,** Sarnia, Goderich, Oshawa, and Thunder Bay.

Since October 1, 1998, the Canadian part of the seaway has been operated by The St. Lawrence Seaway Management Corporation, a not-for-profit organization headquartered in Cornwall.

# Group of Seven

Generally recognized as among the first artists to develop a distinctive Canadian art movement, members of the **Toronto**-based Group of Seven were driven by a great sense of purpose and nationalism. Together, the artists sought to capture the spirit of Canada and express a Canadian identity in their paintings. In the process, they made a deep and lasting impression on the people of central Canada.

The group's roots go back to the early 1900s when Tom Thomson, J.E.H. MacDonald, Arthur Lismer, Frederick Varley, Franz Johnston, and Franklin Carmichael all worked at various times at Grip Limited, a Toronto commercial design firm. While employed at Grip, several of the painters met and discovered their common artistic interests. They also began discussing new directions for Canadian art.

In 1913, they invited A.Y. Jackson to move from Montreal and join them in Toronto. The same year Dr. James MacCallum, a good friend, and fellow artist Lawren S. Harris provided money to build the Studio Building for

Canadian Art, where some of the artists would live and work.

A year later, Thomson left the commercial design firm Rous and Mann to paint and work as a guide in Algonquin Park. Thomson encouraged Lismer, Jackson, and Varley to make several sketching trips to Algonquin Park, where they worked to portray the distinct light of the northern landscape and the intense, bright colours of fall. MacCallum's cottage, on **Georgian Bay,** also became a favourite sketching location for the artists.

During World War I, Harris, Jackson, and Varley all served in the army, Harris at home and Jackson and Varley overseas, eventually as official war artists. Johnston also served at home documenting the activities of the Royal Air Force in Canada. Lismer moved to Halifax to teach, where he recorded the wartime activities of the navy. In 1917, under mysterious circumstances, Thomson drowned at age 39 in Algonquin Park's Canoe Lake while fishing from a canoe. His body was discovered eight days later. He had a gash on his head but there was no water in his lungs, and his canoe was never recovered.

After the war, the artists made several sketching trips from Toronto to the vast Algoma region of **northern Ontario,** where Harris, MacDonald, and Jackson, in particular, were inspired by snow, autumn colours, and waterfalls to create some of their greatest paintings. On several occasions, some of the artists lived in a railway caboose which was shunted from siding to siding. Following the 1919 Algoma trips, the artists decided to organize an exhibition and call themselves the Group of Seven. The seven founding artists were: Harris, MacDonald, Lismer, Varley, Johnston, Carmichael, and Jackson.

Their 1920 exhibition marked an important moment in Canadian art because it represented a growing belief that Canadian art must be inspired by Canada itself. Although initial response to the exhibition was mixed, later exhibitions in the 1920s found increasing acceptance of the Group's work.

By the mid-1920s, Group members had begun to travel throughout Canada. Jackson visited Quebec on a regular basis; Harris and MacDonald travelled to Nova Scotia. Harris, Jackson, and Carmichael journeyed to the north shore of Lake Superior, an area that made a deep impression, especially on Harris, who returned annually for many years.

During the next decade, MacDonald, Jackson, Varley, Lismer, and Harris made many trips to western Canada. In 1927, Jackson, accompanied by Frederick Banting, was the first Group member to visit the Arctic. Jackson later repeated the Arctic trip with Harris, and Varley visited the area in 1938.

*Members of the Group of Seven and some acquaintances gather at the Arts and Letters Club in Toronto in 1929.* (John Vanderpant, National Archives C-85272)

Varley, MacDonald, Carmichael, Lismer, and Johnston were all art teachers. Varley accepted a teaching position at the Vancouver School of Art in 1926. MacDonald held various teaching and administrative positions at the Ontario College of Art. Carmichael left his job as a commercial designer to accept a position as head of the graphic design department at the Ontario College of Art. Lismer became well known as an art educator. From 1927 to 1938 he was the educational supervisor at the Art Gallery of Toronto (now the Art Gallery of Ontario) and from 1941 to 1967, ran the Montreal Children's Art Centre.

Over the years, the Group of Seven became an institution that wielded national influence. Members met formally once or twice a year to plan group exhibitions. After Franz Johnston resigned from the Group in 1926, A.J. Casson was invited to join and became its youngest member. Later members of the Group included Edwin Holgate of Montreal and Lionel LeMoine FitzGerald of Winnipeg.

After the final exhibition in December 1931, and MacDonald's death in 1932, the Group disbanded to make way for the formation of a more broadly based group of artists called the Canadian Group of Painters, which included

Harris, Casson, Lismer, Jackson, and Carmichael as founding members. The Canadian Group of Painters attracted its members from across Canada and, like the Group of Seven, was concerned with many different forms of art, including figure, landscape, and abstract painting.

Group of Seven paintings can be viewed in several locations and galleries, including the **McMichael Canadian Art Collection** at Kleinburg, near Toronto; the **National Gallery of Canada** in **Ottawa**; the Montreal Museum of Fine Art; and the **Art Gallery of Ontario** in Toronto. Toronto's Thomson Gallery, owned by newspaper magnate Ken Thomson, also has a large Group of Seven collection. The public galleries also take their Group of Seven works on cross-country tours several times a year.

Group of Seven paintings rarely change hands but when they do, they're pricey: in 1999, one of Harris's works sold for $1.056 million and in 1986 another went for $450,000.

# Hamilton

The first European visitor to what is now Hamilton was probably Étienne Brûlé in 1616. Early English settlers to the area named it Burlington or Burlington Heights for the south part of the Bay, while the north part was called Head-of-the-Lake or Barton.

Like many parts of Ontario, the area around Hamilton began to grow with the arrival of **United Empire Loyalists,** who moved into what is now Canada during and after the American Revolution. In March 1816, the legislature of Upper Canada passed an act to create the District of Gore and established a courthouse and jail in the new Town of Hamilton. The municipality took its name from George Hamilton, a local politician and entrepreneur who promoted the settlement. By 1823, the population had grown to about 1,000 people, and in the 1830s Hamilton prospered with several public buildings, taverns, and small businesses.

Hamilton benefitted from its large harbour, which was about twice the size then that it is now. The harbour and a new canal built in 1827 helped create new industries and opportunities for settlers to the area. In 1846, Hamilton officially became a city. Although it almost went bankrupt in the 1860s, the opening of the Welland Canal in the 1880s provided a boost to the city, and by the end of the 19th century it had become an industrial hub of south-central Ontario.

The iron and steel industry, for which the city is best known, concentrated in Hamilton for several reasons, including nearby coal supplies, iron ore from **northern Ontario,** and Hamilton's superb harbour on Lake Ontario. The harbour also lent itself to recreational activities such as sailing and skating. By 1913, Hamilton began to boom as new buildings and streets were constructed to keep up with the rapid growth. The city began acquiring land outside its borders, notably the area known to locals as the Mountain, which is part of the **Niagara Escarpment.**

In 1930, McMaster University, which had opened in **Toronto** in 1880 and was rapidly expanding, moved to Hamilton. Initially there were only six buildings on campus, but since locating here the university has thrived and become one of the leading post-secondary institutions in the province.

In 1974, the Regional Municipality of Hamilton-Wentworth came into existence, and regional government evolved over the next 25 years. In late 1999, the provincial government passed a bill calling for the amalgamation of several municipalities in the Hamilton area into one large city, which is to take effect January 1, 2001.

Today, Hamilton continues to be a strong industrial centre in southern Ontario. The city's population totals 330,000, but increases to more than 624,000 when suburbs and bedroom communities are included. Hamilton is home to several tourist attractions, including **Dundurn Castle,** the **Royal Botanical Gardens,** and the **Canadian Football Hall of Fame.**

# Hamilton Tiger-Cats

Hamilton's football team was formed in 1950 as a result of a merger between the Hamilton Tigers of the Ontario Rugby Football Union (ORFU) and the Hamilton Wildcats of the Big Four, also known as the Interprovincial Rugby Union. At that time "rugby" was the name commonly used for football leagues. Prior to the merger, both teams had enjoyed success in their respective leagues and nationally.

The Tigers had played in several Grey Cup championships, dating back to 1910 when they lost 16–7 to the University of Toronto (the first Grey Cup had been played a year earlier when the University of Toronto defeated Toronto Parkdale 26–6). Another team from Hamilton, the Alerts, won the Grey Cup in 1912, defeating the **Toronto Argonauts** 11–4. In 1913, the Tigers defeated Toronto Parkdale 44–2 to win their first Grey Cup, and then won again in 1915 by a score of 13–7 over the Toronto Rowing and Athletic Association team. More than a decade passed before the Tigers returned to contend for the Grey Cup, when they lost 9–6 to Balmy Beach of **Toronto** in 1927.

The Tigers were triumphant in 1928, however, when they defeated the Regina Roughriders 30–0. They played Regina again the next year in the first Grey Cup game that featured the forward pass. The Tigers only passed once in the game, but they still beat Regina 14–3. The two teams next met in 1932, and Hamilton, which had star player Brian Timmis, was victorious again, this time by a score of 25–6. The Tigers played in one more Grey Cup, in 1935, and it was a historic one because Winnipeg defeated them 18–12. This marked the first time a team from the west had won the Grey Cup since it had become an east-west contest in 1921.

The Wildcats were formed in the early 1940s after the Tigers withdrew from their current league. In 1943, the Wildcats won the Grey Cup, defeating the Winnipeg R.C.A.F. Bombers by a score of 23–14. However, the Wildcats lost the Grey Cup the following year 7–6 to the St. Hyacinthe–Donnaconnas from Quebec. Once World War II ended, several football clubs were re-established, and the Tigers returned to give Hamilton two teams until the 1950 merger.

The Tiger-Cats played in the 1953 Grey Cup, where they faced the Winnipeg Blue Bombers. In an exciting game that came down to a last-second play in Hamilton's end zone, the Ti-Cats hung on for a 12–7 victory. This would be the start of a long rivalry in the Grey Cup between Hamilton and Winnipeg, as the two teams met five times in the national final over the next 12 years.

Hamilton and Winnipeg played for the Grey Cup again in 1957, a game Hamilton won 32–7. The championship has become known for the Ray "Bibbles" Bawel incident, in which the Hamilton player was running toward the goal line for a sure touchdown when he was tripped by a fan on the sidelines. The subsequent penalty had little effect on the game's outcome, however. The two teams met again in the Grey Cup the following year in an exciting match that saw Winnipeg win 35–28.

Until 1960, the Ti-Cats had been owned by the city, but in that year a group of 15 men bought the club, making it the final team of the Eastern Football Conference to become privately owned. With such legendary players as Bernie Faloney and Hal Patterson and a dramatic comeback victory over the Toronto Argonauts in the eastern final, Hamilton once again reached the Grey Cup in 1961. In the only championship game that has gone into overtime, the Ti-Cats lost to the Blue Bombers 21–14. The two teams met again the following year in the famous "Fog Bowl" game that had to be played over two days because of poor visibility on the field. Winnipeg won again 28–27.

The 1960s, however, were glory days for the Ti-Cats. They played in four more Grey Cups, winning 21–10 over the B.C. Lions in 1963, losing 34–24 to B.C. in 1964, beating Winnipeg 22–16 in 1965, and defeating the Saskatchewan Roughriders 24–1 in 1967. They were back in the Grey Cup in 1972, beating Saskatchewan again by 13–10 on a last-second field goal. In the 1980s, they played in the Grey Cup five times, losing to Edmonton in 1980 by a score of 48–10, to Winnipeg 47–17 in 1983, and to B.C. 37–24 in 1985. The Ti-Cats won 38–15 over Edmonton in 1986, and lost on a last-second field goal to Saskatchewan 43–40 in 1989, in what many people consider the greatest Grey Cup ever. The Ti-Cats, who came close to folding in the 1990s, returned to the Grey Cup in 1998, but lost in another last-second heartbreaker to the Calgary Stampeders 26–24. In 1999, however, Hamilton got revenge, defeating Calgary 32–21 to win the Grey Cup.

The Ti-Cats play their home games in Ivor Wynne Stadium and have had several owners since 1960, including Harold Ballard, who bought the team in 1978. David Macdonald and George Grant have owned the team since 1995.

# Highway 401

The 401, as most people call it, runs 820 kilometres from the Quebec border to **Windsor,** and forms the spine along which most of the province's growth has taken place in the past 40 years. Highway 401, also known as the Macdonald-Cartier Freeway, has been described by one geography professor as "the most important single development changing the social and economic pattern of Ontario."

The idea for building the 401 originated during World War II, when information gathered from a survey of drivers indicated where such a route should be constructed for ease of travel. Many thought the idea of building a highway to bypass **Toronto** was foolish and that it wouldn't be used. Today, every driver who's ever been stuck in gridlocked traffic on the 401 knows how wrong that assumption was. In fact, a description of the 401 in Toronto from 1956 shows just how much has changed since then—a "motorist's dream," one newspaper report called the route, providing "some of the most soothing scenery in the Metropolitan area."

The highway has a minimum of four lanes throughout its length, but is as wide as 16 lanes in parts of Toronto. A total of 520 bridges span the highway. The 401 was given a formal name in 1965 by Ontario's premier John Robarts to honour two of Canada's Fathers of Confederation—Sir John A. Macdonald and Sir Georges Étienne Cartier. Signs were placed along the highway indicating the name change, but once the signs got older, they were taken down and never replaced.

On a typical day, about 400,000 vehicles use the section of Highway 401 near Highway 400 in Toronto, making it one of the busiest in the world. To help ease congestion on the 401 around Toronto, a toll highway, the 407, was built north of the 401 and opened for business in June 1997.

# Highways

Ontario has more than 16,000 kilometres of highways as well as 145,000 kilometres of municipal, township, and local roads that provide a large, well-developed transportation link throughout the province. **Highway 401,** which runs through southern Ontario from **Windsor** to the Quebec border, is the most famous and certainly the busiest of the province's highways. A toll highway north of the 401, the 407, opened in June 1997 to help reduce traffic on the 401. Highway 407 is the first highway to collect tolls electronically in North America. Highway 2 runs roughly parallel to Highway 401 and is one of the oldest paved roads in Ontario. It traces a route travelled by many early settlers, and several communities in southern Ontario were established because of this road. Highway 400 is a major highway that runs north from Toronto past Barrie. At peak times on Friday evenings when people head to **cottage country,** there are as many as 4,000 cars an hour passing a given point.

The Queen Elizabeth Way, or QEW, was officially opened in June 1939 as Ontario's first superhighway. It runs from Toronto around Lake Ontario to the New York State border. Highway 403 is another four-lane highway that carries vehicles from Woodstock to **Hamilton,** where it joins with the QEW. The 402, running from Sarnia to **London,** is an important Canadian link in what people refer to as the NAFTA (North American Free Trade Agreement) Super Highway because of the amount of goods transported along its four lanes to and from the Michigan border.

Ontario contains 2,325 kilometres, or about 30 percent, of the Trans-Canada Highway's 7,796 kilometres. The main Trans-Canada runs along the northern and central portions of the province from Manitoba to the Quebec border. But there are alternate Trans-Canada routes, one that bypasses Sault Ste. Marie, another that runs eastward from Nipigon to North Bay and another that links **Sudbury** to **Ottawa.** At various places in Ontario the Trans-Canada is known as Highway 17, Highway 69, Highway 12, Highway 11, and Highway 7. Highway 11, which begins as **Yonge Street** in Toronto, runs as far north and west as Rainy River and was an early transportation route for **northern Ontario.** It was known as the Ferguson Highway when it was first built in the 1920s.

# Historical Overview

Before the Europeans arrived in present-day Ontario, **First Nations peoples** had been living here for thousands of years. The two main language and cultural groups of these peoples, by the time of European contact, were Algonquian and Iroquoian. The Algonquian tribes, who were primarily hunters, lived mostly in what is now **northern Ontario,** while two groups of Iroquoians, whose culture was generally based on agriculture, lived along the **St. Lawrence River** and in the southwestern regions. When the Europeans arrived in the 17th century, there were more than 100,000 First Nations people in the area.

The French and English both arrived at around the same time. Henry Hudson began to explore Hudson Bay and **James Bay** in 1610, but his crew mutinied in 1611 and set Hudson, his son, and seven others adrift in a small boat. They were not seen again. Étienne Brûlé was sent by Samuel de Champlain to live among the Hurons near Georgian Bay in 1611. In 1615, Catholic missionaries arrived from France. They travelled up the Ottawa River, along Lake Nipissing and French River to the shores of Lake Huron. The French allied themselves with the Hurons and took part in battles against the Iroquois.

The Catholic missionaries believed it was their duty to convert the various First Nations tribes to Christianity. In 1634, Jesuit Fathers, or "black robes" as they were called, started a mission named St. Joseph on the Penetanguishene peninsula. The other important Jesuit missionary post was the nearby **Ste.-Marie-among-the-Hurons,** founded in 1639. It became the first European community in Ontario, at that time a part of New France. By 1648, about 20 percent of the European **population** of New France lived there.

Although they were able to convert some of the Native people, the Europeans also brought with them diseases that would prove fatal to many. In 1649, the Iroquois tribes to the south attacked the Hurons and killed several missionaries. Disease and Iroquois attacks combined to lead to the disintegration of the Huron Confederacy. The Iroquois also prevented the French from expanding very far west until the 1680s, but with the help of French adventurers known as *coureurs de bois,* portions of the French River, Lake Huron, and Lake Superior were opened for trade.

In the meantime, the English continued to explore the northern regions of the new land, established the Hudson's Bay Company and began trading for furs. The company built forts at James Bay and Hudson Bay to help increase the **fur trade.** The French continued their explorations in the southern half of the province and built Fort Frontenac to guard the entrance to the St. Lawrence River. René-Robert Cavelier, the Sieur de La Salle, explored further inland, becoming the first European to visit **Niagara Falls** in 1675. In the 1680s, the French and English engaged in several skirmishes in the James Bay area, and while the French were able to strengthen their holdings in the southern part of the province, they eventually lost territory in the north.

In 1713, under the Treaty of Utrecht, the colony was partitioned such that the French maintained control of the southern half while the English received jurisdiction over the Hudson Bay lowlands. The French continued to push west-ward and by 1731 had opened a new trading post on the site of Fort William at the top of Lake Superior. They built more settlements in the south along the lower St. Lawrence, as well as on both sides of the Detroit River between Lake Erie and Lake St. Clair.

The French and English waged war several times throughout the early 18th century, but the Seven Years War between the two from 1756 to 1763 estab-lished British control over present-day Ontario once and for all. Another threat to the British followed in 1775, however, as rebels in America pushed for their independence during the American Revolution. Many **United Empire Loyalists,** who did not support the rebels' cause, allied themselves with British troops and fought to protect the colonies north of the St. Lawrence and at places such as Fort Niagara and Fort Detroit. The British, along with Iroquoian allies, were able to protect what was called the "upper country" and, though the British eventually surrendered in 1783 to the Americans, the area along the upper St. Lawrence River and through the **Great Lakes** remained under their control. Many of the Loyalist refugees were now living in a new home, and were granted land on which to settle permanently.

Initial townships were established along the northern shore of the St. Lawrence near Lake Ontario as well as other areas west of the lake. In 1791, the Canada Act, or Constitutional Act, divided the vast region that had been known as the province of Quebec into Upper Canada and Lower Canada (present-day Ontario and Quebec), and John Graves Simcoe was appointed first Lieutenant-Governor of Upper Canada.

Simcoe was keen to ensure the safety and protection of the new province from American invasion and offered new settlers land grants. He hoped to estab-lish a provincial capital in what is now **London,** which he thought was far enough inland to make attack difficult. But the temporary capital was estab-lished in **Toronto** instead in 1793 (which he renamed York). Simcoe was also responsible for starting construction on some key roads across the province, among them today's **Yonge Street.** Settlers, including many Americans, contin-ued to flock to the new province over the next 15 years and by the time of the **War of 1812,** the non-Native population had risen to about 100,000.

Several battles took place on Ontario soil, but the most famous was proba-bly the Battle of Queenston Heights, which was fought on October 13, 1812. It was here that British troops led by General Isaac Brock, and aided by First

Nations warriors, defeated the Americans, but Brock died in doing so. There were also several naval clashes during the war. One of the major ones was the Battle of Lake Erie in September 1813, which the Americans won. The war lasted until Christmas Eve 1814, when it was ended by the Treaty of Ghent, and both sides gave back territory they had captured.

In the years following the war, the province's population grew rapidly, thanks in part to the arrival of immigrants from Britain, and to some extent, America. As new roads and settlements proliferated, **agriculture** became the mainstay of the province. The military also remained a large presence in Ontario until after Confederation in 1867, due to the ever-present concern that the Americans might invade again. In fact, one of the main reasons for building the Rideau Canal from Lake Ontario near **Kingston** to **Ottawa** was to provide an alternate supply route between Upper and Lower Canada in case Americans cut off the St. Lawrence River in a new war (*see* **Canals**).

An elite, privileged group of men essentially ran Upper Canada in the 1820s and '30s. Known to many as the Family Compact, these men were opposed by a growing number of Reformers—some moderate and some radical. The Reformers argued for some form of responsible government, which would establish the supremacy of the legislature over the executive arms of the government. William Lyon Mackenzie and others of the more radical faction led the **Rebellion of 1837,** but it had limited support throughout the province. After a few skirmishes with militia, the rebellion was suppressed. Some of the rebel leaders were hanged, some left for the U.S., while others were sent to penal colonies in Australia.

In 1838, Lord Durham, the Governor General, prepared a report on the grievances and offered suggestions for remedies to the province's troubles, including uniting Upper and Lower Canada. In 1841, Upper and Lower Canada became known as Canada West and Canada East respectively in the United Province of Canada, with Kingston as the new capital.

There were several changes of government throughout the decade, but the **economy** of Ontario continued to grow. The arrival of immigrants from Ireland swelled the population and farms prospered in the early 1850s. The building of **railways**—most notably the Grand Trunk, which by 1859 ran from Montreal to Sarnia—opened up new lands for development. The 1850s was a time of intensive settlement of much of the area below the **Canadian Shield.** Railroads shortened distances and stimulated constellations of integrated villages, towns, and cities. It was in this decade that Toronto rose to prominence, dominating the province economically, politically, and culturally. There remained, however, political differences between the English- and French-speaking populations of the united province and among political leaders, who continued to argue about the evolving shape of democracy.

In 1859, the capital moved from Kingston to Ottawa. By 1861, the population in Canada West was about 1.4 million, slightly higher than that of Canada East. Political leaders such as George Brown, a member of the Reform party, or Grits as they were called, sought representation by population and control over local affairs within the United Province of Canada.

There were also external threats to the province, again coming from south of the border. Some of the Irish people living in North America believed in liberating Ireland and Canada from Great Britain and thought that attacks on Canada West might be used as a bargaining tool in achieving their aim. These Irish patriots, or Fenians, defeated Canadian militia in Ridgeway and Fort Erie in June 1866, but staged no further battles. This perceived threat and the political deadlock in the Union of the Canadas, which was stalling economic development and westward expansion, were instrumental in the development of the Confederation of Canada in 1867.

With Confederation, Canada West was renamed Ontario. Though it remained primarily agricultural for the rest of the 19th century, Ontario soon began to develop new industries and expand existing ones as its population grew, land was colonized, and more and better roads were built. In 1889, the Judicial Committee of the Privy Council ruled in Ontario's favour over a boundary dispute with Manitoba, and Ontario gained 233,000 square kilometres of territory. Under Sir Oliver Mowat, the Liberals, who had evolved from the Reformers, ruled the province for more than 20 years during the last quarter of the 19th century and helped shepherd Ontario into the modern age. Mowat was a staunch believer in provincial rights and clashed several times with the federal government over legal jurisdictions.

By the beginning of the 20th century, Ontario was a place of factories, cities, towns, busy railways, and tremendous untapped potential in its north. The transformation of Ontario from a predominantly small-town, agricultural province into an urban-industrial powerhouse occurred from about 1896 to 1918. As well, the province's limits were again extended, this time north to Hudson Bay, which increased Ontario's size to approximately one million square kilometres.

By 1911, the population had hit 2.5 million and slightly more people were living in urban areas than in rural. Toronto, Ottawa, **Hamilton,** and London were the biggest centres, and with the advent of hydroelectric power, primarily from Niagara Falls, Ontario was becoming a modern and prosperous region. After the Hydro Electric Power Commission was created in 1906, construction and operation of transmission lines linked the provincial power source with municipally owned power systems. Mineral discoveries in northern Ontario before World War I, such as nickel and copper in **Sudbury,** silver in Cobalt, and gold in Timmins, further boosted the province's economy.

World War I brought a demand not only for soldiers but also factories that could mass-produce goods and supplies. Women increasingly began to work to overcome labour shortages and by 1917, they had won the right to vote.

The Conservatives, or Tories, were the dominant political party from 1905 to 1932, but Liberals and even the upstart United Farmers of Ontario both had a taste of power. Between 1919 and 1939, Ontario experienced two depressions and a major economic boom. Perhaps the most surprising event in this period was the 1919 election when the United Farmers of Ontario gained political control. Farmers' groups had great success in Canada at this time, charging that the Liberals and Conservatives had been ignoring agricultural interests for years. The Farmers' party, however, often bickered among themselves and a depression from 1920 to 1922 didn't help. By 1923 they were out of power, and the Conservatives swept into office.

Like the rest of North America, Ontario prospered throughout the rest of the 1920s and increasingly spent money on building roads, hospitals, and schools. Investment flowed in from the United States, and as the automobile boomed, so did that industry and others.

The province was severely hit by the Great Depression, and in 1933 about half a million Ontarians depended on local government for relief. Pockets of prosperity existed throughout the province, but disenchantment with the ruling Conservatives saw the election of the Liberals in 1934. One interesting event during this decade was the birth of the world-famous Dionne Quintuplets in 1934 near North Bay. They became wards of the government and were exploited as a tourist attraction in those years.

The Liberals held onto power until 1943, ushering the province into World War II, but were defeated by the Conservatives that year. It would be more than 40 years before the Liberals returned to power again in Ontario.

Ontario flourished in the years following the war as industry grew, particularly in the area known as the **Golden Horseshoe** around the western edge of Lake Ontario. Thanks in part to the "baby boom," the population grew to 4.6 million in 1951 and 6.2 million ten years later. More schools, roads, and **highways** were built to accommodate the growth, and new sources of energy, particularly nuclear, became increasingly important. The opening of the **Great Lakes–St. Lawrence Seaway System** in 1959 saw ocean-going vessels sailing up as far as **Thunder Bay** on Lake Superior.

Ontario was governed by a Tory dynasty during the post-War decades. Premiers Leslie Frost, John Robarts, and William Davis led their Conservatives to several election victories and shepherded Ontario through mostly strong economic times. The 1960s saw expansion of the province's university system and the building of several community colleges.

The Conservatives remained in power until 1985 when the Liberals under David Peterson, despite having two fewer seats than the Conservatives, were able to negotiate an accord with the New Denocratic Party to rule the province for the next two years. The Peterson-led Liberals then formed a majority government after the 1987 election, and were followed by an NDP majority from 1990 to 1994 under Bob Rae. Led by Mike Harris, the Conservatives won a majority in 1994 and again in 1999.

Regardless of which political party has been in power in recent years, Ontario leaders have generally been key players in strengthening ties between the federal and provincial governments and have argued strongly on behalf of maintaining neighbouring Quebec as an important part of a united Canada. The province now has a population of more than 11 million, about one-third of the country's total population, and remains the industrial heartland of the country.

# Hockey Hall of Fame

In 1943, several decades after hockey came into prominence in Canada, a group of men decided it was time to acknowledge the achievements of the many people who had made outstanding contributions to the game.

Led by Capt. J.T. Sutherland, their vision was the Hockey Hall of Fame, a place under one roof where they would collect, preserve, research, exhibit, and promote sticks, pucks, team sweaters, pads and gloves, trophies, team guidebooks, schedules, and other items that had significance to the

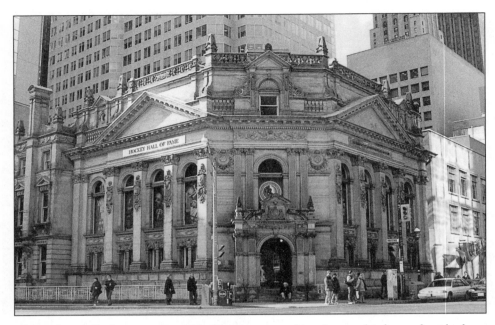

*The Hockey Hall of Fame in Toronto tells visitors everything they need to know about hockey, from the first recorded game in 1875 right up to the present.* (Mark Kearney)

story of ice hockey, in Canada and around the world.

Like many of the teams in the National Hockey League, the Hall of Fame has had its share of homes. When the hall was founded in the 1940s, plans called for construction of a building in **Kingston,** but it was never built. In the late 1950s, with hockey mogul Conn Smythe spearheading the project, the hall moved into its first home in a building at the **Canadian National Exhibition** grounds west of downtown **Toronto,** which was shared with **Canada's Sports Hall of Fame.** In 1961, the hall moved into its own facility on the CNE grounds.

On June 18, 1993, the Hockey Hall of Fame welcomed the public to its current home in BCE Place, a $26 million downtown Toronto facility with 52,000 square feet of space, including 10,000 square feet in the restored Bank of Montreal building at Yonge and Front streets. In its first year of operation, 500,000 visitors passed through the turnstiles to view the largest collection of hockey artifacts and memorabilia in the world.

A tour of the building tells visitors everything there is to know about hockey, from the time of the first recorded game in Montreal in 1875 up to the present. Some highlights of the hall are a full-scale reproduction of the Montreal Canadiens' dressing room in the Montreal Forum; a display that commemorates the buildings played in by the teams known as the NHL's "Original Six"—the Montreal Canadiens, Toronto Maple Leafs, Boston Bruins, New York Rangers, Detroit Red Wings, and Chicago Blackhawks; the Bell Great Hall, with portraits of each of the more than 300 members of the Hockey Hall of Fame; glass cases containing most of hockey's major trophies, including the coveted Stanley Cup; and a 3,500-square-foot exhibit featuring histories and artifacts from 50 International Ice Hockey Federation member countries, such as Sweden, Finland, and Slovakia.

Visitors can also try their luck at hockey trivia, test the speed of their shot, and go between the pipes to test their goaltending skills against simulated shots by Mark Messier and Wayne Gretzky.

# Holland Marsh

About 50 kilometres north of **Toronto** may be found 2,900 hectares of rich, organic soil that is among the most fertile in Canada. Holland Marsh lies in a shallow basin formed by retreating glaciers thousands of years ago, which accumulated dead vegetation at an approximate rate of 30 centimetres every 500 years.

**First Nations peoples** had lived in the area for hundreds of years, but it wasn't until the early 19th century that European settlers began hunting and fishing there. The marsh takes its name from the Holland River, which drains it and which was named after a surveyor, Samuel Holland.

In 1905, officials at the Ontario Agricultural College in Guelph began examining the possibility of draining the marsh and using it to grow vegetables. The marsh had never been considered important economically, and there was little initial support for the idea because most government officials thought the scheme was futile. However, when a small portion of the marsh was drained and used to grow vegetables, officials embraced the idea. Draining on a large scale began in 1925 with a series of **canals** and dikes built around the marsh to divert the Holland River. The project was completed five years later, and by the middle of the 1930s, several Dutch families had settled there and begun developing the marsh as an agricultural community.

Holland Marsh was severely damaged in 1954 by **Hurricane Hazel,** but today it's a fertile agricultural area noted for its flat expanse and dark soil. Among the wealth of vegetables grown and sold are lettuce, carrots, potatoes, onions, parsnips, cauliflower, beets, cabbage, and tomatoes.

**Hudson Bay**. *See* **James Bay**

# Hurricane Hazel

After slicing a deadly path through the Caribbean, Hurricane Hazel blasted the American east coast near Myrtle Beach on the morning of October 15, 1954, then, over the next 12 hours, raced north to southern Ontario where it struck an unprepared **Toronto.**

The storm had been weakened by the overland journey and was technically no longer a hurricane, but after merging with a cold front near Toronto she regained some of her lost fury. Over an 18-hour period, Hurricane Hazel claimed 80 lives, left more than 4,000 families homeless, and caused more than $130 million worth of storm- and flood-related damage.

Packing torrential rains and winds of up to 125 kilometres per hour, the storm washed out bridges, destroyed and damaged homes and businesses, and caused much personal tragedy. The greatest loss of life and property damage occurred in the Humber River Valley and **Holland Marsh,** south of Lake Simcoe, where downpours of up to 178 millimetres saturated soils and produced flash-flooding in rivers and creeks.

In the wake of the hurricane, several flood-control dams and channels were built in and around Toronto. Homes were moved from flood plains in the Toronto area to prevent a repeat of the tragedy.

Other than a two-day storm that flooded parts of Essex County in July 1989, however, no other storm has challenged Hazel's status as the heaviest rainstorm ever to strike southern Ontario, and none has left such tragic memories.

# International Plowing Match and Farm Machinery Show

Plowing matches have been part of Ontario's agricultural history since 1846 when the first provincial agricultural exhibition was held in **Toronto.** A special feature of that event was a plowing match which was held on a farm near the intersection of what today is the area around **Yonge Street** and St. Clair Avenue.

The first official international match took place November 11, 1913, at Sunnybrook Farms, on a site which later became Sunnybrook Hospital. In the early years, plowing matches were sponsored by agricultural societies to give farmers an opportunity to display their skill in the handling of a walking plow and to show off their horses.

These days, the International Plowing Match and Farm Machinery Show is held every September and is sponsored by the Ontario Plowmen's Association, in cooperation with a different host county every year. Involving more than 150 competitors, the show brings the agricultural community together, challenging the abilities of its members, as well as celebrating the history of farming and the latest developments in technology.

The show attracts about 100,000 spectators from across Canada, the United States, and Europe. It is the largest event of its kind in Canada and the second largest in North America.

The idea of plowing competitions is believed to have originated in Europe, as far back as the 16th century when plowing was a great source of rivalry among farmers. During modern International Plowing Matches, competitors plow in their category over the course of several days while judges look for the split, straightness, and uniformity of the crown; the firmness, packing, closeness, and depth of the seed bed; the straightness, neatness, depth, and width of the finish; the burying of grass and stubble; and the straightness and uniformity of the furrows.

(*See also* **Fall Fairs**)

# Invertebrates

Ontario is home to many thousands of invertebrate species, found in every part of the province. They do not have backbones, although many invertebrates—including insects, crustaceans, and mollusks—have a hard outer shell. More than two-thirds of the invertebrates found in the province are insects (members of the arthropod subgroup), which have six legs and often feed on plants, particularly the leaves.

The number of insect species in the province is too numerous to detail, but among the most visible are grasshoppers, beetles, crickets, ants, and termites. Species such as fireflies, which produce light to attract mates by a complex chemical reaction, and butterflies are admired for their beauty or unusual characteristics. Others, such as the spruce budworm and tent caterpillar, are considered pests because they damage forests.

Among the bloodsucking insects that pester humans and animals alike are **mosquitoes,** black flies, horseflies, and deer flies. Although they are a great annoyance to humans, many of these biting flies also transmit parasites to birds and other wildlife. Ducks, for example, can suffer losses among their young each year because of a parasite transmitted by black flies.

Next to mosquitoes, black flies are probably the worst nuisances for humans, especially in areas where people like to spend time outdoors. No other biting flies inspire such apprehension as do black flies. In forested areas of Ontario in June and early July, members of the *Simulium venustum* species can be so numerous and attack so persistently that outdoor activity during the day without some protection is almost impossible.

Black flies often land and take off repeatedly without biting. Their numbers and their tendency to bite increase as sunset approaches. Even when they are not biting, however, their buzzing presence and constant crawling into hair and under clothing is nearly as irritating as the bloodsucking itself. Mercifully, relief comes after dark, for unlike mosquitoes and biting midges, black flies do not attack at night and rarely attack indoors or even in a vehicle.

Approximately 250 species of black flies have been recorded in North

America, with about 70 of these species occurring in Ontario.

Ontario is home to a variety of species of moths and butterflies. The cecropia moth is the largest in North America with a wingspan of about 15 centimetres, while the luna moth is considered by many experts to be among the most beautiful. Unlike moths, butterflies are more commonly seen during the daytime, usually in meadows and at the edges of woodlands. Monarch butterflies are probably the best known, and may sometimes be seen in large numbers as they fly south in autumn to winter in the southern U.S. and Mexico.

Wasps and bees are a common sight in Ontario. Wasps prey on other insects, but are also known for their painful sting. Bees, considered to be among the most intelligent insects, differ from wasps in that they feed their young honey and pollen rather than other small animals. Bumblebees and honeybees are among the most social of invertebrates, living in large colonies. Both types of bee pollinate flowers and eat the nectar, but honeybees also store nectar in the form of honey.

Spiders, typically distinguished by their eight legs and a body with two segments, are also widespread in Ontario. Spiders eat insects, with many species spinning complex silken webs to catch their prey. Others, such as the wolf spider, run down their prey.

Several freshwater invertebrates live in the province, including water mites, dragonflies, water fleas, flatworms, mayflies, water striders, crayfish, and mussels.

(*See also* **Zebra Mussels**)

# Jack Miner Bird Sanctuary

When legendary conservationist Jack Miner drew up his will, he insisted that an admission fee should never be charged at the bird sanctuary that bears his name in South Gosfield Township, east of **Windsor.** He also made it clear that nothing must ever be sold on the property.

"In the name of God, let there be one place on earth where no money changes hands," Miner is said to have told his son Manly.

Remaining true to his words, the patriarch's heirs have never charged for admission to the 152-hectare waterfowl sanctuary, which is now owned by the Jack Miner Migratory Bird Foundation. It was started by Miner in 1904 as a refuge for the thousands of **birds** that migrate annually between breeding grounds about 1,600 kilometres to the north in the Arctic and wintering areas in the southern United States.

When the sanctuary opened, visiting Canada geese numbered fewer than a dozen. Today, peak populations can reach 15,000 in late October, making it a favourite autumn location for bird watchers, tourists, and curious youngsters eager to catch a glimpse of the great North American goose and duck migration.

But there's more to the Jack Miner Bird Sanctuary than its use as a **tourism** hotspot and a stopover for tired birds, including eight species of ducks. Bird banding has always been a part of its raison d'être, in an effort to help biologists decipher the migratory travels of birds and their flight patterns and to assess the survival rates of different sexes and age classes of birds.

The annual goal is to band 1,000 geese and 2,000 ducks. An estimated 200,000 birds have been banded since the process began in 1904. The bands are made of aluminum, stamped with a number and a verse from the bible, such as "Fear God and Give Him Glory—Revelation 14:7." The bands, which have been found on birds downed across North America, have become collector's items, sometimes bringing in $500 apiece at auctions.

When Miner died on November 3, 1944, the federal government designated the week of April 10, which coincides with Miner's birth on April 10, 1865, as National Wildlife Week.

The sanctuary includes a museum, picnic area, nature stadium, and pond area where birds can be hand-fed. It is operated, with no government contributions, through an endowment fund and a charitable foundation. More than 125,000 people visit each year.

# James Bay

Lying south of the much larger Hudson Bay and at the northern extreme of Ontario is James Bay, a 160-kilometre-wide body of **water** that has played an important role in Ontario's and in Canada's history. The water itself is under the jurisdiction of the federal government.

It is believed that the Cree First Nation have lived in the James Bay area for more than 5,000 years, hunting waterfowl, caribou, and other game near its shores. Henry Hudson was the first European to see James Bay in 1610, but it was from English explorer Thomas James, who entered the bay in 1631, that it received its name. James Bay was long the centre of the burgeoning **fur trade** that saw Cree travelling along such rivers as the Albany, Attawapiskat, and Moose to the several Hudson's Bay company posts that had been established on James Bay's shores. One of the key settlements here was Moose Factory, the oldest English-speaking settlement in Ontario.

Cruise ship excursions down the Moose River from Moosonee to James Bay, and stopping at Moose Factory on the return run, attract thousands of tourists each year.

In 1971, the Quebec government announced plans to build a system of hydroelectric dams near James Bay. This led to four years of discussion with the Cree about their rights to continue fishing, hunting, and trapping along James Bay. In 1975, an agreement was signed that outlined how lands were to be divided and what rights the Cree would retain. The original agreement has been altered by several amendments and other related pieces of legislation. The project, and its environmental impact on the region, remains controversial to this day. It is one of the largest energy projects ever proposed in the world. Only the first phase has been completed, costing about $16 billion. Among the environmental concerns raised in Quebec by the Cree were increased methylmercury contamination caused by flooding of the completed reservoir and adverse effects on fish and wildlife populations.

In the 1970s, smaller projects were announced for Ontario along the Moose River basin, but in 1991 Ontario Hydro announced that planning and field studies for all Moose River developments (with the exception of extensions to some existing stations) had been suspended.

James Bay and Hudson Bay are the largest bodies of water in the world that freeze each winter and become ice-free in the summer. The watershed of the two bays covers more than one-third of Canada. Some 60 species of **fish** live in the two bays, while **mammals** include ringed seals, polar bears, and beluga whales. Many **birds** use the coasts of James Bay for breeding and as a migration route, including snow geese, black ducks, mallards, **loons,** common eiders, plovers, and sandpipers.

# Kingston

Kingston is known as the Limestone City for the handsome 19th-century limestone architecture which gives the community a distinct look and feel. It is a city steeped in history and, for more than 50 years, was the home of Sir John A. Macdonald, Canada's first prime minister.

The city's beginnings date back to 1673 when the French sent René-Robert Cavelier, the Sieur de La Salle, up the **St. Lawrence River** to scout for the perfect trading post location. At the eastern end of Lake Ontario, La Salle erected Fort Cataraqui, which eventually became Fort Frontenac, a strategic site on a route travelled by explorers and trappers. It also became an important base for launching exploratory missions along the lakes to the west and military strikes against the Iroquois and the British to the south.

In 1758, the fort was captured by the British, putting an end to French colonization in the area. In 1784, the British negotiated with the Mississauga tribes and obtained lands on which to settle **United Empire Loyalists** from the American colonies. The town was named King's Town, in honour of King George III.

As a stopping-point on the **Great Lakes** route, the town grew prosperous. During the **War of 1812, Fort Henry** was built to provide protection. However, the war had no negative impact on the community, and was in fact an economic stimulus, thanks to the significant naval and military presence. The community's economic prospects were further boosted in 1832 when the Rideau Canal was completed, linking Kingston with **Ottawa.**

Kingston served briefly as the capital of the Province of Canada from 1841–43, but by mid-century its economic stature began to decline as the flow of grain down the St. Lawrence River diminished and larger lake vessels shunned its exposed and shallow harbour. Further blows came with the closure of its naval base in 1852 and the departure of the imperial garrison in 1871.

In the 1880s the city built significant rail links, and in the 1940s and 1950s several large new industries arrived, including Alcan Aluminum, DuPont Nylon, and Celanese Canada. Shipbuilding was important to the **economy** during World War II and for several years after the war ended. The most significant economic stimulus, however, was the growth of Kingston's institutional base, led by Queen's University, the Royal Military College, the National Defence College, several hospitals and provincial government offices, and a number of provincial and **federal penitentiaries** built in the city and surrounding area. The first prison to open was the Kingston Penitentiary, which was built in 1835.

In 1999, with a population of about 113,000, Kingston's economic stars, with the number of employees in brackets, are Canadian Forces Base Kingston (4,787), Queen's (3,800), Limestone District School Board (2,710), Correctional Services Canada (2,670), Kingston General Hospital (2,324), Hotel Dieu Hospital (1,594), and DuPont Canada (1,510).

Waterways and forts that once provided protection and sources of commerce now provide beauty and recreation for locals and more than one million tourists a year, who sink $170 million into the local economy. The **1000 Islands** and the Rideau Canal are nearby, restaurants are numerous, and the city is home to

17 **museums,** seven performing arts venues, five marinas, and a variety of historic sites and limestone buildings that remind visitors and residents of Kingston's rich past.

# Kitchener-Waterloo

These twin cities in southwestern Ontario have developed separately throughout their history, but have shared a socio-economic base.

In 1784, the area where the cities are located was set aside as a reserve for the Six Nations Iroquois tribes, to reward them for their loyalty to Britain during the American Revolution. Led by Joseph Brant, the tribes wanted to sell part of the land to provide themselves an annuity, but the government blocked their efforts. Fourteen years later, the land was subdivided by the government and sold to speculators on behalf of the Six Nations. In some cases, the tribes received the money, while in others funds were misappropriated by government officials.

In the early 1800s, Pennsylvania **Mennonites** who were looking for new land at lower prices began settling here, and German immigrants followed in the 1820s.

Kitchener, which was known as Berlin from 1833 until World War I, grew quickly in the 1820s and '30s to a **population** of about 700 by the 1850s. Like many southern Ontario towns of the 19th century, Kitchener and Waterloo's economic development was aided by their location on a major railway line, the Grand Trunk Railway, which linked them to **Toronto** in 1856. Both communities prospered in the next two decades and were incorporated as towns in 1876. By the 1870s, Waterloo's population had reached about 1,600.

Because of their German flavour, Berlin and Waterloo differed from their neighbouring cities in southern Ontario, whose citizens had strong British origins. In 1865, St. Jerome's College was established in Berlin as a centre for German Catholic education, and by the 1880s Berlin was known as Canada's "German capital." The German artisans, farmers, and tradesmen who settled here boosted the industrial growth of both towns, with insurance becoming an important industry in the late 19th century.

Prominent business people such as J.M. Schneider, a meat packer, and Joseph Seagram, a distiller, got their start in the area and became nationally and internationally known. Furniture making, tanneries, and other industries thrived, thanks to excellent road and rail links and proximity to major American and Canadian markets. Between 1879 and 1912, the number of manufacturers in Berlin jumped from 22 to 76. In the early 20th century, rubber and automotive parts plants further enhanced the area's growth, along with the arrival of hydroelectric power in 1910, the first inland Ontario community to have access to this new source of energy. Berlin was incorporated as a city in 1912, while Waterloo did not attain that status until 1943.

By 1911, about 70 percent of the inhabitants of Berlin and Waterloo had German roots, but with the outbreak of World War I, immigration from Germany ceased, and people in the area began to question whether they should downplay their German heritage. In 1916, Berlin changed its name to Kitchener (in honour of War Minister Lord Horatio H. Kitchener), though not without causing a rift among its citizens.

The strong Lutheran presence in the area led to the establishment of the Waterloo College of Arts in 1924, which was founded by the Lutheran church. The college was affiliated with the University of Western Ontario in **London** until the late 1950s. In 1960, the Waterloo College of Arts became known as Waterloo Lutheran University, until 1973 when it was transferred to control of the provincial government and renamed Wilfrid Laurier University. The University of Waterloo was founded in 1957. It offered Canada's first cooperative education program, in which students alternate their academic careers with practical experience in the workplace.

Kitchener and Waterloo had separate municipal governments from the beginning but shared some services over the years. The arrival of a two-tiered regional government in 1973 led to stronger links between the two cities, with regional government overseeing such services as police and health, as well as some planning and engineering tasks.

Today, Kitchener-Waterloo is an important regional centre in southwestern Ontario with a population of more than 240,000. The residents once again proudly celebrate their German origins with the annual Oktoberfest, the second-largest such festival in the world. **Manufacturing**, retail, and service industries remain the lifeblood of both communities.

# Languages

With a **population** made up of more than 160 cultural groups, it's no surprise to find a broad range of languages spoken in Ontario. However, the primary language of most Ontarians is English. Census figures from 1996 show that 7,694,635 residents, or about 72 percent, consider English to be their first language.

Of the remaining population, 479,285 people state that French is their first language. This is followed by 328,165 who say Chinese is their first language, 305,155 who claim Italian as their first language, and 159,430 whose first language is German.

Other significant linguistic groups in Ontario are: Portuguese, with 150,630 residents claiming it as their first language; Polish, 139,635; Spanish, 100,890; Punjabi, 76,075; Dutch, 71,675; Arabic, 69,210; Tagalog, 67,920; Greek, 64,945; Tamil, 56,425; and Ukrainian, 50,490. Some 21,630 Ontarians claim First Nations languages as their first language, led by Ojibway, with 10,570.

(*See also* **Ethnicity**)

# Legal System

The Canadian Constitution gives each province jurisdiction over the administration of justice in that province, which includes the operation of police forces, the prosecution of most criminal offences, and the administration of the provincial court system.

In Ontario, the court system consists of three divisions: the Court of Appeal for Ontario, the Superior Court of Justice, and the Ontario Court of Justice. The federal government is responsible for the administration of the courts with national jurisdiction, including the Tax Court of Canada, the Federal Court of

Appeal, the Federal Court of Canada, and the Supreme Court of Canada. In addition, the federal government appoints the judges of all superior courts, including courts with national jurisdiction and the Court of Appeal for Ontario. The provincial government appoints the judges of the Ontario Court of Justice. Federal legislative jurisdiction includes matters relating to trade and commerce, banking, bankruptcy, and criminal law.

The three divisions of the court system in Ontario each have different responsibilities. The Court of Appeal is strictly an appellate court for the province, where people can appeal decisions made by other courts in Ontario. Beyond that, appeals must go to the Supreme Court of Canada for a final ruling.

The Superior Court of Justice, which includes three specialized branches, the Divisional Court branch, the Family Court branch, and the Small Claims Court branch, deals with cases involving everything from the most serious criminal offences and civil matters, to small claims for non-payment of bills and recovery of personal property. The Divisional Court hears certain appeals arising from decisions made in the Superior Court of Justice, Family Court, and Small Claims Court, although most appeals proceed directly to the Court of Appeal. Family Court hears cases involving divorce, division of property, adoption, child protection, child and spousal support, custody, and access to children. Small Claims Court has jurisdiction in any action for payment of money or for the recovery of personal property within its monetary jurisdiction, which is limited to $6,000.

The Ontario Court of Justice deals with all but the most serious criminal offences, as well as Young Offenders Act cases. It also deals with certain family and child protection matters.

However, in 1999 a system of unified family courts was gradually being expanded across Ontario to allow family law matters to be dealt with in one court and to provide access to mediation as an alternative to formal court proceedings.

As is the case in all courts in Canada, with the exception of Quebec, Ontario's courts apply the Common Law, the system of law that evolved from the decisions of the English courts.

**Legislative Buildings**. *See* **Queen's Park**

# Liquor Control Board of Ontario

Since June 1, 1927, the Ontario government has been operating liquor stores, and established 16 of them during that first year. Ontario had just come through almost 11 years of prohibition of the sale of liquor, wine, and beer, an economic measure that had been introduced in 1916 to support Canada's involvement in World War I. During this time, the manufacture of these products was legal, and they could be dispensed as a prescription by a qualified medical practitioner.

Within a year of opening its first outlets, the Liquor Control Board of Ontario (LCBO) had 86 stores in operation. From 1919 to 1934, prohibition was in force in the United States, even though it was legal under Canadian law to export alcohol across the border. Ontario's close proximity and easy-to-cross border points led to rampant smuggling of alcohol, or bootlegging, as it was called. Liquor seized in the U.S. often included bottles with counterfeit LCBO seals on them.

Strict rationing in World War II reduced sales in the province, but the post-war period saw more expansion by the LCBO. By 1956, the number of stores had climbed to 215. Anyone buying alcohol filled out a piece of paper and passed it over the counter to a clerk for service. In 1969, the first self-serve store opened in the **Toronto** area, although advertising on the premises was still prohibited. The self-service concept proved so popular, however, that there were more than 500 of them by the mid-1980s.

During the past 15 years, the LCBO has opened more stores, brightened its image, modernized its merchandising, loosened regulations on advertising, staffed some stores with wine consultants, and computerized its inventory and sales system. There are about 600 LCBO stores in Ontario and almost 100 agency stores, which are operated by established retailers in communities not large enough to support a regular operation. Agency stores carry fewer products and have no standard design.

In the late 1990s, the LCBO passed $2 billion in annual net sales for the first time in its history and transferred a record $745 million dividend, excluding taxes, to the province to support schools, hospitals, roads, and other projects. Although there have been suggestions by the current Conservative government to privatize the LCBO, it continues to operate as a Crown agency that reports annually to the Minister of Consumer and Commercial Relations. It was recognized by the Retail Council of Canada as Canada's Innovative Retailer of the Year in both 1997 and 1998.

It is the largest single retailer of beverage alcohol in the world and offers more than 5,000 products for sale from more than 60 countries. The LCBO conducts about 200,000 tests on 11,000 different alcoholic beverages each year as part of its quality assurance programs, to ensure the products it sells meet the LCBO's and the federal Food and Drug Act's standards.

(*See also* **Wineries**)

**Locks.** *See* **Canals**

# London

On March 2, 1793, the Lieutenant-Governor of Upper Canada, John Graves Simcoe, arrived at the forks of the Thames River. He saw before him an area of rich meadow and forest that had been settled by **First Nations peoples** known as the Attawandarons. Simcoe imagined a city rising from this natural beauty— "New London"—which would be the future capital of Upper Canada.

But several factors led Simcoe to choose **Toronto** (then called York) as the capital instead. It wasn't until 1826 that London began to develop as a village when it was selected as the judicial and administrative centre of the London District.

The threat of military raids from Americans gave rise to the designation of London as a garrison town for British troops in the 1830s. The presence of troops led to an expansion of the merchant community, and by the 1840s, improved road links stimulated commercial development and established London as an important regional centre. A fire in 1845 destroyed more than 200 buildings in London, but most had been replaced within two years, when it officially became a town.

By the early 1850s, London had been linked up to the Great Western Railway line (now Canadian National), and on January 1, 1855 it was officially proclaimed a city. With further railway expansion and the discovery of **oil** in 1858 in nearby Lambton County, London's **economy** prospered throughout the rest of the 19th century. Such nationally known companies as London Life Insurance, Canada Trust, and Labatt's all got their start in London at this time and contributed greatly to the growth and stabilization of the city's economy.

London also became home to the University of Western Ontario, which was established in 1878 and continues today to be a major factor in the city's prosperity and identity. By World War I, London was home to some 237 factories and its **population** had grown to approximately 50,000.

During the period from 1918 to 1939, London grew steadily but, like most of Canada, it was affected by the Great Depression. Since World War II, however, London has experienced explosive growth in area and population. A major annexation in 1961 added some 60,000 people. Another annexation of surrounding lands in 1993 added 26,300 hectares to its boundaries and increased London's population to 326,000.

London, also known as the Forest City, is renowned for its tree-lined streets and Victorian-era architecture. Its economy is broad-based with strengths in the **manufacturing** sector, automobile parts, financial services, and food processing. The city is also one of the premier medical centres for research and treatment in Canada and the world, notably for multi-organ transplants. In the early 1950s, the city's medical community pioneered the use of cobalt treatment for cancer.

A variety of cultural activities, festivals, museums, theatres, the university and Fanshawe College, and recreational venues have combined to make London the heart of southwestern Ontario. In the late 1990s, the city was concentrating on revitalizing its downtown. Projects include the construction of a new market resembling London's original 19th-century one, which opened in late 1999; erecting a new downtown arena for its **Ontario Hockey League** team, the London Knights; the strengthening of trade links abroad, particularly in Asia; and preparations for hosting the 2001 Canada Summer Games.

## Loons

It is fitting that the common loon was adopted as Ontario's official bird in June 1994 because the unique cry of this distinctive black and white swimming bird is symbolic of the province's unspoiled wilderness and tree-lined lakes.

Although there are five species of loon worldwide, only four breed in Canada. In Ontario, the common loon (*Gavia immer*) is the most widespread, and probably the most familiar species. Loons breed on freshwater lakes, where their weird, mirthless laugh and eerie wail echoes across the water day and night. They winter along the Atlantic and Pacific coasts of the United States.

Loons eat mainly **fish.** Favoured prey include perch, suckers, sunfish, smelt, and minnows, all common species in Ontario lakes. When fish are scarce, loons eat frogs, newts, crayfish, snails, clams, leeches, and aquatic plants. These birds capture their food underwater. Their legs are placed far back on their body, making them excellent divers and fast swimmers, but clumsy on land.

Loons have been clocked flying at more than 120 kilometres per hour and can dive to a maximum of 30 metres. They have solid, marrow-filled bones (most **birds** have hollow bones), which enable them to dive deeply. Common loons average 4.5 kilograms in weight and the typical loon is about 0.8 metres long, with a wingspan of 1.3 metres.

Loon nests are usually located right next to the water, on a small island or on a mound of vegetation in a marsh, where one or two eggs are laid. The young leave the nest within a day of hatching and often ride on their parents' backs. In Ontario, the number of common loon breeding pairs is estimated to be 100,000.

Most of the loon's breeding range is in the less-populated parts of the country, which have many lakes suitable for breeding. As a result, the loon is not threatened or endangered in Canada as a whole. It does, however, face a variety of threats, including damage to lakes by acid rain, and pressures from habitat loss and human recreational developments.

You may have heard that small lakes never hold more than one pair of loons, and it's true because the birds are solitary nesters. They often chase away birds of other species as well. However, on a larger lake, several pairs may take over different bays.

# Mammals

More than 80 species of mammals may be found in Ontario. Mammals have a number of distinguishing characteristics, including being warm-blooded, and having a body covering of hair and mammary glands that produce milk to nourish their young. The range of mammals in Ontario includes the pygmy shrew— the smallest mammal in North America, several species of **squirrels,** mice, and moles; raccoons; **beavers**; wolves; and large animals such as **moose,** caribou, and black bears.

The black bear is found primarily in the coniferous and deciduous forests of central and northern Ontario. It is noted for its glossy black or dark brown coat, often with a whitish throat patch. An individual's range can vary between 500 and 15,000 hectares, depending on the availability of food. From early November until about April, the black bear stays in its den, often under a brush pile or stump, neither eating nor drinking during its long hibernation. In spring and summer, black bears generally eat carrion and **invertebrates** such as ants and grubs, but also feed on rabbits, **fish,** and a variety of fruits and nuts.

Polar bears can be found in the Hudson Bay area of **northern Ontario.** These huge bears feed mainly on seals, which help them accumulate layers of insulating fat. Polar bears come ashore in July as Hudson Bay melts, making their way back to the ice in late November. The Hudson Bay area is also home to other mammals, including arctic foxes, seals, whales, and walruses.

The Great Lakes–St. Lawrence forest area is home to black bears, lynx, long-tailed weasels, porcupines, several species of bats, eastern chipmunks, moose, and timber wolves. The more northern boreal forest is the habitat for wolverines, otters, caribou, and muskrats, as well as many of the mammals found in the Great Lakes–St. Lawrence region.

In the **Carolinian Zone** of southwestern Ontario, common species include the white-tailed deer, eastern cottontail, red fox, striped skunk, and coyote. Rare species, such as the opossum, Ontario's only marsupial, and the eastern mole, are found in few, if any, other locations in Canada.

The eastern cougar is considered to be the only endangered mammal in Ontario. As well, one species, the eastern elk, has been extinct in Ontario since the early 19th century. Mammals considered vulnerable or threatened are the wolverine, the woodland caribou, the grey fox, the eastern mole, and the southern flying squirrel.

(*See also* **Endangered and Extinct Species**)

# Manitoulin Island

With an area of approximately 2,766 square kilometres, Manitoulin is the world's largest freshwater island. Situated as the dividing point between Lake Huron and **Georgian Bay,** Manitoulin Island has more than 80 inland lakes and a range of topographic characteristics, such as large boulders deposited thousands of years ago by glaciers, limestone plateaus, mossy cliffs, and waterfalls. Manitoulin is primarily made up of limestone, which was sculpted by glaciers thousands of years ago. Its terrain includes rugged cliffs, rivers, rolling farmland, and deep bays.

**First Nations peoples** inhabited Manitoulin for centuries before the Europeans arrived in the 17th century. Manitoulin means "Spirit Island" and to many Native people it was believed to be the home of the Great Spirit or "Kitche Manitou." The Europeans, unfortunately, brought diseases to these people and by the late 1600s the island was mostly deserted. A new Native settlement was established there by the 1830s, however, and a continued influx of European settlers led to new villages on the island by the 1870s.

Because of its location, Manitoulin eventually became an important harbour and site of lighthouses to aid ships sailing on the **Great Lakes.** It also became a thriving turkey production- and sheep-rearing area in the 20th century.

Tourists had begun to visit the island by the 1920s, and today its beaches, fishing spots, and hiking trails continue to make it a popular destination. Manitoulin Island can be reached from the south by ferry from Tobermory on the Bruce Peninsula or from the north via a bridge from Espanola.

# Manufacturing

Ontario is known as Canada's industrial heartland because it is the country's leading manufacturing province, producing more than 50 percent of all Canadian manufactured goods and 80 percent of the nation's manufactured exports. The manufacturing sector provides direct jobs for more than 890,000 Ontarians.

This leadership status was well established at the time of Confederation. Since that time, the trend has been to place industry in Ontario because the province has first-rate transportation links, including railways, major airports, and the **Great Lakes–St. Lawrence Seaway System**; abundant natural resources, such as minerals and trees; widespread access to relatively cheap hydroelectric power; and ready access to more than 300 million consumers in the United States.

The major manufacturing industries in Ontario, based on total value of shipments, are: transportation equipment, $80.9 billion; food processing, $20.2 billion; electrical and electronic products, which includes the fast-growing high-technology sector, $18.5 billion; chemical and chemical products, $15.4 billion; and primary metals, including the steel industry, $14.4 billion.

Nearly all of the transportation equipment sector consists of automobiles and auto parts, which ring up annual sales of more than $80 billion. Automobiles are Ontario's biggest industry, providing more than 110,000 jobs and making up more than 43 percent of the province's international merchandising exports. With the help of modern technologies such as robotics, more than 1.5 million cars and trucks are built every year, with about 85 percent exported, mainly to the U.S.

Major auto factories are located in a number of cities, including Oshawa, Oakville, **Windsor,** St. Catharines, Cambridge, Ingersoll, and Alliston. More than 500 auto parts manufacturing plants are found in Ontario, many near the automobile assembly plants in the southern part of the province.

The food and beverage processing industry, with more than 1,000 processors in Ontario, accounts for 42 percent of Canada's food and beverage shipments. Sixty-five of the 100 largest Canadian food companies are headquartered in Ontario.

The province's electronics and electrical products industries produce a wide range of goods from computers to instrumentation controls, robots, and house-

*Workers build furniture in an Ottawa factory in the early 1900s.* (National Archives PA-42329)

hold appliances. The Ontario **economy** is shifting toward export-oriented, higher value-added industries, with knowledge-based industries such as computers, software, and medical technologies among the fastest growing sectors. The province's main pockets of high-tech industries are located in Ottawa's **Silicon Valley North, Toronto,** Markham, Mississauga, and **Kitchener-Waterloo,** where products range from telephone switching equipment and protective suits worn by bomb squad personnel to Internet firewalls and software that prevents telephone fraud.

The chemical sector is found mainly in Sarnia's **Chemical Valley,** with the industry as a whole accounting for 60 percent of Canadian chemical shipments and 55 percent of employment in Canada's chemical industry. A large variety of products are manufactured in Ontario, including plastics, fertilizer, and rubber.

The primary metals sector, with such large companies as Dofasco, Algoma, and Stelco located in **Hamilton** and Sault Ste. Marie, tallies 80 percent of Canadian steel production, 12 percent of North American production, and 2 percent of all steel produced globally.

Other important manufacturing industries in Ontario include:

• Process machinery, which helps companies produce, process, assemble, or manufacture goods. This sector, which builds robots, printing machinery, mining equipment, compressors, industrial fans, and sawmill and woodworking machinery, among other items, ships about $7 billion worth of products every year and employs more than 37,000 people at 670 establishments in Ontario.

• Plastics production, which includes material suppliers, mould makers, processors, and a variety of end users, including auto assembly companies and construction firms. Typical products include trim and other components found on cars and trucks, flooring, films, and packaging. Ontario accounts for 60 percent of all Canadian shipments and 55 percent of jobs in this industry, which sends 93 percent of its exports to the U.S. Much of the industry is based in the Toronto area.

• The aviation and aerospace industry, with annual sales in the $5.5 billion range, includes companies which are world leaders in the production of aircraft, flight controllers, landing gear, electronic warfare systems, cockpit display systems, and training simulators. Ontario is responsible for about 41 percent of Canada's aerospace sales, making the province the world's sixth-largest aerospace producer, led by 300 companies that provide employment for some 25,000 people. Ontario-made products are used in more than 80 countries in airports and on spacecraft, aircraft, ships, tanks, and other military vehicles.

The United States is Ontario's largest export market, accounting for more than 90 percent of Ontario's total exports in 1997, when Ontario ranked third as an importer into the U.S., behind Japan and China. Ontario's major international markets outside of the U.S. include the United Kingdom, Germany, South Korea, Japan, Brazil, and Mexico.

# Maple Leaf Gardens

Like Toronto's **SkyDome,** Maple Leaf Gardens was an architectural marvel of its time. The arena, which in 1999 ended a 67-year run as home of the National Hockey League's **Toronto Maple Leafs,** was built during the Depression when investment funds were scarce and financiers skeptical. Incredibly, the Gardens was built in five and a half months, less than a quarter the time needed to build the home of the **Toronto Blue Jays** baseball team.

Located on Carlton Street in downtown **Toronto** and owned by Maple Leaf Sports and Entertainment, Maple Leaf Gardens was the pet project of team owner Conn Smythe. He decided his club needed new quarters after it consistently drew up to 8,000 fans at the Mutual Street arena, where the team played until the Gardens opened in 1931. More than 1,200 labourers were employed on the building, which when finished extended 13 storeys above street level.

Opening night, November 12, 1931, saw the Maple Leafs lose 2–1 to the Chicago Blackhawks. The capacity crowd of 13,233 was impressed with the new facility as they paid seat prices ranging from 95 cents to $2.75.

Between the Leafs' first game and the team's departure, the Gardens experienced many changes. Initially, the alterations reflected advancements in technology, such as floodlights installed in 1935, glass to replace link fence along the boards in 1947, and the addition of escalators in 1955. The "blue" sections of seats were added to the north and south ends in 1966–67, setting the capacity at 16,182 spectators for hockey games. Sixty-seven private boxes were completed in 1981, with an additional sixteen "super boxes" added in 1991.

During its run of nearly seven decades, the arena built a string of hockey memories, as well as many that have little to do with sticks and pucks. Among the hockey highlights are: the last Stanley Cup won by the Leafs in 1967; Darryl Sittler's 10-point game in 1976; Rick Vaive's 50th goal in 1982 (he was the first Leaf to hit the 50-mark); the Leafs' 1942 Cup win, when they became the first team in pro sports to win a best-of-seven title after being down 3–0 in games; Harold "Mush" March's goal, the first marker scored in Gardens' history at 2:30 of the first period in the Blackhawks 2–1 win; and play-by-play man Foster Hewitt's radio broadcast of that game.

Non-hockey memories include: boxing matches featuring Muhammad Ali, Floyd Patterson, and Joe Louis; appearances by wrestlers such as Hulk Hogan and Andre the Giant; tennis matches played by such stars as Bjorn Borg and Ilie Nastase; basketball games featuring Wilt Chamberlain and the Los Angeles Lakers; regular appearances by the Harlem Globetrotters; and in 1946 the first professional basketball game of the Basketball Association of America, a forerunner of the National Basketball Association (NBA), when the New York Knickerbockers defeated the Toronto Huskies.

Other activities held in the hockey shrine have featured lacrosse; track and field; speed skating; church services; ballet; circuses; orchestral, operatic, and choral recitals; political rallies; roller derby; bingo; rodeos; softball; and water polo. Music greats who have performed at the Gardens include The Beatles (in 1964 and 1965), Bill Haley and his Comets, Liberace, Frank Sinatra, Chubby Checker, the Rolling Stones, Jimi Hendrix, Bob Dylan, U2, John Mellencamp, and Bruce Springsteen.

Representatives from the world of politics to visit have included Winston Churchill, William Lyon Mackenzie King, Lester Pearson, John Diefenbaker, and

Pierre Trudeau. British royalty came to the Gardens in October of 1951 when Princess Elizabeth visited with her husband Prince Philip.

Although it's no longer the home of the Leafs, the Gardens is still in use as a concert venue and the home of the St. Michael's Majors of the **Ontario Hockey League.** The Leafs still practise there when their new home, the Air Canada Centre, is hosting other attractions. In 2000, the Gardens played host to the Heroes of Hockey game, which is part of the NHL All-Star weekend.

Although many a tear was shed when the Air Canada Centre took over as the Leafs' home, most hockey fans conceded the Gardens was an outdated building that didn't offer the comfort and amenities of the NHL's newer buildings. The Air Canada Centre, where the Leafs also lost their first game to the Chicago Blackhawks (on February 20, 1999), is located about 1.6 kilometres south of the Gardens next to Union Station, and is also the home of the **Toronto Raptors** of the NBA. It seats 19,500 for basketball and 18,500 for hockey. It is equipped with wider seats and more executive boxes than the Gardens, more food kiosks, a food court, a brew pub, and a state-of-the-art sound system and scoreboard/clock.

# Maple Syrup

When **First Nations peoples** began tapping Ontario's sugar maple trees more than 300 years ago, few would have thought the sweet elixir they produced would develop into a multi-million-dollar industry in the province.

Today, Ontario is the fourth-largest maple syrup–producing jurisdiction in the world, following Quebec, Vermont, and New York State. Ontario syrup, which makes its way onto pancakes, toast, and desserts and is used to cure meats and make maple sugar, candies, maple butter, maple cream, taffy, and granulated and hard sugar, accounts for 7 percent of Canada's annual production of 21,000 kilolitres and has a farmgate value of more than $21 million. Quebec accounts for 80 percent of Canadian syrup production.

Ontario has more than 600 production facilities—30 to 40 of which are major enterprises. These businesses tap maple trees every spring to collect sap which is put under intense pressure, then heated and boiled to remove water. The final product is a concentrated syrup that is filtered and canned. It takes 40 litres of sap to make one litre of maple syrup.

Ontario syrup and maple products are exported to Japan, Germany, the

United States, and Europe. In 1999, sap was tapped from about 1.5 million of the province's 70 million tappable sugar maples. Key syrup-producing areas are Lanark County and several surrounding counties in eastern Ontario, as well as areas between **Toronto** and **Kingston** and north and west of Toronto.

But there's more to maple syrup than its commercial value. "Sugar bushes" across the province give people the opportunity to appreciate nature and partic-ipate in a ritual that dates back three centuries. For up to six weeks every spring, when temperatures reach about 5° Celsius in daytime and drop below 0° Celsius at night, the industry provides the public with a special recreational and educational opportunity as Ontarians young and old watch production and sample the results, usually in pancake houses located next to the sugar bushes.

There are about 50 maple syrup producers that open their facilities to visi-tors and almost as many maple syrup festivals. Many producers stay open year round, shipping their products by mail order. In addition, the Maple Syrup Museum of Ontario, located in the village of St. Jacobs, near Kitchener, is pre-serving the heritage of maple syrup–making in the province. The museum col-lects the artifacts of the industry, and offers displays on the history and produc-tion of local maple syrup.

All maple syrup sold in Ontario is required by law to have a sugar content of 66 percent, and no additives are allowed. It is also divided into two grades and four colour classes. Consumers should look for "Maple Syrup" or "Pure Maple Syrup" on the label. The container will also give the name and address of the producer or packer, as well as the volume, grade, and class of syrup.

While maple syrup has been a boon to the Ontario **economy,** the industry suffered a major setback in January 1998, when an ice storm in eastern Ontario damaged or destroyed millions of the province's sugar maples. In some areas, including Lanark County, trees lost 50 to 80 percent of their branches, and syrup production was reduced by up to 80 percent. Thousands of saplings have begun to regenerate in damaged areas, but it will be up to 40 years before these begin producing syrup.

# McMichael Canadian Art Collection

As the only public gallery in Canada dedicated solely to collecting and display-ing 20th-century Canadian art, the McMichael Collection plays a vital role as a national repository for visual culture. Located on 41 hectares of conservation land in Kleinburg, north of **Toronto,** the McMichael Canadian Art Collection owns more than 6,000 permanent works, including those of the **Group of Seven** and Tom Thomson, as well as Inuit and First Nations art. It has custodial care of more than 100,000 works from the Cape Dorset Collection, which are being documented and conserved. This archival collection belonging to the West Baffin Eskimo Co-operative Ltd. in Cape Dorset includes drawings, prints, and sculptures.

The roots of the McMichael collection began in 1951 when Robert and Signe McMichael built a pioneer-style home on 6 hectares in Kleinburg. They began collecting Group of Seven and other Canadian art in 1955, and when word spread about the collection they had assembled, visitors would arrive on their doorstep to look at it. The McMichaels opened their home to the public in the early 1960s, but approached the Ontario government in 1964 about setting up a permanent collection and location for Canadian art. After some negotiations in November 1965, the McMichaels donated their house, property, and 194 works of art to the province in exchange for the government maintaining the grounds and continuing to build the collection. The McMichaels lived in the home until 1981. Robert McMichael worked with the Metropolitan Toronto and Region Conservation Authority to acquire an additional 36 hectares obtained through the purchase, transfer, and lease of lands from the Conservation Authority.

About 40 percent of the gallery's annual $6.4 million budget comes from the Ontario government. In 1998, the McMichael Collection launched a $2 million project to develop a multimedia, interactive CD-ROM called ARTIFICE (Archaeological Research Terminal Intended for Independent Cultural Exploration), which uses art as a primary vehicle to teach 20th-century Canadian history. ARTIFICE was planned for release in 2000.

The McMichael Collection is now housed in an 84,000-square-foot facility that includes 13 exhibition galleries, a restaurant, and a gift shop. There are sculpture trails outdoors and several themed exhibitions. The McMichael's house is still the basis of the building, although it has been refurbished and expanded over the years. Educational programs run throughout the year, and an annual art sale is held each autumn. Some 30,000 students from more than 40 school boards participate annually in the programs.

Six Group of Seven artists are buried on the McMichael grounds: Arthur Lismer, Frederick Varley, Lawren Harris, Franz Johnston, A.Y. Jackson, and A.J. Casson.

# Mennonites

The sight of Old Order Mennonites in their black clothes, driving horsedrawn carriages, is a familiar one in the area around **Kitchener-Waterloo.** However, the 52,600 Mennonites of Ontario, who live throughout the province, form a socially diverse group with a variety of customs and religious practices.

The Mennonites, who were originally known as Anabaptists, date back to the European Protestant Reformation of the 16th century. They separated themselves from Roman Catholics as well as other Protestants by their belief that their relationship with God was an individual decision made in adulthood. They practised adult baptism and for the most part did not pledge allegiance to the church or state.

The Anabaptists were persecuted for their beliefs, and many died as a result, but the movement continued to spread through parts of Europe, particularly in Switzerland, Germany, and Moravia. The Anabaptists, however, were not a

*Old Order Mennonites in horsedrawn carriages are still a common sight near Kitchener.*
(© 2000 Ontario Tourism)

uniform group, with a diversity in beliefs and practices almost from the start. The Mennonites take their name from Menno Simons, a Dutch Catholic priest who renounced his beliefs in 1536 and embraced the Anabaptist faith. He wrote influential books on **religion** and advocated a life of pacifism. Because of their belief in peace and refusal to fight for their country, the Mennonites and other similar sects continued to be persecuted by religious and civil leaders throughout the 17th century. Many Mennonites remained in central Europe during this time, but fled to safer places, such as the Alsace and Prussia.

By the late 17th and early 18th centuries, Mennonites began immigrating to North America, particularly to Pennsylvania, where they could practise their religion without persecution. The American Revolution, however, led some Mennonites to move to Ontario, where land was plentiful and the British government promised religious freedom and a continuance of their German culture.

The first Mennonites in Ontario settled in the Niagara Region, but in 1800 a few families located in Waterloo. They were soon followed by others, who began purchasing large blocks of land in the area and establishing permanent settlements. For the most part, Mennonites owned their houses and land as individuals rather than as a group or colony. By the 1840s, more than 5,000 Mennonites were scattered throughout southern and southwestern Ontario.

About the same time the first Mennonites came to Canada, Dutch-German Mennonites in Europe began moving to southern Russia (Ukraine), where they were able to live in colonies that were allowed a high level of self-government. In the 1870s, some of these privileges were threatened.

The Mennonite **population** in Canada swelled at this point when many Mennonites from Russia immigrated to a new land with guaranteed privileges. Though helped by the Ontario Mennonites, most of these newcomers settled in Manitoba where farmers were needed. One of the attractions of living in Canada was a promise that Mennonites would be exempt from military service. This promise was kept through World War I, when about 13,000 Mennonites lived in Ontario, but there were strong anti-German feelings in the country at that time, and many citizens spoke out publicly against this special treatment. In 1919, the Canadian government passed an Order-in-Council prohibiting immigration into the country by such religious groups as the Mennonites and Hutterites, but the ban was lifted four years later. The majority of Mennonites continued to practise pacifism in World War II, though many provided alternative service on farms, in hospitals, and at logging camps, while more than

4,000 voluntarily enlisted in the armed forces.

Mennonites were primarily involved in **agriculture** from their beginnings in Canada, but fewer than 20 percent of them farm today. While some farmers have adapted to new mechanization and changes in society, others, particularly the more traditional Old Order Mennonites, have resisted, preferring to use the methods that have served them well in the past. Some continue to live in close-knit rural communities, and members of the Old Order Mennonites are often distinguished by their plain dress. But more than half of Ontario's Mennonites now live in cities, and members have developed outreach programs in foreign relief, homes for the aged, nursing homes, and other service organizations.

(*See also* **Religion**)

# Metric System

Ontario, like the rest of Canada, uses the metric system of measurement.

The Canadian government made the decision to change from the historic British imperial system of units (based on yards, pounds, and gallons) to a metric system in 1971. The metric system chosen is known as the Système international d'unites (SI). Rapidly advancing technology and expanding worldwide trade prompted the conversion to metric, because it was clear that a country as dependent upon import and export trade as Canada needed an international measurement system.

Converting to the metric system in Canada was gradual, to allow for the re-education of a public used to the British imperial system. The first use of metric unit measure in everyday Canadian life was unfortunately introduced on April Fool's Day (April 1), 1975, when all temperature announcements were given only in degrees Celsius during weather forecasts. In September 1977, road signs showed distances in kilometres and speed limits in kilometres per hour. At border crossings in Ontario, signs showing how to convert from miles to kilometres were posted to alert American drivers to the new system. The national process of converting to metric was completed in December 1983.

The adoption of the metric system has been controversial from the beginning, both because of the mandatory nature of the government regulations and the fact that many Canadians saw it as an attack on British-Canadian heritage. During the mid- to late 1980s, regulations were relaxed so that the two measures could be posted side by side and small businesses could continue to operate to a limited degree using the imperial system. The metric system is clearly here to stay, however.

The following chart shows common conversions.

| To change | To | Multiply by |
|---|---|---|
| centimetres | inches | .39 |
| metres | feet | 3.28 |
| kilometres | miles | .62 |
| square metres | square yards | 1.20 |
| square kilometres | square miles | .39 |
| hectares | acres | 2.47 |
| kilograms | pounds | 2.21 |
| kilometres | nautical miles | .54 |
| inches | centimetres | 2.54 |
| feet | metres | .30 |
| miles | kilometres | 1.61 |
| square yards | square metres | .84 |
| square miles | square kilometres | 2.59 |
| acres | hectares | .41 |
| pounds | kilograms | .45 |
| nautical miles | kilometres | 1.85 |

# Mining Industry

For more than a century, Ontario has been one of the world's leading mineral producers. In 1999, the value of mineral production was more than $5 billion from 50 operating mines, yielding about 50 different minerals, from precious metals such as gold and platinum to industrial minerals, including salt, gypsum, and talc.

Since 1900, the province has produced nearly 140 million ounces of gold, more than 1 billion ounces of silver, 12 million tonnes of copper, more than 9 million tonnes of nickel, and nearly 9 million tonnes of zinc. Ontario is also a major producer of cement, stone, sand, and gravel. The province's granite, marble, and limestone grace many prominent buildings in Canada, including the legislative buildings in Toronto and the **Parliament Buildings** in **Ottawa**, as well as buildings around the world, such as the Canadian Embassy in Washington.

In addition, more than 300 companies supply more than $1 billion a year worth of mining equipment and services to hundreds of exploration and development projects in Ontario and dozens of countries. The province boasts top experts in technology and metallurgy. On average, mining companies spend more than $300 million annually in Ontario on exploration and development.

The mining and metallurgical sector employs approximately 18,000 people in mines and associated smelters and refineries, with another 5,000 employed in quarries and sand and gravel operations.

Early prospecting opened up much of the northern part of the province. Had it not been for mining, such communities as New Liskeard, Cobalt, Red Lake, Timmins, **Sudbury,** and Wawa might never have made it onto the map of Ontario.

The Sudbury Basin, with 17 operating mines, produces about one-third of the world's nickel. Ontario is Canada's leading source of gold, with three mines at Hemlo on the north shore of Lake Superior accounting for about 25 percent

*After finishing their shift at the 540-metre level at a mine near Timmins, miners wait for a cage that will take them to the surface.* (William James Topley Collection, National Archives, PA-17570)

of Canada's gold and approximately 2 percent of world production. In 1997, the province produced about two-thirds of Canada's salt and more than one-third of its copper. The Sifto salt mine in Goderich, northwest of **London**, is the world's largest, producing more than five million tonnes of salt in 1999. The salt from this operation is primarily used on roads. Ontario also produces more than 80 percent of Canada's cobalt as a byproduct of nickel-copper mining.

On average, more than 136 million tonnes of structural materials are extracted annually in Ontario, including dolostone, shale, sand, and gravel, and the province's stone industry produces more than 36 million tonnes of granite, marble, and limestone. Active quarries in the Kenora, Vermilion Bay, and Sudbury areas deliver high-quality stone to world markets.

Among Ontario's newest mines, all of which came into production in 1997, are Placer Dome's Musselwhite site 500 kilometres north of **Thunder Bay,** which is expected to produce 200,000 ounces of gold a year; River Gold Mines' Edwards mine near Wawa, with potential annual gold production of up to 20,000 ounces a year; and Tomclid Iron Mines open-pit iron mine, about 100 kilometres west of Ottawa, with an estimated capacity of 25,000 tonnes.

Proper care of the environment is an important challenge faced by the mining sector in an era when environmental management is high on the agenda of many Ontarians. The province's mining firms spend about $50 million a year on environmental programs to run operations that are energy efficient and that minimize harmful effects on their surroundings. Fly-in operations, which do not require road construction, reduce the impact of mining in wilderness areas; in the Sudbury area, companies have spent more than $1 billion on sulphur-abatement programs and have planted more than three million trees to rejuvenate land scarred by years of mining. In recent years, mining companies have been required by the provincial government to develop closure plans to restore lands to their natural state upon completion of exploration and mining activities.

# Mississauga Train Derailment

Just before midnight on November 10, 1979, a 106-car freight train carrying explosive and poisonous chemicals derailed in Mississauga, west of **Toronto.**

The mishap, which occurred on what should have been an uneventful run between **Windsor** and Toronto, sparked the largest non-wartime evacuation of people in Canadian history and placed the city in the international spotlight.

Canadian Pacific Train 54, hauling a cargo that included caustic soda, propane, chlorine, styrene, and toluene, was rolling through Ontario's rich farmland and heavily populated areas en route to railyards in Toronto when a bearing overheated, causing a tanker car to lose an axle.

In a light-industrial area about 30 kilometres from downtown Toronto, the car and 23 other rail cars left the tracks. Several that were carrying propane burst into flames. Tankers containing styrene and toluene were punctured, spilling their loads and causing a massive explosion. The yellowish-orange fire rose more than 1,000 metres into the air and could be seen 100 kilometres away.

As firefighters made preliminary plans to battle the fire, several more tankers blew up. Soon after, it was confirmed that some of the derailed cars were carrying chlorine, a deadly chemical that causes suffocation if inhaled.

Over a 20-hour period, emergency officials evacuated nearly 220,000 people—including residents of six nursing homes and staff and patients at three hospitals. The southern part of Mississauga, Canada's ninth-largest city, with a population of 284,000 at the time, was a virtual ghost town.

With the city closed down and commuter traffic to Toronto routed around the evacuated area, fire crews brought several fires under control and eventually affixed a steel patch to a tanker that was leaking chlorine. Gradually, evacuees were returned to their lodgings, with the exception of some who lived close to the derailment or in the path of winds carrying the deadly gas.

On Thursday, November 15, officials announced that there was little leakage and that a small quantity of escaped chlorine gas had dispersed harmlessly over Lake Ontario. A day later, most of the chlorine had been pumped into trucks and shipped safely away and by early evening on November 16, all remaining residents were back in their homes. Miraculously, no one was killed or seriously injured.

In the aftermath, experts from around the world came to Mississauga to determine why the mass evacuation had gone so smoothly. Most credited the police for sealing off the evacuation area, and the efficient network of roads that allowed vehicles to be moved in and out quickly. CP Rail paid more than $1.3 million to cover out-of-pocket expenses evacuees incurred during the derailment, and the federal Department of Transport launched a public inquiry into the accident. A 200-page report highlighted outdated government regulations for transporting potentially dangerous chemicals and pointed to a need for more comprehensive disaster strategies. The accident ultimately led to the development of the federal Transportation of Dangerous Goods Act and assisted in the development of a model for emergency evacuations, which is now in place around the world.

# Moose

This largest member of the deer family, generally greyish or reddish-brown in colour, is found in northern Europe, Asia, and North America, usually in boreal forests that have shrubby growth or young trees. They are most prevalent in Ontario north of the **Great Lakes,** particularly in Quetico Provincial Park west of **Thunder Bay.** In the summer, moose will also live in swamps, marshes, or thickets close to **water**. Their territory may range from 2 to 20 square kilometres.

Their diet consists of young leaves, particularly those of the maple, birch, and aspen, but in summer they also eat water lilies, rushes, and other aquatic plants. Their winter diet consists mainly of buds and twigs.

Moose are relatively inactive during the day, foraging primarily at dawn and dusk, then retiring to a quiet spot to chew their cud. They are skilled swimmers and, despite weighing between 300 and 500 kilograms, can travel as fast as 55 kilometres per hour on land. Moose have a strong sense of hearing and smell, but poor vision.

Breeding season for moose is in September and October. During rutting season, moose call loudly to attract mates, and the males can be unpredictable and dangerous. While they tend to avoid humans, some bulls have been known to charge people, horses, and cars. One or two young are born in late spring. Young moose remain with their mother for about a year. Females begin mating at three years old and will continue to do so for about the next 15 years.

White-tailed deer, which have spread northward into the moose's habitat, have brought with them a parasitic worm that can cause paralysis, blindness, and death in moose. Winter ticks also affect moose, irritating them so much that the mammals will lick, scratch, and rub themselves to the point that they suffer from extensive hair loss. If the weather is cold enough in early spring, some moose may die of hypothermia.

Humans and wolves are the main predators of moose, although bears will attack young moose. Despite the hazards, moose can live to almost 30 years.

# Mosport International Raceway

In the 1950s, a 184-hectare tract of land northeast of **Toronto** near the community of Bowmanville consisted of rolling farmland, groves of trees, and little else. By 1961, this pastoral setting had been converted into Mosport (a contraction of the words motor and sport), one of the most challenging motor racing tracks in the world.

Most definitely, it was a case of "build it and they will come."

Since opening in May 1961 with a clubman's race organized by the Oakville Trafalgar Light Car Club, Mosport has played host to dozens of car racing legends, including Gilles Villeneuve, Bruce McLaren, A.J. Foyt, Jackie Stewart, Bobby Unser, Emmerson Fitapaldi, stock car king Richard Petty, and Stirling Moss, the British racing great whose name is tacked to Moss Corner, two challenging turns on the track.

The 8.4-metre-wide, 3.95-kilometre track, which features fast, sweeping bends that rise and fall over the contours of the site, has featured Formula One cars, Indy cars, Can-Am stock cars, World Endurance, Formula 5000, Formula Atlantic, and Super Vee, as well as Formula Fords, GT cars, superbikes, go-karts, snowmobiles, and off-road machines. The site has also hosted rock concerts, air shows, and sky diving.

Mosport, one of only three tracks in the world to have hosted Formula One, Can-Am, and Indy Car events, also includes an 800-metre paved oval, known as Mosport International Speedway, and a one-kilometre kart track.

# Mosquitoes

Mosquitoes are found in most parts of Canada, and Ontario is no exception—just ask anyone who spends time outdoors in **cottage country,** or even in city backyards, which are often swarming with these annoying pests. Other biting flies can be severe pests in certain areas, but mosquitoes can be encountered both day and night, from early spring until late summer, giving no respite even in autumn in some years.

Of the 74 species in Canada, 57 are found in Ontario. Worldwide, there are more than 3,000 mosquito species, with most occurring in the tropics.

Dominant species in Ontario are from the genus *Aedes*. Three species, *A. provocans, A. stimulans,* and *A. communis,* arrive in spring, usually after breeding in temporary woodland pools and ponds flooded with rain and meltwater. The larvae hatch and develop quickly. These early species account for the great surge in numbers of mosquitoes as soon as leaves appear on the trees.

The first mosquitoes to arrive in Ontario, however, are the *Culiseta impatens,* large mosquitoes that hibernate as adults in woodpiles and other protected areas. These mosquitoes usually appear on warm days in the earliest part of spring.

In June and July, the most common and most bothersome species is *Aedes vexans,* which lays its eggs in damp, open depressions. The drying up of breeding pools in summer is of no consequence once adults have emerged from them, because their eggs can survive until water returns, sometimes for many years. Known as Canada's worst pest mosquito, *Aedes vexans* is capable of repeated rapid breeding during hot weather and may become unbelievably abundant during summers with heavy rainfall, resulting in a severe reduction in livestock gains and milk production.

Also significant are five species from the genus *Anopheles.* These breed in temporary water-filled basins, such as tires and tree holes, and can carry malaria, although none is known to be a carrier of the disease in Canada at this time. *Culex pipiens* is also common in southern Ontario, hatching throughout the summer in puddles and roadside ditches and generally preferring **birds** rather than people. This species is a primary carrier of St. Louis encephalitis, which can sicken people and be carried by birds, which are not adversely affected. However, there has been no outbreak of this disease in Ontario for several years.

Mosquitoes are not the only species of bloodsucking flies that harass people and livestock in Ontario: others are black flies, biting midges (also called no-see-ums, punkies, or sand flies), horse flies and deer flies (collectively called tabanids), horn flies, and stable flies.

(*See also* **Invertebrates**)

# Museums

If you're a museum fanatic, Ontario is the place to be—just don't plan on seeing every museum in the province in one lifetime.

As more than one museum-goer has learned, Ontario is a goldmine of unique, educational, world-class—and, yes, weird—museums and collections. In fact, there are more than 600 nonprofit museums and another 200 commercial venues where you will find everything from reconstructed dinosaurs, shoes,

*The Canadian Museum of Nature in Ottawa is one of the more than 800 Ontario museums where visitors will find everything from reconstructed dinosaurs and contraceptives to paintings and antique cars. (Randy Ray)*

sports artifacts, and contraceptives, to paintings, animals, guns, skis, stamps, trophies, caricatures, antique cars, and state-of-the-art movie theatres.

**Toronto** alone has more than 50 institutions that the Ontario Museum Association defines as "museums," including halls of fame, libraries, historic homes, archives, art galleries, and castles, while **Ottawa** has more than 20. All are publicly accessible and have either a collection of some sort, or a display of Canada's heritage or culture.

Among the largest and most popular are **Casa Loma,** the **Hockey Hall of Fame,** the **Royal Ontario Museum** and Black Creek Pioneer Village in Toronto; the Canadian Museum of Nature, the National Museum of Science and Technology, and the Royal Canadian Mint in Ottawa; the **Canadian Football Hall of Fame** in **Hamilton**; **Upper Canada Village** in Morrisburg; **Science North** in **Sudbury,** and **Fort Henry** in **Kingston.**

Some of the interesting smaller facilities include: the Agricultural Museum in barns on the grounds of Ottawa's **Central Experimental Farm**; Dressler House, home of Canadian-born actress Marie Dressler; the Dionne Quints Museum in North Bay; the Algonquin Park Logging Museum in Whitney; the

Oil Museum of Canada in Oil Springs; and the Maple Syrup Museum of Ontario in St. Jacobs. The Canadian Canoe Museum in Peterborough has the largest collection in the world of canoes, kayaks, and other self-propelled watercraft.

And, of course, Ontario has its share of off-the-wall museums. One is Louis Tussaud's Waxworks in **Niagara Falls,** where, in the tradition of Madame Tussaud's in England, you'll find a waxy crowd of famous people, including John Lennon, George Burns, and Pablo Picasso. Another is the Museum of Contraception, in Toronto, which includes hundreds of artifacts used from 1850 B.C. until today, including crocodile dung and intrauterine devices.

# National Gallery of Canada

Built on Nepean Point, a promontory overlooking the Ottawa River and in full view of Parliament Hill, the National Gallery of Canada offers its glass-vaulted Great Hall as one of the most recent additions to the capital city's skyline. In its current quarters since 1988, the gallery's collection houses Canadian, European, American, and Asian works of art, including paintings, photographs, prints, drawings, sculpture, and a contemporary collection of film, video, and multimedia by Canadian and international artists, such as the **Group of Seven,** Van Gogh, Picasso, Andy Warhol, Betty Goodwin, and Mark Rothko.

But its history dates back to 1880 when the first gallery was housed in the Clarendon Hotel in downtown **Ottawa.** Among its other temporary homes was a remodelled workshop on Parliament Hill, where it shared space with the Supreme Court of Canada.

The gallery's early works included *Sunrise on Saguenay* (1980) by Lucius O'Brien, the first president of the Royal Canadian Academy; *Gulf of Naples* by European artist Vilhelm Melbye; and *A Venetian Bather* (1889) by Canadian artist

Paul Peel. Over the years, the gallery has acquired paintings by the Group of Seven, Tom Thomson, Cézanne, Picasso, Rembrandt, Benjamin West, and Barnett Newman, whose controversial painting *Voice of Fire* raised an uproar in 1990.

Perhaps the gallery's most important role is as the home of 800 Canadian paintings, sculpture, and decorative works, with the world's most comprehensive collection of paintings by Tom Thomson and the Group of Seven, including Thomson's *The Jack Pine* (1917), A.Y. Jackson's *The Red Maple* (1914), and Lawren Harris's *North Shore Lake Superior* (1926). Paintings by Emily Carr, Jean-Paul Riopelle, and Edwin Holgate, and works by many Inuit artists are also part of the Canadian collection.

The gallery is well known for its ambitious program of special exhibitions from around the world, which have included the works of Picasso, Cézanne, Renoir, and Monet. A notable exhibition was "Van Gogh's Irises: Masterpiece in Focus," in the summer of 1999.

**National Parks.** *See* **Bruce Peninsula National Park**; **Fathom Five National Marine Park**; **Georgian Bay Islands National Park**; **Point Pelee National Park**; **Pukaskwa National Park**; **St. Lawrence Islands National Park**

# Niagara Escarpment

As one of Ontario's most scenic landforms, the Niagara Escarpment winds some 725 kilometres from Queenston to the islands of **Fathom Five National Marine Park** in **Georgian Bay.** It then runs underwater to **Manitoulin Island** and continues across the northern edge of Michigan.

The escarpment originated more than 450 million years ago as the shore of an ancient body of water. Skeletons of primitive sea animals were added to layers of sediment over time to create the shale, sandstone, and limestone of the escarpment. Nature has sculpted the rock over millions of years into the wonderful landscape seen today.

Within the escarpment lie wetlands, rivers, creeks, streams, and an abundance of wildlife. Its old-growth **forests** harbour some eastern white cedars that are among the oldest living trees in eastern North America. Some experts believe the escarpment is the most diverse ecosystem in the province.

More than six million people live within an hour's drive of the escarpment, and in recent years there have been concerns about overdevelopment of the land around it. In response, the Ontario government approved the Niagara Escarpment Plan in 1985 and revised it in 1994 as a way of preserving the natural environment of the area. The plan calls for promoting land stewardship and conservation, funding the restoration of natural habitats, and educating the public on environmental matters.

More than 100 public parks and natural areas are contained in the escarpment. In 1990, the United Nations Educational, Scientific and Cultural Organization (UNESCO) designated it an International Biosphere Reserve, for its successful balance of conservation and preservation of an ecosystem with surrounding development. The escarpment is one of only six such reserves in Canada. The popular **Bruce Trail** runs along the length of the escarpment, allowing people to enjoy its natural beauty.

# Niagara Falls

Known as the "Honeymoon Capital of the World," Niagara Falls and the surrounding area have intrigued humans for thousands of years. The falls were created some 12,500 years ago during the retreat of Ontario's last ice age. The word Niagara may come from the Iroquois *Onguiaahra,* meaning "the strait," although other sources say it's a Neutral Iroquoian word meaning "thunder of water."

Although Europeans first visited the falls in the early 17th century, the first man to write about the cataract was a priest, Father Louis Hennepin, who arrived there in December 1678. He described the falls as "frightful" and that he "could not behold [them] without a shudder." The falls sit on the border between Ontario and New York State. The Canadian or Horseshoe Falls are 54 metres high and 675 metres wide, while the American Falls are 64 metres high and 305 metres wide.

The falls have been a tourist attraction since about the 1820s. In 1846 the first *Maid of the Mist,* a boat that gives visitors a close-up look at the falls, began taking sightseers to the base of the American Falls. The arrival of the railway in the 1860s brought visitors from across North America and people also came from around the world. A decade later, **tourism** was the area's dominant industry. The falls have also long been the subject of paintings and photographs. The first-known photographs ever taken in Canada were of Niagara Falls. Hugh Lee

*The "honeymoon capital of the world" has also been a source of power for much of Ontario for almost a century. (© 2000 Ontario Tourism)*

Pattinson, a British scientist, visited in April 1840 and took several daguerreotypes (an early form of photography) while there.

The **water** of the falls has been used as a source of energy since the 1750s, when French settlers used the rapids above the falls to turn mill wheels. By the late 1880s, Americans were trying to harness the waterfall to run turbines that could generate electrical power. Canadians, in particular Sir Adam Beck, began working to utilize the falls' power in the early 1900s, and the first power plants were built in 1905–1906. Two hydro plants there today are named in his honour.

The growth of power companies in the area, however, threatened the falls as a tourist attraction, and today an international agreement calls for diverting only about half the water that would flow over the falls to the two hydroelectric stations on the Canadian side and the one on the American side. The three plants produce more than 31 million kilowatts and fuel many of the industries in northeast North America.

On several occasions, the falls have actually run dry, most notably in March 1838 when an ice jam blocked the flow of water to the falls for about 30 hours. Frozen conditions also stopped the falls a few times in the 20th century, and in 1969 the American Falls were manually stopped for five months so military engineers could examine the eroding face.

The falls have attracted their share of daredevils who have either tried to survive going over the falls in barrels or, like Jean Francois Gravelet, also known as

Blondin, walked across on tightropes. As one of the great natural wonders of the world, Niagara Falls attracts about 12 million visitors annually.

# Northern Ontario

Fewer than 8 percent of Ontarians live in northern Ontario, but the region's contribution to the province's economic and social fabric is immense. So large, in fact, that many residents of this ruggedly beautiful part of the province consider themselves and their region distinct from the rest of Ontario.

Ontario's north is a diverse 81-million-hectare area of forests, lakes, minerals, wetlands, prime agricultural land, and modern communities. Measuring roughly 1,000 kilometres from north to south and 1,100 kilometres from east to west at its widest point, it makes up more than 75 percent of Ontario's land mass, spans two time zones, Eastern and Central, and lies in two climatic zones, boreal forest and subarctic.

Northern Ontario's southern boundary follows the Canada–U.S. border from Lake of the Woods to **Manitoulin Island,** then travels east across the southern limits of Parry Sound and Nipissing districts to the Quebec border. It is bounded in the east by Quebec, in the west by Manitoba, and in the north by Hudson and James bays.

The region contains 163 incorporated municipalities, consisting of five major cities (**Thunder Bay, Sudbury,** North Bay, Timmins, and Sault Ste. Marie) and scores of smaller communities. There are also 441 unincorporated communities and organizations without municipal structure that deliver local services. Thunder Bay and Sudbury provide specialized health, educational, financial, and commercial services for northwestern and northeastern Ontario respectively.

Northern Ontario has 11,000 kilometres of provincial **highways,** more than 7,000 kilometres of rail lines, a 10-million-tonne **Great Lakes** port facility at Thunder Bay, and 63 publicly owned airports. In remote areas, **air travel** plays an important role in delivering goods, ferrying tourists, and evacuating the sick. The region is dotted with countless lakes and rivers, which had been used as travel routes by **First Nations peoples** for centuries before the arrival of Europeans. In the 17th century, they became main routes for the English and French explorers, early settlers, and fur traders, who travelled along the Mattawa and French rivers toward the **Great Lakes.** Today, northern Ontario's lakes and rivers are a popular destination for canoeing, kayaking, powerboating, white-water rafting, fishing, and sailing.

In relation to the south, northern Ontario has always been sparsely populated. In 1871, just 15,000 people lived in the north, most of them in communities clinging to the shores of Lake Huron, including Sault Ste. Marie, Batchawana, Bruce Mines, Manitoulin Island, Spanish River, Killarney, and Lake Timiskaming. Today, northern Ontario's 826,000 residents represent 7.7 percent of the province's total **population,** with more than half living in the north's five major cities.

About 68 percent of northerners speak English as their first language and 17 percent grew up speaking French. In all, northern Ontario is home to 31 percent of Ontario's francophone population.

More than 45 percent of Ontario's First Nations population lives in northern Ontario, where Native people make up 8 percent of the total population. About 7 percent of the region's population came to Canada from another country. The greatest growth spurt in the history of northern Ontario occurred in the 1950s during a period of unprecedented economic prosperity. The boom, mostly in the mining sector, pushed the population from 536,000 in 1951 to 722,000 by 1961.

The north's labour force totalled 413,200 in 1998, up from 403,600 in 1997. Fifty-seven percent are employed in services, 15 percent in mining, 12 percent in forest products, 8 percent in tourism, 7 percent in **manufacturing,** and 1 percent in **agriculture.**

Long before Confederation, animal furs were the north's major resource. First Nations peoples trapped, prepared, and traded furs to Europeans for tools, weapons, and other goods. Gradually, the appeal of fur gave way to silk as a favoured fashion material, and by the 1840s timber and minerals were the resources of interest. Initially, huge virgin stands of white pine forest were harvested around Nipissing and Timiskaming in the northeast and the Fort Frances area in the northwest. Later, the area prospered with mineral discoveries at Bruce Mines, Michipicoten, and Red Lake, and Silver Mountain and Silver Islet near Thunder Bay.

At the end of the 20th century, the northern **economy** owed much of its prosperity to the forestry and mining industries, along with **railways,** which played a key role in the founding of most northern communities. These resource-based industries, plus tourism, contribute more than $13 billion annually to the provincial economy and provide about 75,000 direct jobs.

Other industries play an important role too. According to the most recent figures available, $9.8 billion worth of manufactured goods (including forest and mining products) was shipped from northern Ontario in one year, while farm cash sales, mainly from beef and dairy farming, totalled more than $100 million. In recent years, the region has seen considerable growth in the emerging telecommunications and information technology sectors, in particular companies that provide telecom services, such as local Internet service providers, call centres, Web site developers, and on-line businesses.

Although it was not always the case, the provincial government now recognizes the importance of northern Ontario. The first cabinet minister from northern Ontario was appointed in 1905. Over the years various branches and ministries were created to develop the north and give the region a voice at **Queen's Park** in **Toronto.** In 2000, the region has two ministers in the provincial cabinet and is also represented by the Ministry of Northern Development and Mines.

# Nuclear Power

Twenty of Canada's 22 nuclear power reactors are located in Ontario. Eight are at the Pickering Nuclear Generating Station, four at the Darlington Nuclear Generating Station, both east of **Toronto,** and eight are at Bruce Nuclear Generating Stations A and B at the Bruce Nuclear Power Development near Kincardine.

Together, they are capable of supplying more than 70 percent of the province's electricity needs. In 1999, however, eight of the reactors were not operating. As a result, nuclear power was providing Ontario with only 41 percent of its electricity.

The facilities are operated by Ontario Power Generation, formerly Ontario Hydro, which runs another 67 hydroelectric and fossil fuel generation stations to meet the province's remaining electrical needs. The three nuclear power stations employ about 9,000 people.

Nuclear power was introduced in Ontario when the federal government built a nuclear reactor for research purposes at Chalk River on the Ottawa River following World War II. In the late 1950s, when it became apparent that the residential and industrial power needs of the rapidly expanding province could not be met by hydroelectric and fossil fuel–powered generating stations, Atomic

Energy Canada Limited (AECL) began designing a nuclear reactor for Ontario Hydro.

The decision to go nuclear was also based on the fact that much of the coal needed to fire fossil fuel stations was located in the United States, where labour disputes often threatened access to the resource. In addition, the fluctuating value of the Canadian dollar against its American counterpart had the potential to make coal costs prohibitive. Another factor was that uranium, the fuel source for nuclear reactors, was plentiful in Canada, thereby reducing the province's dependence on outside fuel sources. And because the power plants could be built in southern Ontario, close to the people who would use the power, the cost of electricity would generally be less than other forms of energy production.

In 1962, the first Ontario Hydro/AECL reactor went into operation at the Douglas Point Nuclear Generating Station midway between the towns of Port Elgin and Kincardine on Lake Huron. Canadian General Electric was also a partner in the venture, which cost $34.5 million. The station used CANDU (CANada Deuterium Uranium) reactors fired by natural uranium fuel to boil water into steam, which turns turbines and drives generators that produce power.

In 1971, Pickering Unit 1 was the first Ontario Hydro commercial nuclear reactor built in Canada. Today's Pickering Nuclear Generating Station on the shore of Lake Ontario is built around eight CANDU reactors that enable the facility to produce its enormous electrical output for a whole year with no more fuel than would fill a two-car garage. When all eight reactors are in operation, the Pickering station is capable of producing about 20 percent of all the electricity consumed in Ontario, enough to serve a city of two million people.

The Darlington Generating Station is Ontario's newest CANDU nuclear generating station, located on a 485-hectare site 70 kilometres east of Toronto. It opened in 1992 and provides about 20 percent of Ontario's electricity needs.

Since 1995, four reactors at the Bruce Nuclear Generating Station have been removed from service, and in 1997, four reactors at Pickering were also stopped. All were shut down when the utility's board of directors decided to focus its staff and resources on its 12 newest reactors. The eight non-operational reactors are expected to be put back in service between 2003 and 2009, although in 1999 the Ontario government was attempting to sell the Bruce facility or find investors to run it as a joint venture with the province.

Many people remain skeptical about the safety of nuclear power and methods of storing spent nuclear fuel—in part because of several accidents at the facilities, such as spills of heavy water, in which the hydrogen atom is replaced by deuterium, a heavier isotope of hydrogen. However, the utility maintains that the utmost in safety features have been installed at each nuclear power facility and also notes that Ontario's nuclear plants have never been involved in a serious accident. An aggressive program of inspection and maintenance keeps equipment in peak working order.

Nuclear supporters also point out that nuclear power has clear environmental benefits because it does not pollute the air. They also say that nuclear waste is compact and easy to store, although the perfect method of storage is still being sought. The waste, which can remain radioactive for more than a thousand years, is stored at each of the reactor sites and at a larger storage facility at the Bruce Nuclear Power Development.

# Oil

In the summer of 1858, James Miller Williams, a carriage maker from **Hamilton,** struck oil more than 15 metres below the ground near Oil Springs in southwestern Ontario. With this discovery and the subsequent pumping, transportation, and marketing of the product, Oil Springs can lay claim to being the birthplace of Canada's modern petroleum industry.

The discovery was important because by 1850 geologists and chemists had agreed that crude oil would be superior to the dwindling supplies of whale oil used for illumination and lubrication. North America was becoming increasingly urbanized, the population was better educated and reading more than previous generations, and the lighting of cities and homes was becoming an essential part of 19th-century society. Prior to the well dug by Williams, oil had been used only if it bubbled to the surface. Although Americans claim the first well was in

Titusville, Pennsylvania, in 1859, the Oil Springs discovery predates it by a year.

As Williams began to sell the oil, he found clients throughout Ontario and New York. He formed a partnership with other Hamilton entrepreneurs and opened a refinery in 1860 called the Canadian Oil Company. They would eventually sell lamp fuel to customers in Europe, South America, and Asia. The discovery of oil set off a boom around Oil Springs as people moved to the area to dig more and deeper wells. In the early 1860s, the demand for oil increased, and one well in the area was said to be generating 7,500 barrels a day. For a short time Canada was the world leader in the petroleum industry.

When production in Oil Springs began to drop, new wells opened in nearby Petrolia, and that town's population began to swell. Both towns were named for their connections to the industry. During the 1860s and 1870s, **London** was oil's business centre. That soon changed, however, as the first refinery in Sarnia was established by 1871, leading eventually to the development of that city's **Chemical Valley,** a collection of refining companies that would thrive in the 20th century.

A revival of the industry in Oil Springs in the 1880s and continued steady production in Petrolia helped the oil business in Ontario mature. Many people grew wealthy because of oil, and the region became known for its wealth of drilling expertise. Drillers who called themselves "Hard Oilers" began taking their knowledge abroad in the late 19th century and well into the 20th century. They were crucial to the opening of oil fields in such places as Indonesia, southeast Asia, Russia, the Ukraine, South America, and the Middle

*An oil well near Petrolia shoots the black liquid skyward.* (National Archives, C-30224)

East. Few oil fields in the world were without the expertise of Ontario drillers.

In the early 20th century, the oil fields of Petrolia began to dry up and the refinery business became even more firmly established in Sarnia. Today, however, there is still a scattering of oil wells in the Petrolia–Oil Springs area. The jerker rods that pump the oil from historic wells can be seen in fields in southwestern Ontario, but they produce only about 75,000 barrels annually. The province's total oil industry is relatively small, producing about 1.7 million barrels annually, about the equivalent of one day of production in Alberta. Ontario's oil industry peaked in 1995, when 1.8 million barrels were pumped, and revenues from oil were their highest in 1996 at $47 million.

The Oil Museum of Canada in Oil Springs and the Petrolia Discovery Site, which is a working oil field in Petrolia, tell the story of this important part of Ontario's past.

## Ontario Boundary Dispute

At the time of Confederation in 1867, Ontario's boundaries were declared to remain what they had been when the province was known as Upper Canada. Unfortunately, those boundaries had never been specifically defined in the north and west. When the federal government purchased the Hudson's Bay Company's lands in 1869, a dispute over the province's boundaries developed between the two levels of government.

The federal government believed Ontario's northern boundary to be the height of land that marked the Hudson Bay watershed, while the western boundary was considered to be west of Fort William (now **Thunder Bay**). Ontario's premiers during this time, notably Oliver Mowat, disagreed. They wanted Ontario's boundaries to be at **James Bay** and the Albany River in the north, and Lake of the Woods in the west. In 1878, a federal commission agreed to the northern boundary of the Albany and a western one that included Lake of the Woods. But the federal government under Sir John A. Macdonald didn't want to comply. The federal government further complicated the matter by declaring in 1881 that Manitoba's boundaries would be extended eastward to include the region between Fort William and Lake of the Woods.

Because of this disagreement, Ontario and Manitoba each kept a municipal government and police force for two years in what is now Kenora. Both provinces also held provincial elections in the same jurisdiction. Finally, the dispute over who owned what went to the Judicial Committee of the Privy Council at Westminster, England, in 1884. The committee ruled in favour of Mowat and Ontario, but it would take another five years before the Ontario Boundary Act was passed by the federal government, giving Ontario full possession of its resources and lands in the disputed area. The province's boundaries were further expanded north and west in 1912, so that its total area is now more than one million square kilometres.

# Ontario Hockey League

The Ontario Hockey League—with teams in 18 Ontario communities and two cities in the United States—is renowned for feeding young hockey players to the National Hockey League.

Since the first NHL entry draft in 1968, 1,644 players have been selected from the OHL, more than from any other talent source in the world. An average of 50 OHL players are drafted every year by such NHL teams as the **Toronto Maple Leafs,** Montreal Canadiens, and St. Louis Blues. In most seasons, 30 percent of the players on NHL teams' active rosters hail from the OHL.

OHL graduates include Eric Lindros of the Philadelphia Flyers; Wayne Gretzky, who played with the Edmonton Oilers, Los Angeles Kings, St. Louis Blues, and New York Rangers; Doug Gilmour, whose NHL clubs have included St. Louis, Toronto, New Jersey Devils, and Chicago Blackhawks; and Bobby Orr, the great Boston Bruins' defenceman. The OHL, which is for players 16 to 20 years old, has also produced its share of top NHL coaches, including Scotty Bowman and Roger Neilson, who coached the Peterborough Petes, and Terry Crisp, who coached in Sault Ste. Marie and played in **Niagara Falls.**

The OHL's roots date back to the 1890s when the first junior hockey was played in Ontario. The OHL became an independent league in 1974. Today's teams play a 68-game schedule during which they vie for the right to play in the Memorial Cup Tournament, the national championship of the Canadian Hockey League (CHL). The CHL is the umbrella group for junior hockey in Canada and also includes the Quebec Major Junior Hockey League and the Western Hockey League. The 1999–2000 season marked the first time inter-league games were held between the OHL and the Quebec Major Junior Hockey League.

OHL teams are: Belleville Bulls, Kingston Frontenacs, Oshawa Generals, Ottawa 67's, Peterborough Petes, Barrie Colts, Mississauga IceDogs, North Bay

Centennials, Sudbury Wolves, Toronto St. Michael's Majors, Brampton Battalion, Erie Otters (based in Erie, Pennsylvania), Guelph Storm, Kitchener Rangers, Owen Sound Platers, London Knights, Plymouth Whalers (based in Plymouth Township, Michigan), Sarnia Sting, Soo Greyhounds, and Windsor Spitfires.

On average, more than two million fans attend OHL games every season.

# Ontario Place

With a variety of rides, mini-golf, an IMAX theatre, waterslides, and an amphitheatre for concerts, there is no shortage of ways to amuse yourself at Toronto's Ontario Place.

The $29 million venue opened on May 22, 1971, near the **Canadian National Exhibition** on the city's waterfront, spread over three artificial islands that covered 38 hectares with 5.5 kilometres of pathways.

Response to the site was immediately positive, as Ontario Place won a variety of architectural awards for its design. The Forum concert venue attracted top musical acts, while Cinesphere was the world's first commercial IMAX theatre. Also on site since the beginning was the H.M.C.S. *Haida,* a destroyer which was commissioned in 1943 and sunk more enemy tonnage than any other ship in the Royal Canadian Navy.

*Thrill seekers enjoy the log ride at Ontario Place.*
(© 2000 Ontario Tourism)

Each year since its opening, Ontario Place, which now sits on about 48 hectares of parkland, has added new features to keep visitors coming back. Among the additions over the years have been the Children's Village, the Wilderness Adventure Ride, the Hydrofuge waterslide, Sea-Trek, a deep-sea submarine simulator, and Cool Hoops, a state-of-the-art basketball challenge. In 1995, the Molson Amphitheatre opened on the site with seating for 16,000 and an additional 7,000 on the lawn. New in 1999 was Mahogany Harbour, an interactive wooden boat museum that offers boat building, sailing, rowing, and regatta.

Ontario Place, which is an agency of the provincial government's Ministry of Economic Development, Trade and Tourism, is open each year from the long weekend in May to early September. It attracts about 2 million visitors annually.

# Ontario Provincial Police

The Ontario Provincial Police (OPP) provides province-wide general policing services to more than 2.3 million people, a number that swells to 3.6 million every summer. The OPP area of responsibility encompasses nearly the entire province—approximately 993,000 square kilometres of land and 174,000 square kilometres of Ontario's waterways.

In accordance with Ontario's Police Services Act, OPP responsibilities include front-line municipal and First Nations policing, traffic patrol on all 400 series and King's **highways,** patrol of waterways and snowmobile trails, policing of **provincial parks,** specialized criminal investigative services, and provincial emergency assistance.

The OPP also maintains the provincial serial predator Violent Crimes Linkage Analysis System and the provincial firearms registry, administers the Private Investigators and Security Guards Act, and provides security at **Queen's Park** and for key Ontario government officials and visiting dignitaries.

Founded in 1909 with a complement of 51 men, the OPP is now one of North America's largest police agencies. It maintains 82 detachments and 106 satellite offices in six regions throughout the province. Its broad range of services is made possible through the use of thousands of mobile units, including helicopters, snow vehicles, boats, motorcycles, and cars. In 1999, the OPP's 6,450 uniformed and civilian employees served as patrol officers, scuba divers, marine operators, canine handlers, and helicopter and fixed-wing pilots.

Members of the OPP also investigate major crime cases and provide technical identification expertise. Special teams are trained to handle incidents requiring emergency response, tactical, and rescue expertise, including bomb and explosive occurrences. Other members work closely with their communities through classroom education and community organizations. The effectiveness of the OPP also relies upon its civilian employees, who work in areas such as telecommunications, technology, forensics, research, and human resources, and upon the OPP Auxiliary, whose 837 members make it the largest police auxiliary in Ontario.

In 1995, the OPP relocated its general headquarters from downtown **Toronto** to Orillia, a city of 27,000 people about 120 kilometres north of Toronto. Orillia is also the site of one of the OPP's six regional headquarters. The others are in **London,** Aurora, North Bay, Smiths Falls, and **Thunder Bay.**

(*See also* **Public Safety**)

# Ontario Science Centre

The Ontario government decided in 1964 to build a science centre for the province as a Centennial project. A site just off the Don Valley Parkway in **Toronto** was chosen, and construction began in 1966. Premier John Robarts officially opened the Ontario Science Centre on September 27, 1969, and since that time more than 35 million people from around the world have visited it.

The Science Centre, which houses more than 800 hands-on exhibits in a variety of halls within the building, has featured a wide range of demonstration projects and exhibits over the years. Among the highlights in its 30-year history have been the first World Crafts Exhibition in 1974, which featured artisans from 50 countries; a demonstration of First Nations heritage in 1976; the popular "China: 7000 Years of Discovery" in 1982; the Mindworks exhibition in 1991, which was a collaboration with the American Psychological Association; and the Living Earth exhibit on challenges to the natural environment, which opened in 1993. Other popular exhibits have included the science behind roller coasters, an examination of infectious diseases, the latest information technology, different modes of transportation, the science of sport, and programs on weather, geology, physics, and engineering.

Visitors can also see daily live demonstrations, such as the effects of static electricity, the chemical impacts of extreme temperatures, paper making, and a trip through the solar system in the Starlab. The 320-seat Shoppers Drug Mart OMNIMAX Theatre opened in the centre in December 1996, the first of its kind in Ontario. The films shown on the 24-metre wrap-around dome screen have entertained more than 700,000 visitors.

Each year about 200,000 Canadian school students visit the centre, and 56 high school students from across Ontario are selected each year to study for a semester in the centre's own Science School, which was established in 1982. A report by Tourism Toronto in 1998 showed that the centre is the fastest-growing tourist attraction in the Greater Toronto Area. The Science Centre also reaches out to millions of people outside Toronto by marketing its exhibits and expertise around the world.

(*See also* **Science North**)

# Ontario's Name

The name Ontario was first used by Europeans beginning in the 16th century to describe the area they explored along the **Great Lakes.** But in 1791, when Quebec was divided, the western portion was called Upper Canada. That name was changed in 1841 to Canada West, which lasted until Confederation in 1867, when Ontario became the name of the new province.

According to research from the Archives of Ontario, the name derives from an Iroquois word; however, there are several possible explanations of its origin. One theory says the name is a variation of the word *kanadario,* which means "sparkling or beautiful water." The name was first used to describe the body of **water** known as Lake Ontario and it then came to include the land along the shores. Another explanation is that the name derives from *Onitariio,* meaning "beautiful lake," while a third possibility is that it came from *Skanadario,* meaning "very pretty lake."

It's also been argued that the concept of beauty being applied to a geographical feature was alien to the Iroquois, and that Ontario may just have meant "a large body of water."

# Order of Ontario

The Order of Ontario is the province's highest and most prestigious annual award. Established by Order-in-Council in December 1986, the award recognizes individuals who have shown the highest degree of excellence and achievement in any field and whose contributions have enriched others' lives, bettered their communities, and helped improve society.

More than 240 people have been invested in the Order of Ontario since its inception, including dancer Karen Kain, scientist and astronaut Dr. Roberta

Bondar, and author Margaret Atwood. Award winners receive a white and green medal in the shape of a **trillium,** which bears in its centre the province's coat of arms surmounted by a crown.

Each year the Ministry of Citizenship, Culture and Recreation researches and verifies nominations for the Order, and an advisory council prepares a short list of recommended recipients. Nominees must be residents of Ontario and not currently holding political office. Members of the Order of Ontario have the right to use the letters "O.Ont." after their names.

# Ottawa

From the outside, Ottawa has long been perceived as a stable city, where major change is the exception rather than the rule. This notion has been fuelled by its image as a "one-horse town" dominated by the federal government.

In fact, the nation's capital, like many large Canadian cities, has undergone its share of alterations over the years. As the 20th century drew to a close, Ottawa was well into perhaps its greatest change ever, the swing from what was essentially a single-industry government city to one with a burgeoning high-technology industry that had mayors and economic development officials in other municipalities green with envy.

In the middle of the 19th century, a similar transition occurred when this booming frontier lumber town with a generation of growth behind it was named the capital of Canada. Government was a large but minority player in the life of the city and for more than a generation it did little to shape the community. But as the lumber industry began to decline at the end of the century, government began its 20th-century ascension to dominance.

Ottawa was established in 1826 by Lieutenant-Colonel John By near the mouths of the Rideau and Gatineau rivers. It began as an unnamed campsite set up as a construction base for the Rideau Canal, which by 1832 would link Ottawa and **Kingston.** By 1827, a considerable settlement named Bytown had sprung up, and in the 1830s the timber trade to Britain became the focus of economic activity. By the middle of the century, trade in squared timber, large milling operations, and Bytown's connection to the Grand Trunk Railway and American rail networks were driving the community's **economy.** Major entrepreneurs of the period included Thomas McKay, J.R. Booth, and Erskine Bronson, whose names can be found on streets and buildings in Ottawa today.

In 1855, the community's name was changed to Ottawa, which is thought to derive from a First Nations tribe of the same name. Two years later, it was selected by Queen Victoria as the permanent capital of the United Province of Canada. Construction of the **Parliament Buildings** began in 1859 on a plot of land overlooking the Ottawa River, and in 1865 some 500 politicians and civil servants moved from Quebec City to Ottawa. In 1867, the city became the capital of the new Dominion of Canada, fortunately for Ottawa, since the sawn lumber industry would decline significantly in the 20th century.

The growth of the federal government gave the city a sense of permanence that could never be guaranteed by the volatile lumber industry. It also brought a well-paid civil service and inspired a building boom which produced hundreds of homes, government buildings, churches, post offices, fire halls, and schools. In 1901, there were about 1,000 civil servants employed in Ottawa and by 1921, close to 10,000.

The early 1900s marked the end of Ottawa as a lumber town, as the government evolved and grew in size to deal with important issues that faced the growing country. These included the sorry state of Canada's economy in the Depression era, its involvement in World Wars I and II, and the development of programs to deal with the unemployed and the aged, as well as health care and financial aid to families. As a result, job growth in the federal government boomed in the 1950s and '60s, and the number of civil servants jumped from 38,000 to about 105,000 in the 1970s. By the 1980s, some 120,000 employees were on the federal payroll in the Ottawa area.

Synonymous with the rise of government was the growing municipality's desire to develop parks and parkways and preserve the natural heritage of the city and region. Beginning in 1958, the National Capital Commission created a 17,600-hectare greenbelt, which runs in a continuous 44.8-kilometre arc on the outer edge of the Ottawa urban area and has since been expanded to more than 20,000 hectares.

At about the same time, the Ottawa landscape further changed with the assembly of tracts of land circling the city core. On these, the government built decentralized government offices, including Tunney's Pasture and Confederation Heights, usually about four or five kilometres from Parliament Hill. Eventually, inner-city railway lines were removed, an automobile freeway known as the Queensway was built, and scenic parkways were built along the Rideau Canal and Ottawa River.

Key developments from the 1960s onwards included highrise developments in the city centre; the closure of Sparks Street (a main east-west downtown thoroughfare) to vehicular traffic to become the Sparks Street Mall; the evolution of world-class hospitals; construction of the Rideau Centre, a downtown shopping complex linked to hotel and convention facilities; and the rapid growth of the suburban communities of Nepean, Gloucester, and Kanata in Ontario, and Gatineau and Aylmer across the Ottawa River in Quebec.

In 1969, the Regional Municipality of Ottawa-Carleton was established as a means to provide major infrastructure services to the expanding urban area. It was the first regional government created in Ontario. By 1981, the Ottawa Region had a population of 717,978, and in 1996 it crossed the one million mark. The region's current population is approximately 1.1 million, of whom 44 percent speak both French and English. In 2000, Ottawa and its surrounding municipalities were slated to be amalgamated into a single city.

As Ottawa enters the 21st century, it is a more vibrant city than ever before. Once mocked as a community that rolled up its streets after 5 p.m., it now has an extensive entertainment, cultural, and social scene with restaurants, nightclubs, theatres, galleries, **museums,** numerous **festivals,** and professional sports. Although the city lost the Ottawa Rough Riders Canadian Football League team in the 1990s, it gained National Hockey League status in 1992–93 with the arrival of the **Ottawa Senators,** who returned to the city after a 58-year absence.

But the most significant change relates to the region's labour force. With the rise of the high-technology industry, the government's role as the dominant employer has slowly been diminished: in 1976, the government accounted for more than 32 percent of all jobs in the region and the technology sector only 3.1 percent. But by the late 1990s, just 18 percent of all workers were employed by the government and 10 percent in the technology field. The Ottawa Economic Development Corporation in late 1999 predicted that the high-tech sector would catch and surpass the government as the region's primary source of jobs by 2002.

The transition has occurred for two reasons. In the mid-1990s, federal government belt-tightening reduced the civil service workforce by 15,000 people. And between the 1970s and '90s, a high-technology corridor now known as **Silicon Valley North** sprang up, stretching from downtown Ottawa through the city's west end, across the neighbouring City of Nepean and into Kanata, where more than 900 high-tech companies have built facilities.

The Ottawa area is also the site of world-leading research and development laboratories, including the National Research Council and the Communications Research Centre, four universities, and two advanced technical colleges. A strong life sciences sector includes such fields as biotechnology, medical technology, and health-related systems. Twenty-four research institutes in the region focus on the life sciences and invest approximately $300 million a year in research and development.

The federal government remains the foundation stone of the region's success, however. Including Crown corporations and government agencies, it continues to employ more than 100,000 people and its presence contributes to Ottawa's high-technology culture by purchasing goods and services, acting as a training ground for future high-tech employees and entrepreneurs, and serving as an incubator for ideas, which are often developed as products and services by the technology sector. Each year the federal government spends about $8 billion on goods and services and, as a major landowner, landlord, and tenant, contributes to the stability of the local real estate market.

Despite the many changes, the Ottawa region has maintained its reputation as a safe, clean, and dynamic place to live, work, and visit, due in part to its 57 recreational parks, 47 golf courses, 15 beaches, wide variety of festivals, and many nearby resorts. More than 5.5 million tourists and business travellers visit Ottawa annually, generating about $1 billion worth of yearly economic activity and firmly establishing **tourism** as the city's number-three industry behind the federal government and technology.

# Ottawa Senators

After a 58-year absence from the National Hockey League, the Ottawa Senators returned to the NHL for the 1992–93 season. Not since 1934, when the New York Americans defeated the Senators 3–2 before 6,500 fans, had **Ottawa** had its own NHL team. The first version of the Senators won nine Stanley Cups between 1903 and 1927.

Professional hockey's long road back to the national capital began in 1989, when Terrace Investments of Ottawa filed a letter of intent with the NHL for an expansion team and later unveiled plans for a new arena in Kanata, a city on the western outskirts of Ottawa. In December 1990, Ottawa was awarded the franchise.

With former Philadelphia Flyer player Mel Bridgman as general manager and Rick Bowness as head coach, the Senators played their first regular season home game in temporary quarters at the Ottawa Civic Centre on October 8, 1992. They beat the Montreal Canadiens 5–3, but the victory was not a sign of what was to come, not in the team's early years, at least.

The first few seasons for the new Ottawa Senators were tough ones: Ottawa ended its initial season with a dismal record of 10 wins, 70 losses, and 4 ties. But things gradually improved and by 1996–97 the team made the playoffs for the first time, and it took the Buffalo Sabres seven games to knock the Senators out of the Eastern Conference quarter-final series. That season, the Senators moved into their new rink, the Palladium, later renamed the Corel Centre.

In 1997–98, the club finished the regular season with 83 points, establishing a club record for most points in a season. The following year, the Senators finished with 103 points and earned their first regular-season Northeast Division title. Fans were stunned, however, when the team was knocked out of the first round of the playoffs after losing four straight games to the Sabres.

In 2000, the Senators were a Stanley Cup contender and owed much of their success to a handful of front-line players, including wingers Daniel Alfredsson, Shawn McEachern, and Marian Hossa; defencemen Wade Redden and Chris Phillips; and goalie Ron Tugnutt. Head coach Jacques Martin, NHL coach of the year in 1998–99, also deserves plenty of credit. High-scoring Russian centre Alexei Yashin was a hold-out in the 1999–2000 season because of a contract dispute.

The Senators entered the 1999–2000 season with Marshall Johnston as their new general manager.

# Ottawa Valley

You know you've arrived in the Ottawa Valley when you stop for gas or a snack and you're greeted with the phrase, "G'day, g'day."

It's the way folks say hello to one another up and down this wide glacial valley, which stretches from the North Bay area to just north of **Ottawa** where it merges with the Laurentian Lowlands.

Although there has been much debate about its boundaries over the years, much of the Ottawa Valley sits within Renfrew County, with a population of 91,000 and an area of 4.8 million hectares. Its boundaries are roughly: on the north and east, the Ottawa River from Arnprior to North Bay; on the south and west, an irregular line along the edge of Algonquin Park to Whitney, through Madawaska, Barry's Bay, Combermere, Denbigh, and Calabogie.

The Valley, as it's commonly referred to, was first visited by Europeans in the early 17th century, when it was the home of the Algonquians who called the Ottawa River *Kichesippi* (Grand River). For a few years in the late 17th century, another First Nations tribe—the Ottawas—traded on the river, and its name was changed to the Ottawa at that time.

Sporadic European settlement began late in the 18th century, primarily in the area in and around what is now the National Capital Region. By the 1840s the Valley had become a major lumber supplier, based on a vast supply of tall white pine trees. British and some French settlers had moved into the low-lying areas where the soil was suitable for agriculture. In the latter part of the 18th century, many German immigrants arrived in the Valley.

Today, the **economy** of the Ottawa Valley relies on logging, **agriculture, tourism,** a Canadian Forces Base with a contingent of 4,800 military personnel at Petawawa, and a **nuclear power** research facility at Chalk River. Its largest urban areas are Petawawa, with a population of 15,000, and Pembroke, with about 13,500 people.

The Valley is well known for its pristine waterways, rolling woodlands, and dramatic landforms, and for its simple pleasures and old-fashioned values. It's also home to some of the best whitewater rafting in the province.

And it's not without its heroes and legends. Five men who played with the Renfrew Millionaires hockey team in the early 1900s—Frank and Lester Patrick, Fred Taylor, Newsy Lalonde, and Fred Whitcroft—are members of the **Hockey Hall of Fame** in **Toronto,** as are former Pembroke residents Frank Nighbor, Harvey Cameron, and Hugh Lehman, who also played professional hockey. Local folklore has it that Mussie, a six-metre monster, lives in Muskrat Lake at Cobden, and Big Joe Mufferaw, also known as Canada's gentle giant, is a mythical lumberjack brought to life by local raconteur Bernie Bedore.

# Paramount Canada's Wonderland

It's no exaggeration to say that Paramount Canada's Wonderland is this country's Disneyland. It may not have the year-round sunshine that Disney sites south of the border can offer and it's not open 12 months of the year, but it is one of Canada's premier theme parks.

Located 30 minutes north of downtown **Toronto,** Wonderland, as it's known for short, features nine themed areas and more than 180 attractions that bring more than 3 million people every year. The 120-hectare park is open daily from late May until early September, and weekends only during early May and into early October.

When Wonderland first popped out of the ground in 1981 on a block of farmland next to busy Highway 400, it was owned 75 percent by Taft Broadcasting and 25 percent by Great West Life. It was purchased by Paramount in 1992, and since 1994 has been owned by Viacom Inc., a developer and operator of regional theme parks and other entertainment attractions across North America.

At the core of Wonderland's many activities are its thrill rides, including the greatest variety of roller coasters in North America. Among the 11 coasters found at the park are The Fly, Top Gun, the Mighty Canadian Minebuster, and the Bat, a backward-looping coaster. Other thrill rides include Drop Zone, a 23-storey free-fall plunge, and Xtreme Flyer, Canada's largest free-fall swing.

If that's not enough, there's also an 8-hectare water park, games, go-karts, live shows, fireworks, laser shows, concerts featuring such big-name performers as Amanda Marshall and Fleetwood Mac, two themed areas for children, and a seemingly endless supply of shops, eateries, souvenir outlets, and costumed characters strolling the grounds.

Paramount Canada's Wonderland is also a generator of jobs, employing more than 3,700 seasonal employees and 160 year-round workers.

# Parliament Buildings

"If anyone in the country really wants to feel like a Canadian, this little group of stone buildings is the place to visit." These words, penned in 1996 by an **Ottawa** writer, say it all about Canada's Parliament Buildings. Rare is the Canadian who hasn't felt a patriotic thrill on visiting Parliament Hill for the first time.

For more than 130 years, the Parliament Buildings have been the venue where prime ministers, members of parliament (MPs), senators, and bureaucrats have developed, debated, and finalized the laws and policies that govern the lives of all Canadians. Issues dealt with on the Hill have included income tax rates, health care programs, capital punishment, conscription, trade agreements, the Goods and Services Tax, and political scandals.

*Whether you are a tourist or a politician, the Centre Block is where you'll find most of the action at Parliament Hill.* (Andrew Ray)

The main parliamentary edifices—consisting of the Centre Block, with the Parliamentary Library attached at the rear, and the east and west blocks at either side—occupy a parcel of land 350 metres by 350 metres, 60 metres above the Ottawa River. The Centre Block and library were first designed by Thomas Fuller and Chilion Jones in 1859, and reworked in 1863 by Fuller and Charles Baillairgé. The east and west blocks were designed by Thomas Stent and Augustus Laver. The Parliament Buildings were built between 1859 and 1867 (except for the library, which was completed in 1877) on property originally known as Barracks Hill, which once changed hands for a paltry £12. The government set aside $480,000 to cover construction costs, but by the time the job was complete, the bill had mushroomed to 10 times that.

The Parliament Buildings officially opened in June 1866, nine years after Ottawa was selected by Queen Victoria as the permanent capital of the United Province of Canada. The Dominion Parliament held its first session in 1867, the same year that Ottawa became capital of the Dominion of Canada.

The Parliament Buildings provide space for the House of Commons and Senate to meet, as well as offices for the prime minister, MPs, senators, the Speaker of the House of Commons, bureaucrats, administrators, and office staff. They also house committee rooms, cafeterias, a gift shop, the library, a reading room, the Memorial Chapel, and part of the Parliamentary Press Gallery. As Canada's premier landmark, the Parliament Buildings attract approximately 500,000 visitors every year.

Other buildings have been added to the Parliamentary complex over the years, all located on Wellington Street, which runs in front of Parliament Hill: the Confederation Building built in 1927, a few minutes' walk west of the Centre Block and now used to house MPs, cabinet ministers, and government officials; the Langevin Block across the street from Parliament Hill, built between 1883 and 1889 as a departmental building, but now used as offices for the Privy Council and the prime minister; and the Wellington Building across Wellington Street from the West Block, built in 1925 as the Canadian head office for the Metropolitan Life Insurance Company and now providing office space for MPs, the House of Commons human resources department, and a host of others who help Parliament run smoothly.

Although there have been several renovations and restorations over the years, each of the buildings is original, with the exception of the Centre Block, which was badly damaged in a spectacular fire in 1916. The block took 10 years and $12 million to reconstruct, and when finished was wider, longer, and one storey higher, with a taller and more slender central clock tower, dubbed the Victoria Tower like its predecessor. In 1933, it was renamed the Peace Tower.

Architecturally, the Parliament Buildings represent Canada's best example of Gothic revival style, with pointed arches, lancet windows, prominent and exposed buttresses, and variegated stonework set off by brick trim. The Centre Block, including the library and the 92.2-metre-high Peace Tower with its 53-bell carillon, is the most impressive of the buildings. Unfortunately, visitors rarely see beyond its first floor visitors' centre, the legislative chambers, the Peace Tower, and the library. That's not bad though, because that's where most of the action is.

# Pelee Island

Located in Lake Erie, Pelee Island is the southernmost inhabited part of Canada and home to about 275 residents year round, with about 1,000 in the summer. Humans have lived on Pelee Island for about 10,000 years, but it was the 17th-century French traders who gave the island its present name ("pelée" means bald or barren).

In 1823, William McCormick bought the island for $500 from a settler named Alexander McKee. McCormick eventually moved his family here and began clearing the land and farming it. Grape growing for wine began in the 1860s, and today the island is noted for its vineyards, with Pelee Island wines considered among the best in Canada (see **Wineries**).

Pelee Island was home to several animals that are now extinct, including the American mastodon and the passenger pigeon. Although the biodiversity of the island has diminished over time, it is still inhabited by such rare-to-Canada species as the Lake Erie water snake and Blanchard's cricket frog.

In addition to **agriculture,** the island, which is approximately 14.5 kilometres long and 5.6 kilometres wide (about 4,000 hectares), has a long-established fishing industry. Today its unspoiled beaches and **forests** make it a popular spot for cottagers and tourists. The island is reached by ferry, which runs from Kingsville to Scudder Dock in the north of the island, or by airplane from **Windsor.**

(*See also* **Point Pelee National Park**)

# Peterborough Lift Lock

This 19.8-metre-high concrete structure is as much a part of Peterborough as Peter Robinson, the city's namesake and the man who directed settlement in the central Ontario community in the early 1800s.

Built between 1896 and 1904, it is the world's highest hydraulic lift lock and one of the city's most popular tourist attractions. With the ability to raise and lower vessels in two water-filled chambers, the lock is an essential component of the 370-kilometre-long Trent-Severn Waterway as it enables boaters to overcome a considerable rise in the Trent River between Little Lake and the Otonabee River at Nassau Mills.

Richard B. Rogers, the engineer who constructed the lock, expected the single lift to decrease lockage time for commercial traffic. The waterway, which connects Lake Ontario at Trenton to **Georgian Bay** at Port Severn, was intended to become a commercial passageway between Lake Ontario and the upper **Great Lakes** and western Canada.

Average transfer time through the lock is 10 minutes and an average of 3,900 boats pass through each year. The lock consists of nearly 20,000 cubic metres of concrete poured without a single piece of reinforcing steel, largely because the use of steel rod was viewed with skepticism when the lock was built. To this day, it is considered an engineering marvel.

(*See also* **Canals**)

# Petroglyph Provincial Park

Deep within a forest northeast of Peterborough lies Petroglyph Provincial Park, the site of an extraordinary collection of "picture-words" called petroglyphs that depict turtles, snakes, humans, and other animals and objects. About 900 markings, which had deep spiritual meaning to their carvers, constitute one of the largest concentrations of First Nations rock art in North America and are regarded as an archaeological treasure.

It is generally agreed that the glyphs were carved on a 60-metre by 35-metre slab of crystalline limestone by Algonquian-speaking peoples 500 to 1,000 years ago. However, it is not known when the site was abandoned, or how long it slept in the woods undisturbed by humanity before being discovered in 1924 by Charles Kingam, a member of the Peterborough Historical Society.

The provincial park was established in 1976 and a glass enclosure was erected in 1984 to protect against the effects of acid rain, algae, frost, and vandals.

# Point Pelee National Park

Despite its small size (20 square kilometres), Point Pelee National Park, the southernmost point of mainland Canada, contains a variety of terrain that few parks can equal. As well as having one of the last large freshwater marshes on the **Great Lakes,** Point Pelee features a blend of **forests,** fields, and beaches, that meet to form a sandy southern tip that changes its shape based on winds, waves, and currents.

Part of the **Carolinian Zone,** the park contains five distinct habitats: the marsh, the Carolinian forest, the cedar savannah, the beach, and the swamp forest. In addition to its many species of **birds,** Point Pelee is home to several **reptiles** and **amphibians,** butterflies, and **mammals,** including the southern flying squirrel, which was re-introduced in 1993. Because of its southern location and the moderating influence of Lake Erie, Point Pelee shelters a variety of plants and animals rarely seen elsewhere in Canada. Among the rare species found here are the native honey locust, green milkweed, prickly pear cactus, the prothonotary warbler, and the five-lined skink.

Evidence of First Nations settlements go back to 600 A.D. In the 1790s, several First Nations families lived on the point and grew corn there. At about the same time, the British declared the southern portion of Point Pelee a naval reserve to ensure that its forests of oak and white pine were available for shipbuilding. As more European settlers moved into the area in the 1830s, farming such crops as apples, peaches, and grapes became important, and commercial fishing enterprises sprang up. Although there had been about 100 Chippewas living in the area in 1850, their population dwindled, and in the 1871 census no First Nations people were recorded.

In the late 1800s, several citizens led by W.E. Saunders, a young naturalist, became interested in studying the number of birds that migrated and nested in the area. In the spring of 1901, Point Pelee became the first site in Canada to report a nesting pair of cardinals. Those birds have since spread northward throughout many parts of southern Ontario.

As more people became interested in the birds and other wildlife of Point Pelee, they began lobbying the federal government to protect the area. Thanks to their efforts, Point Pelee became Canada's ninth national park on May 29, 1918. All hunting and trapping were now regulated by the government, and the area effectively became a game sanctuary. Point Pelee, however, continued for many years to be the only national park in Canada where sport hunting was allowed.

**Camping** and other recreational activities at the park have been popular since the early 1900s, and by the 1930s more than 250,000 visitors came to Point Pelee annually. The high level of visitor and vehicular traffic and the desire from some quarters to develop the land for cottages all put strains on the park, but the government resisted attempts to overpopulate Point Pelee. Like some other national parks, however, two hotels were built here, the Post Hotel and the Aviation Inn, which operated until the 1960s. Several conservationists argued that the national park should be preserved more for its unique flora and fauna than for the recreation of visitors, but throughout the 1940s and '50s more facilities were built and parking lots were added. Annual visits climbed to more than 700,000 by the early 1960s.

Point Pelee came close to losing its national park status at this time, but in 1972 a Master Plan for the park was introduced and approved. It called for returning all privately owned lands within the park's boundaries to the public, to ban camping, and to create a transit system that would reduce the number of parked cars at the southern tip. The reduction in car traffic has benefitted the park and led to the development of about 12 kilometres of trails in the park for hiking, biking, and cross-country skiing.

Today, Point Pelee National Park remains a popular place for birdwatchers and nature enthusiasts. Group camping only is available to registered educational and nonprofit groups. The park also features a visitors' centre, several workshops, theatre programs, and interactive presentations. Its popularity has caused some environmental problems, however. In December 1999, the Canadian Nature Federation published a report stating that Point Pelee was the second most endangered national park in Canada because of the high number of visitors.

In July 1999, the Nature Conservancy of Canada bought back Middle Island, the southernmost part of Canada, from a private American owner for $1.3 million. The island, which lies about 3.5 kilometres south of **Pelee Island,** at the same latitude as the northern boundary of California, is to become a national park run in conjunction with Point Pelee National Park.

# Polar Bear Express

One of the most popular excursions in **northern Ontario** is the 299-kilometre (one-way) rail journey known as the Polar Bear Express. This day-long train ride runs six days a week in the summer from Cochrane to Moosonee, Ontario's only saltwater port, and takes travellers along the Arctic watershed, crossing such historic rivers as the Moose and Abitibi, which were vital links in the province's **fur trade.**

The excursion is operated by Ontario Northland Railway, a provincially owned enterprise originally known as the Temiskaming and Northern Ontario Railway. The railway was built in the early 1900s to link small towns in the areas of Lake Timiskaming and Lake Nipissing but wasn't connected to Moosonee until 1931. The Polar Bear Express has been running since 1964.

The railcars that carry passengers along the route have large windows so tourists can enjoy the lakes, forests, and muskeg that make up much of this part of the province. What passengers don't see are polar bears, which are not found in this region.

Moosonee's waterfront is the point of departure for large barges that take building supplies and other goods to communities farther north. Across the Moose River is Moose Factory, the oldest English-speaking settlement in Ontario, founded as a trading post for the Hudson's Bay Company in 1673.

Over the past five years, more than 16,000 passengers annually have ridden the Polar Bear Express.

# Population

In 1861, just over 500,000 people lived in Ontario. In 1901, the population was two million. Since then, the number has grown steadily and in 1999 was headed toward the 12 million mark, one-third of Canada's population.

Census data shows that more than 80 percent of Ontarians live in towns and cities, while only 8 percent live in the vast expanse of **northern Ontario.** Half of the province's residents live along the western end of Lake Ontario, between St. Catharines and Oshawa, an agricultural, commercial, and industrial belt known as the **Golden Horseshoe.** The largest city is **Toronto,** with a population of 2.4 million. When residents in the surrounding regions of Peel, York, Halton, and Durham are added in, the total population is 4.6 million. The entire area is called the Greater Toronto Area, or the GTA for short.

Other large cities in Ontario, with 1999 populations in brackets, are Mississauga (544,382), **Hamilton** (317,000), Brampton (285,000), Oshawa (134,364), and St. Catharines (130,000) in the south; **London** (330,258), **Windsor** (200,062), Kitchener (181,703), Cambridge (103,000), and Waterloo (83,000) in the southwest; **Ottawa** (330,228) and **Kingston** (110,327) in the east; and **Thunder Bay** (116,965), **Sudbury** (91,056), and Sault Ste. Marie (80,054) in the north.

Many of the province's 500 municipalities developed along lakes and rivers, near railway lines, at mine sites, and in other areas where resources and jobs were plentiful. Immigration has been an important factor in Ontario's population growth throughout the province's history. In 1783 and 1784, **United Empire Loyalists** fleeing the American Revolution were the first large group of immigrants to arrive in Ontario. During the 19th and early 20th centuries, they were joined by people from the British Isles. There was also localized immigration from Quebec into eastern Ontario. After 1945, immigration from continental Europe, the West Indies, East Asia, and a handful of African countries had a discernible impact on the most populous areas of the province. Where earlier immigrants fanned out across primarily rural areas, by the late 20th century they were settling in Toronto and other major southern Ontario cities.

In the late 1990s, more than 210,000 newcomers were arriving in Canada every year, with about 54 percent settling in Ontario. According to the most recent Statistics Canada survey, the main sources of immigrants to Ontario between 1991 and 1996 have been Hong Kong (9.1 percent); China (7.4 percent); India, the Philippines, and Sri Lanka (all 6.8 percent); Poland (4.8 percent); and Jamaica (3.4 percent). People born in the United Kingdom still form the majority of Ontario's total immigrant population (13.6 percent), followed by those born in Italy (8.1 percent), Poland and India (both 4.5 percent), and Hong Kong (4.4 percent).

**First Nations peoples,** who until the 17th century were the dominant inhabitants of the province, now constitute about one percent of the province's residents, living on reserves, in settlements on Crown land, or in towns and cities.

The median age of Ontario residents is 35.2, which means the province has the second-oldest population in Canada, behind Quebec, with a median age of 36.2. By comparison, the youngest population in Canada is found in the

Northwest Territories, where the median age is 25.7 years old.

Ontarians are among the best-educated people in Canada, with 41.1 percent of residents holding a post-secondary certificate, diploma, or university degree, compared to the Canadian average of 40.1 percent.

# Post-Secondary Education

There are 18 universities in Ontario, including the Ontario College of Art and Design. Each university offers undergraduate (bachelor's) degrees, and most offer graduate (master's and doctoral) degrees. More than 300,000 Ontario students are enrolled in undergraduate studies.

Each university operates independently and determines its own academic and admissions policies, programs, and staff appointments, but the Ministry of Training, Colleges and Universities provides funding and gives the institutions degree-granting authority. There are also 25 colleges of applied arts and technology, as well as agricultural colleges, colleges of health sciences and of art, a military college, privately funded degree-granting institutions, and registered private vocational schools.

Ontario's colleges of applied arts and technology have more than 100 campuses across the province and offer approximately 169,000 students the opportunity to develop skills in a variety of areas, including business; applied arts such as advertising and design, horticulture, and graphic arts; technology; and health sciences. Most college programs are either diploma programs (which may be two or three years in length) or certificate programs (which run one year or less). Some courses of study lead to official certification in skilled trades that are regulated by professional associations. In some cases, colleges and universities have joint programs that allow students to earn a university degree and a college diploma simultaneously. One example is a program offered by Conestoga College and the University of Waterloo that allows students to work toward a bachelor of arts degree and a diploma in journalism at the same time.

Ontario's and Canada's largest university is the University of Toronto, with more than 38,000 full-time students. It offers more than 50 degree programs at the bachelor, master, and doctoral level, as well as more than 30 diplomas and certificates. Other large post-secondary institutions include York University, also in **Toronto,** with more than 28,000 full-time students; the University of Western Ontario in **London,** with more than 21,000 students; and the University of

Waterloo, which features North America's largest co-operative education program and has about 17,000 students. Queen's University in **Kingston,** though slightly smaller with about 11,000 full-time students, is one of the province's oldest and most prestigious post-secondary institutions, offering degrees from the bachelor to the doctoral level.

Total costs for an academic year at a post-secondary institution vary from approximately $3,000 for a student who lives at home and attends a college of applied arts and technology to $10,000 or more for a university student living on campus or other lodging away from home. Those studying specialized programs such as engineering, medicine, business administration, or dentistry may spend even more.

Colleges and universities establish their own policies for international students. Many post-secondary institutions in Ontario also offer distance education courses that students can complete at home for credits.

# Provincial Parks

Ontario's provincial parks system—now numbering 272 parks covering 7.1 million hectares—was born when the provincial government under Premier Oliver Mowat created **Algonquin Provincial Park,** about 200 kilometres north of **Toronto,** in 1893 to satisfy a growing conservation movement in the province.

Originally known as Algonquin National Park, it consisted of 18 designated townships placed under the control and management of the Department of Crown Lands. As recommended by a royal commission, title to the Algonquin Park land remained with the Crown, settlement was prohibited, hunting and trapping were banned, angling was limited to rod and line under permit, a short-term lease policy was established for hotels and summer residences, and timber harvesting was restricted to mature pine trees.

As the movement to preserve and conserve grew stronger, more provincial parks were created. By 1944 seven others had been established: Rondeau in 1894, Quetico in 1913, Long Point in 1921, Presqu'ile in 1922, Ipperwash in 1938, Sibley in 1944, and Lake Superior in 1944.

In 1954, three decades of significant parkland expansion began when Premier Leslie Frost created the Division of Parks within the Ontario Department of Lands and Forests. By 1989, there were 261 parks, embracing some of the most scenic and historically and recreationally valuable land in Ontario, totalling more than 6.3 million hectares.

Since then, the provincial parks system has grown to 272 parks, managed by Ontario Parks and categorized as follows: 94 nature reserve parks, protected for educational purposes, scientific research, and genetic conservation; 8 wilderness parks, large areas of land left in their natural state where visitors can travel only on foot or by canoe to enjoy solitude and physical challenge; 4 historical parks that protect important features of Ontario's history and culture; 29 waterway parks for canoeists in search of high-quality recreation and historical river travel; 71 recreation parks with sand, sun, surf, and a wide variety of outdoor activities; and 66 natural environment parks, which offer recreational opportunities in places of outstanding natural or historical interest, including waterfalls, geological formations, and old-growth **forests**.

The largest park in Ontario is Polar Bear Provincial Park, a wilderness park in northeastern Ontario that covers 2.4 million hectares. Algonquin, by comparison, covers 772,300 hectares. Other popular parks include: Killarney, on the north shore of Georgian Bay, southeast of Sudbury, which was a favourite subject of A.J. Casson of the **Group of Seven** and today is still a mecca for painters; Sleeping Giant, on the Sibley Peninsula, which juts into Lake Superior, south of **Thunder Bay**, and takes its name from a rock formation that eerily resembles the profile of a sleeping giant; and Sandbanks on Lake Ontario, near Picton, which is known for its giant sand dunes and outstanding beaches.

More than 8.3 million people visited Ontario's provincial parks in 1997, including 1.5 million who camped at 18,747 developed campsites.

(*See also* **Algonquin Provincial Park**; **Petroglyphs Provincial Park**; **Wasaga Beach**)

# Public Safety

Under Ontario's Police Services Act, each of the province's 500 municipalities is responsible for providing police services by establishing a municipal police force, joining with other municipalities to provide protection, or by contracting the **Ontario Provincial Police** (OPP).

Most small Ontario communities are served by the OPP, which has 82 detachments and 4,900 uniformed officers in the province, while more than 75 municipalities have their own police services, employing about 16,000 uniformed personnel in total.

Self-policed communities include large cities and regions, such as **Toronto, Ottawa, Hamilton, Windsor, London, Kingston,** Peel Region, and York Region, and smaller communities, including Aylmer, Carleton Place, and Atikokan. The Toronto police department, with 4,904 uniformed officers, is the largest force in the province.

Fire protection in Ontario is provided by a network of 602 fire departments. Twenty-nine of these use full-time staff, 147 combine full-time and volunteer staff, and 426 are run exclusively by volunteers.

There are approximately 9,000 full-time firefighters in Ontario and 17,000 volunteers. In addition to firefighting, these personnel provide communities with a range of other services, including emergency rescue, extrication of auto-mobile accident victims, hazardous materials response, first aid, fire safety inspections, and public fire safety education.

Most communities in Ontario operate 9-1-1 telephone services for police, fire, and ambulance emergencies.

# Pukaskwa National Park

Located where the **Canadian Shield** meets Lake Superior near Marathon, Pukaskwa National Park comprises 2,000 square kilometres of wilderness, shoreline, hiking trails, and hilly terrain. The Anishnabe First Nation has lived in this region for some 3,000 years. The area around the park has also been home to voyageurs, missionaries, traders, and miners, and in the 1880s, to a thriving commercial logging industry along the Pukaskwa River. The park itself, however, has been spared most commercial and industrial pursuits over the years, making its large tract of boreal forest important to Ontario's biodiversity (*see* **Forests**).

Founded in 1978, Ontario's largest national park plays a key role in pre-serving resources within the Lake Superior basin. Its purpose is to protect a portion of the central boreal upland, a subregion of the boreal forest, and **Great Lakes** shoreline. The park provides a variety of education programs that emphasize dune ecology, First Nations culture, and predator/prey research. Park officials have been conducting research into the woodland caribou that live there, as well as studying the interaction among the caribou, **moose,** and wolves and their use of park habitats. The park is also home to black bears, and has several species of arctic plants growing within its boundaries that are not normally found as far south as Lake Superior.

Because of the park's long association with **First Nations peoples,** there is also a strong emphasis on interpretive programs that allow visitors to experience Native culture. No clear explanation exists for the meaning of the word *Pukaskwa* but theories of its origins include "eaters of fish," "safe harbour," or a term associated with cooking the marrow inside animal bones.

The park is open year round, but full service is available only from May to September. In addition to the **camping** sites at Hattie Cove within the park, there is also a visitor centre and a range of recreational activities, such as guided hikes, canoeing, and sailing.

# Purple Loosestrife

This purple-spiked plant has become a familiar sight throughout Ontario in recent years, particularly in roadside ditches, swamps, meadows, and marshes. A perennial herb that has caused some negative environmental and economic impacts, it can grow as high as two metres in favourable wetland conditions.

Native to Eurasia, purple loosestrife has traditionally been used for dyes and a variety of medical uses. The plant has existed in North America for almost 200 years and is most commonly found in the northeastern U.S. and southern Canada. Experts believe the plant has spread widely because of the increase in road construction and accompanying ditches, which provide continuous stretches of cleared habitat. If moisture is adequate, purple loosestrife will proliferate.

This invasive plant has created several environmental concerns. It has reduced wetland habitat for native aquatic vegetation, threatened some endangered species, and clogged irrigation and drainage ditches. Purple loosestrife has been controlled to some extent by hand pulling, cutting, mowing, and burning, but all of these methods are limited in their effectiveness. Three types of beetles introduced from Europe, however, are proving effective in attacking the roots, leaves, and seeds of the plants.

# Queen's Park

The main legislative building of Ontario, known as Queen's Park or affectionately as "the Pink Palace" by those who work there, was officially opened on
April 4, 1893, when Sir Oliver Mowat was premier of the province. Prior to its
construction, the government of Ontario had met in several buildings in
**Toronto** to enact legislation. In fact, when the first legislative building was
burned down during the **War of 1812**, politicians even met for a time at
Jordan's Hotel on King Street.

*Ontario's main legislative building in Queen's Park is known as "the Pink Palace."*
(Mark Kearney)

In 1859, the University of Toronto transferred some of its land to the city under a 999-year lease. A year later, the Prince of Wales, later King Edward VII, officially dedicated this land as Queen's Park, in honour of Queen Victoria. Both Toronto and the province were growing rapidly in the 1860s, and there was a consensus among politicians that a new legislative building should be erected. Queen's Park seemed a logical choice because Toronto was already expanding northwards from Lake Ontario. The government decided in April 1880 to hold a competition for designing the new building. Reaching an agreement on the winner proved difficult, but Richard Waite of Buffalo, New York, who was a friend both of cabinet ministers and one of the competition judges, was ultimately given the project.

Waite signed a contract in 1886 to erect the legislative building for $750,000. In fact, it would take seven years and more than $1.4 million before the building was opened. The legislature was designed in a style known as Richardson Romanesque, which emphasized rugged stone walls on a large scale. The frontage was 147 metres, with a depth of 88 metres, enclosing approximately 7,093 square metres with some 200 rooms. The main walls were made of sandstone from the nearby Credit Valley. The ornate main chamber was built near the entrance, which was unusual for the time.

The centre and west wings were used for parliamentary activities, and included several reception rooms and a library. The east wing was more functional, used for the day-to-day operations of the government and by civil servants. Modifications were already underway by 1897 to create more working space.

Although the building had its critics, thousands of people visited it on opening day and praise was almost universal. By the end of the 19th century, the legislature had become something of a tourist attraction and the subject of many photographs. A fire in 1909 destroyed the legislative library and much of the west wing. That section of the building was rebuilt and made more fireproof, but with the addition of a third and fourth floor the building became even more asymmetrical than it had been originally. The sandstone for the rebuilt portion came from Sackville, New Brunswick, which gave it a slightly different hue from the original edifice. A new north wing was also added at about this time to house the library.

In March 1928, a new $2.5 million six-storey east block, today known as the Whitney Block, officially opened and helped consolidate the government offices that had been scattered throughout the city. The new grey limestone building was done in the neo-Gothic style popular at the time. Several other government buildings have been constructed in the park since the 1960s, and the main legislative building itself underwent a restoration starting in 1992. The legislative chamber was refurbished in 1999.

As Toronto grew throughout the 20th century and more construction took place in the vicinity of Queen's Park, the main legislative building and the greenspace around it became a popular venue for rallies, marches, demonstrations, and several royal visits. The name Queen's Park has become synonymous with the legislature and the parkland around it, and the area remains a major focal point of Toronto today.

## Railways

Although the face of rail service changed dramatically in Ontario in the 1990s, the province continues to have an extensive and efficient rail service that is widely applauded by passengers and industrial customers alike.

The major change was a move in the mid-1990s by large carriers, primarily Canadian National Railway (CNR) and Canadian Pacific Railway (CPR), to abandon less profitable branch lines and focus on their strength—long-haul freight service on high-volume lines. Between 1996 and 1998, CNR and CPR discontinued 262 kilometres of track in Ontario and transferred another 1,760 kilometres to new operators.

As the national rail companies gave up branch lines—and in the wake of federal legislation adopted in 1996 which deregulated the rail industry—a number of entrepreneurs and regional carriers took over much of the track. These carriers, some of which are American-owned, have enjoyed considerable success because they have a lower cost base than the national operators, are locally managed and have flexible workforces. These advantages enable them to be highly responsive to the needs of their customers.

Despite these changes, Ontario, with 13,351 kilometres of track, continues to have more active lines than any other province, with links to the west and east coasts of Canada. Ontario is also the principal gateway by rail to the United States, with 80 percent of rail cars travelling to and from the U.S. crossing the border in Ontario, most at Fort Erie, **Windsor,** or Sarnia.

The province is served by more than a dozen railways, of which CPR, CNR, and Via Rail are the largest carriers.

CPR operates on approximately 5,440 kilometres of track plus another 1,656 kilometres of siding and yard track that stretches from Quebec to Manitoba. Working with its eastern subsidiary, the St. Lawrence and Hudson Railway, CPR maintains links with the American northeast and midwest. CNR runs on about 4,800 kilometres of track, also stretching from Quebec to the Manitoba border and running through the southern part of the province where it connects to the U.S. at Sarnia, Windsor, and Fort Erie. CNR is a major carrier of the province's natural resources and manufactured goods, moving approximately 50 million tonnes of freight in Ontario every year.

The bulk of passenger train service is provided by VIA Rail Canada, which relies on Ontario for more than 3.2 million of the 3.8 million passengers it carries annually in Canada. In Ontario, VIA serves more than 105 communities, links passengers with Canada's eastern and western provinces, and works with

*An electric locomotive owned by the St. Clair Tunnel Company of Sarnia, circa 1905.* (Andrew Merrilees Collection, PA-164305)

American rail line Amtrak to connect passengers to New York and Chicago. The Greater Toronto Transit Authority's GO Transit (formerly run by the Ontario government) provides intercity commuter rail and bus services to an 8,000-square-kilometre region covering the Greater Toronto Area and some surrounding communities. GO trains carry more than 28 million riders a year on 361 kilometres of track, making GO Transit the fifth-busiest commuter rail system in North America.

In **northern Ontario,** North Bay–based Ontario Northland Railway provides a mix of passenger and freight service on 1,120 kilometres of mainline track, which stretches from North Bay as far as Moosonee on **James Bay** and Hearst to the northwest. It is an important carrier of northeastern Ontario's resource products and also provides freight service between northern Ontario and Rouyn-Noranda, Quebec. Passenger service is provided south from Cochrane to **Toronto** and north from Cochrane to Moosonee. Its annual passenger load is about 72,000, including 16,000 riders on its **Polar Bear Express,** a seasonal train that runs between Cochrane and Moosonee. ONR carries about 41,000 carloads of freight annually.

Ontario's smaller railways include Algoma Central Railway, a 515-kilometre regional carrier owned by Wisconsin Central Transportation, running between Sault Ste. Marie and Hearst, with a branch to Michipicoten; Goderich-Exeter Railway, owned by RailTex Inc. of San Antonio, Texas, and operating on 110 kilometres of former CN track in southern Ontario; Trillium Railway, a short-line operator affiliated with three short lines in the U.S., which has operated the 12-kilometre Port Colborne Harbour Railway since 1997; and Ontario L'Original Railway, which runs on 43 kilometres of track in a loop connecting Hawkesbury, L'Original, and Glen Robertson. It is a subsidiary of Cape Breton and Central Nova Scotia Railway and operates on former CN Lines.

(*See also* **Agawa Canyon**; **Mississauga Train Derailment**)

# Rebellion of 1837

Although it lasted only a few days, the Rebellion of 1837 was a decisive step in the political development of Ontario and Canada. Throughout the 1820s and '30s, Upper Canada (Ontario) was governed by an elite, privileged group of men known as the Family Compact. Their control was far-reaching, and they often rewarded their friends with official jobs and public works contracts. They were opposed by a growing number of Reformers who believed the province should have some form of responsible government, with the elected legislature having power over the executive arms of the government.

Reform support was concentrated in the central and some eastern portions of the province, and small pockets in the west, while the Family Compact generally had its strength in the east. Family Compact supporters believed that responsible government would destroy the British traditions already in place and become dangerously similar to the American style of democracy.

William Lyon Mackenzie, who had become mayor of **Toronto** in 1834, was a key critic of the Family Compact. He and others of the more radical faction of the Reformers had seen similar rebellions take place in Lower Canada (Quebec) and in Texas and, frustrated by the government's power, believed a change was also needed in Upper Canada.

Mackenzie and his followers gathered north of Toronto in early December 1837, then marched down Yonge Street, where they skirmished with government troops and burned some buildings. A similar insurrection took place near Brantford. The Rebellion of 1837 had limited support throughout the province, however, and was quickly quashed by government forces. A few other unsuccessful uprisings took place in various spots in the province the following year.

Some of the rebel leaders were hanged; some, including Mackenzie, escaped to the U.S., while others were sent to penal colonies in Australia. The Rebellion did have the effect, however, of convincing British authorities that something should be done about government in the Canadian colonies. In 1838, Lord Durham, the Governor General, began writing a report on the grievances and offered suggestions to address the province's troubles that endorsed some of the Reformers' policies. He also advocated uniting Upper and Lower Canada to try to alleviate French-English antagonism, and on July 23, 1840, the British Parliament passed the Act of Union which created the United Province of Canada.

(*See also* **Historical Overview**)

# Religion

The predominant religion in Ontario is Christian, as it has been for at least two centuries. According to the latest Statistics Canada figures, approximately 3.5 million Ontarians identify themselves as Roman Catholics, while 4.4 million are Protestants. The Protestants are divided into several denominations, with the largest being the United Church (1.4 million adherents), followed closely by Anglicans at just over one million. The numbers drop significantly for other denominations, with 422,000 Presbyterians, 264,600 Baptists, 227,900 Lutherans, and 167,200 Pentecostals. There are, however, 876,000 people who identify themselves as Other Protestants. Approximately 187,900 people are Eastern Orthodox. A significant number of Ontarians—1.24 million—claim to have no religious affiliation.

Several non-Christian religions are practised in the province. Among these are Jewish at 175,600, Islamic with 145,600, Hindu at 106,700, Buddhist at 65,300, Sikh at 50,100, and a number of others with fewer members.

# Reptiles

There are 24 species of reptiles native to Ontario, 15 of which are snakes, eight are turtles, and one a lizard.

Of the 15 snakes slithering around the province, seven lay eggs and eight have live births. Most of the snakes are found in the south and central parts of Ontario, but the eastern garter snake ranges through much of the north as well. In addition to the eastern garter, the province is host to the northern brown, northern redbelly, northern water, queen, butler's garter, northern ribbon, eastern hognose, northern ringneck, smooth green, blue racer, black rat, eastern fox, eastern milk, and eastern massasauga rattlesnake.

Ontario's only venomous snake, the eastern massasauga is found near the shores of Lake Huron, Lake St. Clair, and **Georgian Bay.** It is distinguished by the segmented rattle at the end of its tail and its venomous fangs. It usually kills prey such as frogs and mice by injecting them with venom. The eastern massasauga doesn't always rattle its tail as a warning and doesn't always inject venom when it bites. This snake has caused few human deaths over the years.

The black rat snake, which feeds on small rodents and **birds,** is Ontario's largest snake at between 100 and 200 centimetres. Usually seen in pastures, this snake is able to climb trees to find food. A threatened species, the black rat snake hibernates under rocks, in old buildings, or rotting stumps and will hiss and flatten its neck when disturbed.

The eastern fox snake is also a large species, between 60 and 140 centimetres, and is distinguished by its yellowish brown colour and brown splotches on its back. Usually found in woodlands and marshes, it eats frogs, birds, mice, and **squirrels.**

The eastern garter is the most common and widely seen snake in Ontario. It can grow up to about 70 centimetres, is black with yellow stripes, and is active from spring to late autumn. The eastern garter will eat toads, frogs, birds, and **fish.** It is an adaptable survivor because females give birth to about 30 live snakes annually, and they have the ability to store sperm over the hibernating season. Butler's garter is less common, found only in the most southerly sections of southwestern Ontario. Smaller than the eastern garter, it prefers to live in marshes and wet meadows, and feeds on fish, frogs, and worms.

The northern ribbon snake is similar in colour to the garter, and is usually found in woodlands or near ponds, bogs, and streams. This species preys on tadpoles, salamanders, and frogs.

The smooth green snake lives mostly in meadows and can climb up small bushes. It eats spiders, grasshoppers, and caterpillars and is most active during the day.

The blue racer, Ontario's rarest snake, is considered an endangered species in the province. It's found only on **Pelee Island** and in prairie lands around **Windsor.** A swift and alert snake, it feeds on birds, mice, frogs, and other snakes, but changes in **climate** and agricultural techniques have reduced the habitat for this bluish-grey reptile.

The northern brown, northern redbelly, and northern ringneck snakes are the smallest species found in Ontario, ranging in length from about 20 to 35 centimetres. All three tend to be nocturnal and are rarely seen. The northern brown, also known as DeKay's snake, feeds on slugs and earthworms, as does the northern redbelly—so named because of its orange-red underside. The northern ringneck, which has a yellow collar around its neck, lives near woodland marshes and bogs and tends to feed on salamanders.

The northern water snake is aquatic and eats fish, tadpoles, and frogs. A common sight in Ontario's **cottage country,** it can reach up to 100 centimetres in length, and is known to bite. The queen snake is also aquatic, found mostly in rivers around lakes Huron and Erie. It feeds primarily on crayfish and is most active at night.

The eastern hognose snake has a thick body, a pointed and slightly upturned snout, and a short tail. It's known to hiss loudly when approached, and if that fails to scare off intruders the snake will then lie on its back and play dead. It feeds mostly on toads but occasionally also eats frogs.

The eastern milk snake is mostly nocturnal and is characterized by its reddish brown colour. The eastern milk snake eats rodents and other snakes and is often found in urban areas. It takes its name from an old belief that it could milk cows.

Turtles are the other group of reptiles commonly seen in Ontario. All turtles have an upper shell, known as a carapace, and a lower shell, called the plastron, which are fused at the side. The snapping turtle, at 20 to 40 centimetres, is the largest species in Ontario and is found mostly in the southern half of the province. It has a rough carapace and a large tail and head. Snapping turtles are usually found in slow-moving waters, preferably those with a muddy bottom. Although they can be aggressive on land and snap their jaws as a warning, in **water** they tend to be timid and avoid contact with humans. These turtles are primarily carnivorous, feeding on mollusks, fish, and even ducklings, but they will eat aquatic plants and algae on occasion.

The other large species are Blanding's turtle, the eastern spiny softshell, and the wood turtle. Blanding's turtle is about 15 to 25 centimetres in size and has a brown-black shell with yellow specks. This species tends to be found in secluded bays and lakes, and open marshes in southern Ontario. It eats frogs, snails, crayfish, and aquatic insects.

The eastern spiny softshell is a rare and endangered species in Ontario, with a leathery carapace and piglike snout. The females are about twice the size of the males and have thicker, longer tails. The spiny softshell tends to stay in the water and is a powerful swimmer, catching fish, tadpoles, and aquatic insects.

The wood turtle is usually found on land in meadows and floodplains, but hibernates in winter in rivers with gravel bottoms. It has a rough, brown carapace and grows to between 13 and 20 centimetres. As a mainly terrestrial turtle, this species eats fruits, flowers, worms, insects, and frogs. They are preyed upon by raccoons.

Medium-sized species include the map and painted turtles. The map turtle, found in southern Ontario, has a brown carapace with yellowish lines throughout. The males are smaller than the females. Map turtles prey on fish, aquatic insects, and snails, but the female, with its larger jaw, also feeds on clams.

The painted turtle has an olive-coloured upper shell with red lines around the edge and a yellow-striped head, neck, and tail. There are two subspecies of painted turtle: the midland painted turtle, found in central and southern

Ontario, and the western painted turtle found north and west of Lake Superior. Painted turtles are omnivorous, eating snails, insects, algae, and submerged plants. They prefer rivers, ponds, and lakes but are often seen basking on tree stumps and logs.

The smallest species in Ontario are the stinkpot and spotted turtles. The stinkpot, found in southern Ontario, is so named because of the musky smell it gives off when handled. It's generally 8 to 13 centimetres in size and is found in bays, marshes, and weedy streams. Rarely seen out of the water, the stinkpot is nocturnal, feeding on tadpoles as well as insects, leeches, and algae. The hatchlings often bury themselves in the mud or the roots of aquatic plants as a way of avoiding predators.

Spotted turtles are about the same size as stinkpots and have a black upper shell with bright yellow spots. This species prefers bogs and marshes, but will bask on logs and shorelines in the summer. Spotted turtles eat snails, fish, tadpoles, insects, and some aquatic plants. Female spotted turtles are able to store sperm from fall breeding, which allows them to fertilize their eggs in the spring.

The only lizard in Ontario is the five-lined skink. It has a brilliant blue tail and cream-coloured stripes that run along its shiny black body. The skink is usually found near rocks, shores, and woodlands and feeds on such insects as grasshoppers and flies. Female skinks lay about 6 to 10 eggs annually that hatch in August or September.

# Rideau Hall

Rideau Hall, the **Ottawa** residence of Canada's governor general, was built in 1838 on a site just east of Parliament Hill, not far from the home of the prime minister, who resides at **24 Sussex Drive.**

The original structure was built by local industrialist Thomas MacKay, a key figure in the construction of the Rideau Canal. While it served as a home for MacKay's family, it was known as MacKay's Castle. In 1864, less than a decade after the city of Bytown had been renamed Ottawa and designated as the new capital of the United Province of Canada, Rideau Hall was leased to the government as a residence for Lord Monck, then Governor General of British North America and later Canada's first Governor General.

In 1868, the house and grounds were purchased by the government of Canada for $82,000. Over the years, a variety of renovations have been undertaken and several wings have been added, including the posh Tent Room and a lavish ballroom.

Rideau Hall is a popular Ottawa tourist attraction. Walking tours are offered from April to October, and occasional garden parties and levies are open to the public. The ceremony of changing the guard takes place at the site daily during the summer.

# Royal Agricultural Winter Fair

Each November, more than 350,000 people visit the Royal Agricultural Winter Fair at the **Canadian National Exhibition** grounds in **Toronto.** They get a close-up look at cattle, pigs, rabbits, sheep, horses, and other farm animals from across Canada and around the world, all competing for ribbons at the fair.

The first fair was held in 1922 after the $1 million Coliseum was built to house the activities. The fair was the idea of W.A. Dryden, who owned a short-horn breeding farm in Brooklin, northeast of Toronto. He and three other men decided to attract the best animal breeds and agricultural products from every province by featuring competitions in a variety of classes. The first fair featured livestock from across Canada and visitors from as far away as Prince Edward Island. More than 22,000 people visited on the opening day.

In 1997, the "Royal" celebrated its 75th anniversary by moving into the new $180 million National Trade Centre, and today it is the world's largest indoor agricultural, horticultural, and equestrian competition. More than 400 tonnes of hay are eaten by 5,000 animals during the fair, and more than 30,000 litres of milk are produced during the dairy cattle show. Some 162 kilograms of butter are used by Ontario College of Art students to create their popular butter sculptures.

The Royal Agricultural Winter Fair also features educational programs and intimate views of rural life. In addition to the food and livestock competitions, the Royal Horse Show is a popular highlight of the fair. Show jumping and dressage competitions attract teams from around the world and offer more than $750,000 in prize money.

The fair occupies one million square feet of space on the CNE grounds and attracts visitors from more than 50 countries annually. Themed gardens designed for the fair reflect the landscape, culture, and cultural diversity of Canada.

# Royal Botanical Gardens

Located at the western end of **Hamilton,** the Royal Botanical Gardens is an 1100-hectare oasis of flowers, trees, and other plants. Not only does it offer a decorative entrance to the city but it also acts as a centre of recreation and research.

The gardens feature more than 100,000 flowering bulbs, the world's largest collection of lilacs, 250,000 irises, and nearly a hectare of roses. There is also an indoor Mediterranean garden and 30 kilometres of walking trails.

The gardens were the dream of Thomas Baker McQuesten, a member of the city's board of parks management, who wanted a place in Hamilton similar to Kew Gardens in Edinburgh, which would provide a sanctuary for **birds,** wildlife, and various plant species. In 1927, the board acquired 160 hectares of land in the Westdale area of Hamilton, near McMaster University, and decided that a public botanical park would beautify the area. Work on the Rock Garden began in November 1929 and took three years to complete. In 1930, the gardens received permission from King George V to use the term "Royal" and a year later more land at the north end of the site became available. The park was first opened to the public in 1932.

Over the years, the gardens have continued to expand, add new plants and become more popular as a tourist attraction. The Royal Botanical Gardens were officially created by legislation in April 1941. McQuesten, who became minister of highways, transferred another 205 hectares of land owned by his ministry to the site. It cost the Royal Botanical Gardens $500. In 1946, the gardens began to sell memberships as a way to raise funds. By the late 1940s, the gardens had grown to about 650 hectares.

Despite provincial grants to help offset costs, the Royal Botanical Gardens faced financial problems from the 1950s through the 1970s because of the high cost of maintaining the grounds. Nonetheless, they continued to expand, increase the variety of plant life, and erect new buildings. On the park's 50th anniversary, the gardens introduced admission fees.

The gardens, with more than 8,000 different varieties of plants, continue to be one of the tourist gems in the Hamilton area, attracting some 400,000 visitors annually. In 1998, it was recognized as a National Historical and Architectural Site. The gardens feature annual plant sales, demonstration areas, and educational programs.

# Royal Canadian Henley Regatta

Each summer in St. Catharines, rowers from around the world come to compete in one of the oldest and most prestigious athletic events in North America, the Royal Canadian Henley Regatta. The tradition began in 1880 when the Canadian Association of Amateur Oarsmen (now called the Canadian Amateur Rowing Association) staged its first championship.

For the first 22 years of the event, several venues across Canada were used. The first championship was held in **Toronto,** but Montreal, Brockville, and Barrie were sites in other years. The association decided in 1903 that the Henley should have a permanent home and chose Martindale Pond in St. Catharines. In the early years, the course covered one mile and 550 yards, the same distance as the English Henley event, but in 1964 the distance was changed to 2,000 metres, the international racing standard.

Women first raced in a demonstration event in 1947, but it wasn't until 1972 that they became a permanent fixture at the Henley. The female rowers initially raced 1,000 metres, but the distance was changed to 2,000 metres in 1985.

The Henley site was completely renovated in 1966, which involved dredging the course, building a shellhouse, a finish tower, adding adjustable starting gates, and building a bridge to Reid Island, which is now called Henley Island. More refurbishing of the course and facilities was needed in 1999 because the Henley course was also the site of the World Rowing Championships that year.

The regatta relies on hundreds of volunteers to help stage the annual event, which takes place over five days. The 1999 regatta attracted more than 2,000 rowers who took part in more than 120 regular and masters class races. Several other regattas are held on the course during the rowing season, including the Canadian Schoolboy Championships in May.

# Royal Ontario Museum

As one of the few museums in the world to combine art, **archaeology,** and science in one building, Toronto's Royal Ontario Museum, or "the ROM" as it's known by many, is the largest museum in Canada. More than 700,000 visitors a year enjoy the ROM's exhibits, which span human and natural history throughout the ages and around the world.

Among the museum's highlights are an impressive Chinese collection; the

Ancient Egypt Gallery; the Sigmund Samuel Canadiana Gallery, which houses the world's premier collection of early Canadian decorative arts and historical paintings; the Samuel European Galleries; and the S.R. Perren Gem and Gold Room. The ROM also has 13 dinosaur skeletons, a bat cave, and the Discovery Gallery, a 1,981-square-metre facility that uses theatrical settings, hands-on activities, and artifacts aimed at children. Visitors to the Discovery Gallery can roll up their sleeves and dig for dinosaur bones, walk through a crystal cave, dress up in armour, or learn how research is done from museum curators.

The ROM was created in 1912 by an act of the Ontario legislature and opened its doors to the public on March 19, 1914. The two men most responsible for the ROM's creation were Sir Byron Edmund Walker, a bank executive and amateur palaeontologist, and Dr. Charles Trick Currelly, an archaeologist and the museum's first director of archaeology.

The museum was expanded in 1933, and in 1955 the ROM, which had operated as five separate **museums** devoted to archaeology, geology, mineralogy, palaeontology, and zoology, became a single entity.

In 1968, the McLaughlin Planetarium opened as part of the ROM, and in that same year the museum's annual attendance exceeded one million for the first time. The ROM closed the planetarium in November 1995 because of a reduction in the museum's operating grant, but was exploring ways to redevelop the planetarium site into a revenue-producing attraction in the year 2000.

The ROM went through a $55 million renovation in 1978 to house its greatly expanded research operations and collections. Today, the ROM is a major research institution pursuing human and natural history projects throughout the world. The museum's education department also provides hands-on learning to some 200,000 visiting students annually and serves about a quarter of a million people across Ontario through travelling exhibits, lectures, and school resources.

(*See also* **Museums**)

# St. Lawrence Islands National Park

St. Lawrence Islands National Park was established in 1904 in the heart of the **1000 Islands** as the first Canadian national park east of the Rocky Mountains. Primarily an island park with **water** the main recreational attraction, it is Canada's smallest national park.

The park began with nine federally owned islands in the St. Lawrence River and a small piece of waterfront granted to the federal government by the Mallory family, with the stipulation that it be used for park purposes. Over the years, 12 more islands and land parcels were annexed and today St. Lawrence Islands National Park consists of all or part of 21 islands and some 90 islets scattered between **Kingston** and Brockville, as well as a 41-hectare mainland base at Mallorytown.

The presence of the **Great Lakes** to the west moderates the climate in the area, allowing many plants and animals that are rare in the rest of Canada to live there. Notable examples include the black rat snake, Canada's largest reptile; pitch pine trees; and the least bittern, a wading bird.

The park is the site of the preserved hull of a British gunboat from the **War of 1812,** raised from the **St. Lawrence River** near Mallorytown Landing in 1867. The islands are a popular stopping-point for power- and sailboaters cruising the St. Lawrence River. Scuba diving and sea kayaking are also gaining in popularity in the area.

In December 1999, a report by the Canadian Nature Federation rated this park as the third most endangered in Canada because of air and water pollution from outside sources.

# St. Lawrence River

Explored by Jacques Cartier in 1534 for France, the St. Lawrence River was named in 1604 by Samuel de Champlain, the founder of Quebec City. Although only a small portion of the watercourse lies within Ontario's boundaries, the river has always been key to the province's development, primarily because it acts as a gateway to the heart of North America.

In Ontario, the St. Lawrence extends from the eastern end of Lake Ontario near **Kingston** to the Ontario-Quebec border. Communities that dot its north shore in Ontario include Kingston, Gananoque, Brockville, Prescott, Iroquois, Morrisburg, and Cornwall.

In part of southeastern Ontario, the river defines the border between Canada and the United States, but much more than that, it is a vital part of the **Great Lakes–St. Lawrence Seaway** system. This great waterway penetrates 3,700 kilometres into the heart of North America, serving both as transportation route and drainage basin.

The river itself covers 1,224 kilometres from Lake Ontario to the Gulf of St. Lawrence, including about 201 kilometres in Ontario. Because it drains the entire **Great Lakes** system, the St. Lawrence is considered to originate in the forests of Minnesota and to flow almost 4,025 kilometres to the Gulf of St. Lawrence.

Geologically speaking, the St. Lawrence is a young river, whose bed is described in *The Canadian Encyclopedia* as "a deep gash in the earth's crust" which was exposed about 10,000 years ago when glaciers receded from North America.

As the route taken by explorers, the river played a prominent role in Canada's early history and served as an important passage for fur traders. Many historians have argued that the east-west axis of the river made it possible for Canada to be settled. Today its shores are home to several million people. It remains Canada's most important commercial waterway, as well as a source of hydroelectric power, **fish,** and drinking **water.** The river provides a stopover for migrating waterfowl and a playground for tourists who marvel at its beauty.

The average flow of water is about 13,000 cubic metres per second, with relatively minor fluctuations because of the reservoir effect of the Great Lakes. Little sedimentation takes place, but economic growth along the river has resulted in local biochemical pollution.

Below Lake Ontario, the river can be divided into two parts—the river proper, which flows to just beyond Quebec City, and the estuary, extending to the Gaspé Peninsula. As the river leaves Lake Ontario, the wide channel flows around the **1000 Islands** between Ontario and New York State. From the islands to Montreal, it forms a series of pools and rapids, dropping 68 metres over the course of 293 kilometres.

Navigation for ocean-going ships has always been possible upstream as far as Montreal. Although the Welland Canal between lakes Ontario and Erie opened the entire Great Lakes system to large ships, the rapids above Montreal continued to prevent their passage to the sea. This obstacle was eliminated in 1959 with completion of the **canals** and locks that opened the St. Lawrence Seaway. Every year, the seaway handles about 40 million tonnes of goods and more than 4,000 pleasure boats. A bonus when the seaway was built was the hydroelectric power it produced, which accelerated growth in the existing industrial and agricultural area along the river.

The St. Lawrence is one of the longest rivers in Canada, second only to the Mackenzie, and the 17th longest river in the world.

# Sainte-Marie-among-the-Hurons

The first European community in Ontario was established on this site near Midland. Founded in 1639 by French Jesuit missionaries in the territory of the Hurons on the Wye River, it was part of an attempt to convert some 25,000 **First Nations peoples** in the area to Christianity.

The fortified mission, which eventually contained more than 20 buildings, including a hospital, functioned as a retreat for missionaries. Eventually, other French settlers arrived, bringing livestock, tools, and weapons to trade with the Hurons. The community thrived for about a decade, but the presence of the French brought such diseases as influenza, measles, and smallpox, which were deadly to the Hurons. By 1647, the French population at the mission had grown to 18 priests and 24 laypeople, which represented more than 10 percent of the total European population in what was then the entire colony of New France.

Rivalry between the Hurons and the Iroquois to the south culminated in attacks on several villages by the Iroquois. Five priests were killed during this time and became revered as martyrs to the cause of spreading Christianity. In 1649, the Jesuits and Hurons abandoned Sainte-Marie-among-the-Hurons and later burned it so the Iroquois couldn't attack it. A second community was set up at nearby Christian Island, but it was abandoned in 1650, and the Jesuits returned to Quebec.

Although amateur archaeologists examined the site in the 19th century, it was not until after World War II that professional excavation was undertaken. The province began reconstructing Sainte-Marie-among-the-Hurons in 1955, and it was restored to its 17th-century likeness in 1967. Included in the village are wooden palisades, stables, houses, wigwams, and gardens. The village is now an interpretive museum staffed by people dressed in period costume, which attracts thousands of visitors annually.

Also nearby is Martyr's Shrine Church, which was built in 1926 as a tribute to the 17th-century Jesuits. The shrine is one of four in Canada and honours the pioneering religious leaders who were martyred, as well as the Hurons who accepted and lived the Christian faith. Thousands of people from around the world visit the shrine annually.

# Santa Claus Parade

If there's a tradition in **Toronto** that is universally loved, it's the Santa Claus Parade, which winds through the city's downtown streets every November. There are other Santa parades in Ontario, but none compares to Toronto's, which has been an annual event since Sunday, December 2, 1905, when the Jolly Old Fellow appeared in his first parade, sponsored by the T. Eaton Co. That year's event was a one-man show, featuring only Santa. Eventually floats were added, gradually increasing to about 25. Costumes and volunteers are also a huge part of the parade, both numbering more than 1,300 in the 1999 extravaganza.

On his first trip, Santa arrived in Toronto by rail. He then transferred to his special automobile and rode through downtown streets, handing out souvenirs and surprise packages along the way. In 1906, Santa arrived in a coach drawn by four white horses, and in 1923, he drove down **Yonge Street** in a sled pulled by eight live reindeer from Labrador.

In the 1920s and '30s, Santa switched to more modern means of transportation, such as motorized floats, a huge airplane, and the caboose of a train. In 1953, he came to town on a more conventional style of mechanized float—a sleigh and eight white reindeer leaping over the housetops. This has been his trademark ever since.

In 1982, a nonprofit organization was established when 20 corporations decided to jointly sponsor the parade, after Eaton's announced it would no longer foot the total bill.

The Santa Claus Parade has become one of the biggest productions of its kind in North America. The 1999 parade was broadcast on the Global Television Network to major cities across Canada, as well as to a number of local stations. The parade was also broadcast internationally.

# Science North

Science North is one of the treasures of **northern Ontario.** Located on the shores of **Sudbury's** Ramsey Lake, it is internationally renowned for the originality and accessibility of its science exhibits, which enable visitors to identify minerals, learn about animals and the latest technology and software, see how earthquakes form, and even test their fitness level. The facility opened to the public on June 19, 1984, and now attracts about 200,000 visitors every year.

The premier attraction at Science North is the Science Centre, a four-floor exhibit building that houses hands-on exhibits, designed to encourage visitors to play and explore. The first level features the INCO Cavern Theatre, an underground theatre with 3-D movies. Visitors young and old can have hours of fun in the Waterworks area on the second floor, and trade for treasures in the Swap Shop. The third floor's Northern Ecosystem involves the visitor in the natural world. Animal habitats, a stream table, a rock xylophone, and fossil beds are just a few of the exhibits that help visitors discover the natural world.

The fourth floor takes visitors deeper into human exploration: the human body, our technical environment, and our quest for knowledge about space. The Science North IMAX Theatre—with its five-storey-high, 21-metre-wide screen and 6,400 watts of surround-sound—give viewers a taste of what it's like to ride the world's scariest rides, climb to the summit of Mount Everest, and prospect for gold in the Yukon.

Science North's Virtual Voyages adventure ride synchronizes film, sound, and computer-controlled motion to deliver the sensation of virtual reality. Visitors can also cruise Ramsey Lake aboard the Cortina, a 70-passenger boat that offers a one-hour scenic tour of the lake.

Ten minutes away, and also operated by Science North, is the Big Nickel Mine, which offers the opportunity to experience the environment of a miner's

*Science North on Sudbury's Ramsey Lake is a must-see for visitors to northern Ontario.*
*About 200,000 people visit annually, to see its internationally renowned science exhibits.*
(Science North)

workplace. A 45-minute guided underground tour is complemented by surface exhibits, which include Sudbury's most famous landmark, a nine-metre-high, 61-centimetre-thick replica of the Canadian commemorative five-cent piece.

Science North was first conceived as a mining museum in the mid-1950s, but by the late 1970s the emphasis had changed toward a centre for science. Once the idea was put on paper in November 1980, money began flowing in to finance the project, led by a $5 million donation from INCO Ltd., a major figure in Sudbury's mining sector. Work began on June 29, 1981.

The architecture of Science North captures two images of the Sudbury Basin, a snowflake settling over a crater. The Sudbury Basin was created two million years ago as the result of a meteorite impact, while the snowflake symbolizes the glaciation and the **climate** that have sculpted the northern landscape.

Since its doors first swung open, Science North has continued to evolve. In the spring of 2000, a 1,000-square-foot butterfly gallery was scheduled to open, and construction was underway on a hall for travelling science exhibits.

(*See also* **Ontario Science Centre**)

# Shaw Festival

As the only theatre in the world that specializes in the plays of George Bernard Shaw and his contemporaries, the Shaw Festival is an interesting and vital part of Ontario's arts and **tourism** sectors. Each year plays are presented in three distinctive theatres in the historic town of Niagara-on-the-Lake, attracting more than 300,000 visitors who come primarily from Canada and the United States.

The festival was founded in 1962, when Niagara-on-the-Lake lawyer Brian Doherty presented eight weekend performances of Shaw's *Don Juan in Hell* and *Candida* in the assembly hall of the town's old courthouse. Doherty helped establish the Shaw Festival Theatre Foundation the following year as a nonprofit society with an elected board of governors. The mandate states that the festival stages only plays written during Shaw's lifetime (1856–1950).

With the appointment of Paxton Whitehead as artistic director in 1967, the festival began to gain national and international prominence, and today it is one of the largest and most successful theatre companies in North America. As the festival grew, however, the 324-seat courthouse was not large enough to accommodate theatregoers. Construction on the 861-seat Festival Theatre began in 1972, and it opened the following year. Its proscenium-arch style and advanced technical facilities provide the ideal venue for the festival's large-scale productions. In 1980, the festival acquired the Royal George Theatre, a former vaudeville house and cinema which seats 328. That same year, Christopher Newton became artistic director, a position he still holds, and has since helped the festival attract worldwide attention for its stylish productions.

The festival's 1999 operating budget was $14.9 million, of which 74 percent came primarily from ticket sales, 19 percent from private sector funding, and 7 percent from government grants. Twelve plays were staged from April to November, involving more than 70 actors.

The Shaw has also gained a reputation for research and development, not only of the works of the British playwright but also of Victorian drama and plays of continental Europe rarely staged elsewhere, classic musicals, and mystery and suspense plays. The festival also offers outreach programs and tours for the public and a residency program for established Canadian string quartets. A series of musical performances takes place throughout the season.

(*See also* **Stratford Festival**)

# Silicon Valley North

Once thought of as a "one-horse" region almost totally reliant on the federal government for jobs, **Ottawa** and its surrounding municipalities, particularly Kanata, have won the designation of "Silicon Valley North" thanks to the area's burgeoning high-technology industry.

The Ottawa area is home to 75 percent of all scientists and engineers in Canada. It's the site of 75 percent of Canada's telecom research and development, and more than 900 technology companies are located in the area, providing jobs for more than 50,000 people. Between 1994 and 1999, the number of high-tech companies has grown by 70 percent. Not surprisingly, the area has the highest proportion of computers per household in Canada.

World-class companies located in the Ottawa area include Newbridge Networks, Mitel Corporation, Corel Corporation, QNX Software, Computing Devices Canada, JetForm Corporation, DY 4 Systems Inc., Iogen Corp., World Heart Corp., Simware Inc., Telesat Canada, and Nortel, which in 1999 employed 13,000 people at 21 sites in the area.

These and many others have built the high-tech sector into a $12-billion industry. In addition to advanced technology research, the industry develops and sells a variety of products and services in the fields of telecommunications, networking, life sciences, health care, aerospace, and defence. Goods and services originating in the Ottawa area are exported around the world.

# SkyDome

Near the shore of Lake Ontario in the shadow of the **CN Tower,** a few minutes' stroll from downtown **Toronto,** is SkyDome, one of the world's most advanced entertainment venues. It has served as a model for domed stadiums around the world.

The complex, which opened in 1989 as home of the **Toronto Blue Jays** baseball club and the **Toronto Argonauts** football team (it also served for three seasons as the temporary home of the **Toronto Raptors** basketball team), sits on 5.14 hectares of land. The building itself covers 4.66 hectares and consists of 135,000 cubic metres of concrete, twice the amount used to build the CN Tower and enough to lay a sidewalk from Toronto to St. Louis.

The field can easily contain any of the following: the Roman Coliseum, 516

African elephants, eight Boeing 747s, the entire Eaton Centre Shopping Mall in Toronto, or a 32-house subdivision. SkyDome accommodates 51,517 fans for baseball; 53,506 for football; up to 55,000 for concerts; and 33,276 for events when a system of tents known as SkyTent is utilized. Its full capacity is 65,673.

SkyDome's fully retractable roof, the first of its kind in the world, rises to a height of 82 metres, high enough to house a 31-storey building at centre field. The four-section roof covers 3.2 hectares and opens or closes in 20 minutes. Another SkyDome feature is its JumboTron, one of the world's largest videoboards, measuring 33 metres wide by about 10 metres high, to bring fans closer to the action. The screen is lit with 67,200 lights.

In addition to sporting events, SkyDome hosts ice shows, monster truck meets, rock concerts, and trade shows.

Total cost of the facility was $532 million, including the stadium, the attached 346-room SkyDome Hotel, a health club, the cost of demolishing Toronto's main water pumping station and reconstructing a new one across the street, and building new streets, bridges, and other infrastructure.

With more than six million visitors annually, it is one of Toronto's top three tourist attractions. It is estimated that SkyDome contributes $326 million annually to the Toronto economy and a further $45 million per year to the provincial economy.

Although SkyDome has been seen as a technological marvel from the day it opened, its financial viability has been dubious from the beginning. Private-sector partners have lost a lot of money over the years, and Ontario taxpayers were stung for $263 million before governments severed their ties with the complex.

# Snowbelts

Ontario's snowbelts are well known—among skiers who swarm to them on weekends and for winter vacations and among commuters who curse every time high winds and deep snow close roads and play havoc with their drive to work. Snowbelt areas include the highlands south of Parry Sound and northeast of Sault Ste. Marie, as well as areas along the **St. Lawrence River** and north of **London.**

On the upland slopes facing Lake Huron, **Georgian Bay,** and Lake Superior, snowfalls in the 300- to 400-centimetre range occur during most winters, with much of the white stuff coming from the prevailing winds blowing off the open lakes.

The snow forms when cold air is warmed and moistened as it travels over the **water.** It is then forced to ascend the highlands, triggering heavy snowfalls. More snow arrives on the backs of winter storms as they rise over the province's higher terrain. Known as the orographic effect, this contributes about 17 centimetres of snow for each 30-metre rise in elevation.

Ontario snowstorms have been known to pack a heavy punch. One of the worst took place in the London area between December 7 and 9, 1977, when 101 centimetres of snow fell, with winds howling at 100 kilometres per hour. Drifting snow necessitated a state of emergency and the mobilization of the armed forces to restore essential services but, as is often the case, some cities and towns less than 30 minutes away were bathed in sunshine and never felt the effects of the storm. One of the worst blizzards in recent memory occurred in **Toronto** in January 1999 when a string of storms dumped 112 centimetres of snow in a two-week period, choking the city's downtown core for several days. The heavy snow caused Mayor Mel Lastman to declare an emergency snow removal plan and call on the armed forces for help. The snowstorm broke a longstanding record and ate up much of Toronto's $31.4-million snow-clearing budget.

Snowfall accounts for about 33 percent of the year's total precipitation in the snowbelt regions, compared to just 12 percent in snow-sparse regions such as the area around Chatham and **Windsor.**

## Snowmobiling

Joseph-Armand Bombardier may be not be an Ontarian, but the snowmobile he invented has certainly had an impact on Ontario. Since Bombardier unveiled the first commercially viable version of a snowmobile in Quebec in the mid-1930s, with its sprocket wheel and double, endless track, snowmobiling has become a huge economic contributor to the province. Some say it is Ontario's fastest-growing winter sport.

At the end of the 20th century, snowmobile trails were generating more than $1 billion in annual economic activity in Ontario, including $73 million in provincial taxes. The Ontario Federation of Snowmobile Clubs (OFSC), an umbrella group for more than 280 member clubs, estimates there are 175,000 active snowmobiles in the province that are ridden every winter by about 225,000 snowmobilers.

Ontario has 49,500 kilometres of marked and groomed trails, maintained by local clubs and the OFSC, including the federation's 18,000-kilometre Trans-Ontario Provincial (TOP) trail network, which enables snowmobilers to travel from Manitoba to the Quebec border without having to backtrack. TOP raises money through the sale of trail permits and distributes the proceeds among the member clubs for maintenance and equipment.

Ontario has the longest managed snowmobile trail system in the world, well ahead of Vermont, the leading American state, which has 19,000 kilometres of managed trails. Among the most popular snowmobile areas in the province are Muskoka, including areas near Gravenhurst, Huntsville, and Bracebridge; the Kawarthas, including Buckhorn, Apsley, and Bancroft; the North Bay area; New Liskeard; Haileybury; and Kirkland Lake; and the **Ottawa Valley** and **Thunder Bay** areas.

In Ontario, snowmobile use is regulated under the Motorized Snow Vehicles Act, which means that unless the machines are operated solely on private land, snowmobiles must have a licence, obtained by paying an annual vehicle registration fee to the province. Despite regulation and safety programs offered by snowmobile clubs, a number of snowmobilers die every year, usually when their machines break through ice-covered lakes or collide with vehicles while crossing roads.

# Squirrels

In the city, countryside, and the average backyard, squirrels are a very visible part of the Ontario landscape. Four species of tree squirrels live in Ontario—the grey or black, the red, the southern flying, and the northern flying. Other members of the squirrel family found in Ontario include the eastern chipmunk, the least chipmunk, and the woodchuck or groundhog (see **Wiarton Willie**).

The grey squirrel is the most familiar to southern Ontarians, in varying shades of grey, dark brown, or black. Although the myth still persists that grey and black squirrels are different species, they are in fact the same. These sociable animals live near deciduous forests and spend much of their time in trees. The long bushy tail helps squirrels keep their balance when aloft.

Squirrels have been noted for making significant migrations from one territory to the next, but they are usually found where there is ample foliage and a good supply of nuts and seeds. Grey squirrels eat a variety of buds, flowers, fruits, and berries. These squirrels horde food for the winter and forage to supplement their supply. The average lifespan for a grey squirrel is about six years.

Red squirrels are found throughout Ontario, often in the same habitat as the grey. Although they eat most of the same kinds of food, they are more carnivorous than other squirrels and have been known to eat mice, robins, and orioles. Red squirrels are smaller than greys and spend even less time on the ground. They are gifted climbers, territorial, and noisy. Their lifespan is about three years.

The southern flying squirrel is found mostly along the lower **Great Lakes** and **St. Lawrence River,** but may be seen as far north as **Sudbury.** A loose fold of skin attached to its wrists and ankles allows it to glide. It can be differentiated from the northern flying squirrel by the pale fur of its belly (the northern has a grey belly) and smaller size. Both species are nocturnal and highly sociable, with an average lifespan of three to four years. The southern flying squirrel has been known to glide for as long as 30 metres in the air from tree to tree. It lives among deciduous trees, eating nuts, seeds, and fruits, as well as night-flying insects.

The northern flying squirrel, found throughout Ontario, is much larger than its southern counterpart. It generally lives among coniferous trees, adding insects and **birds** to the typical squirrel diet. This species tends to adapt to winter more successfully than the southern flying squirrel.

# Stratford Festival

Renowned across North America and around the world, the Stratford Festival has been delighting audiences with plays by William Shakespeare and other playwrights for almost 50 years. The plays are now presented in three venues, the Festival Theatre, the Avon Theatre, and the Tom Patterson Theatre, all located in Stratford. Operating with an annual budget of almost $30 million, the Stratford Festival draws more than 450,000 theatregoers from North America and 50 other countries to its plays, musicals, and concerts.

The festival was the inspiration of Stratford-born journalist Tom Patterson, who, with the help of respected British stage director Tyrone Guthrie and renowned designer Tanya Moiseiwitsch, decided in 1952 that a festival of Shakespearean theatre should be established here. On July 13, 1953, actor Alec Guinness stepped onto a revolutionary thrust stage, erected under a specially constructed canvas tent, and began the festival with his performance of *Richard III*. The other play produced that year was *All's Well That Ends Well*. The stage revolutionized the performance of Shakespeare in the 20th century and inspired the designs of more than a dozen major theatres around the world.

Guthrie remained artistic director until 1955, attracting talented actors and crews and expanding the repertoire of the festival each year. There have been eight artistic directors in the festival's history since that time, all bringing their vision to the productions and offering plays from other great dramatists of the past, including Samuel Beckett and Eugene O'Neill. The festival also features operettas, musical theatre, and works by contemporary Canadian playwrights such as Timothy Findley, Elliott Hayes, and Michel Tremblay.

The canvas tent that was home to the festival in the early years was replaced by the Festival Theatre, which was dedicated on June 30, 1957. The first production in the new theatre, which overlooks parkland and the Avon River, was *Hamlet*. A multi-million-dollar renovation of the theatre took place in 1996 and was opened by Queen Elizabeth II on June 28, 1997. The theatre seats 1,836.

The Avon Theatre had been built in 1901 and used as a vaudeville house, a venue for local amateur theatre, and later as a cinema. The festival began renting the theatre in 1956 and bought it in 1963. Remodelled with an enlarged stage, the theatre currently seats 1,083 people.

The Tom Patterson Theatre evolved from a 1971 festival innovation called the Third Stage. This theatre has been used for workshops and performances of new Canadian plays and experimental productions. It was closed and re-opened several times in the late 1970s and early '80s. Now seating 487, it was renamed the Tom Patterson Theatre in 1991.

The Stratford Festival continues to be a not-for-profit operation and is committed to attracting and training the world's best talent, developing new audiences through such projects as its school programs and backstage tours, and to providing a venue for a range of contemporary and classical plays.

(*See also* **Shaw Festival**)

# Sudbury

Like many Canadian communities, Sudbury's roots are tied to the railway. The city began as a temporary work camp for the Canadian Pacific Railway in the spring of 1883 and was named Sudbury Junction by CPR chief James

*The big nickel is Sudbury's most famous landmark. It's a nine-metre-high replica of the commemorative five-cent piece.* (© 2000 Ontario Tourism)

Worthington, to honour his wife's birthplace in England.

"Rough and rugged in the extreme," was how Provincial Land Surveyor Francis Bolger in 1883 described the area's terrain, which was dominated by gigantic rock outcrops, interspersed with extensive swamps, endless lakes, and large areas burned out by bush fires.

In its early years, most expected Sudbury would remain a railway and lumbering community with moderate growth at best. But during construction of the railroad, a blacksmith named Tom Flanagan collected copper ore samples from rock outcroppings. His discovery sparked a prospecting boom and the development of Sudbury's prosperous **mining industry.**

First to go into production was the Canadian Copper Company's Copper Cliff mine, in 1886. Two years later, vast nickel deposits were discovered, and Sudbury became known around the world for its mines, which also contained sizeable deposits of uranium. Later, Canadian Copper merged with Orford Refining Company to become International Nickel (INCO) Ltd.

In 1893, the community of 1,400 people, 390 kilometres north of **Toronto,** became an organized town with an elected mayor and council and many of the features of a thriving municipality, including a newspaper, schools, churches, and 35 shops. By 1900, its population was 2,027. When World War I broke out, more than 1,000 people worked in the mines.

On July 28, 1930, Sudbury gained city status, with a population of over

18,000 people. In 1973, Sudbury joined six area municipalities to become the Regional Municipality of Sudbury, and by 1981 its population had swelled to 91,829. Located at the intersection of Trans-Canada Highway 17 and Highway 69, the Regional Municipality of Sudbury had a 1999 population of about 165,000.

Once almost totally reliant on the mining industry, Sudbury's economic viability is no longer dependent on minerals, thanks to an aggressive 20-year diversification plan. Although mining continues to play an important role in the local **economy**—and the skyline continues to be dominated by the lofty INCO smokestack—city leaders have actively pursued telecommunications/technology initiatives that have positioned Sudbury as one of Ontario's leading-edge communities. A broadband telecommunications network based on fibre optics has been installed and has attracted a wealth of new business and employment opportunities to the area.

Mining companies, including INCO and Falconbridge Ltd., remain among the city's largest employers, along with the Sudbury Regional Hospital Corporation, Laurentian University, and Revenue Canada.

**Tourism** is also a big part of the local economy, led by a handful of key attractions, including the Big Nickel underground mine tour; **Science North,** a world-class science centre on Ramsey Lake; and five **provincial parks** within an hour's drive of the city.

Although some people suggest Sudbury is somewhat lacking in charm, due largely to scars left on the landscape by years of mining, much has been done over the years to reclaim 17,400 hectares of so-called "lunar landscape." In 1978, the municipality initiated a large land reclamation program and by 1997, 3,200 hectares of badly damaged land had been re-vegetated with grass cover. More than 3.5 million evergreen trees were planted as part of the program.

# Symbols

Ontario has several emblems and symbols that reflect the province's natural and historic heritage.

The coat of arms consists of a green shield with three gold maple leaves and the Banner of St. George, a red cross on a silver background, above it. The banner indicates the province's close ties with Britain. Green and gold are Ontario's official colours, with green symbolizing the land. Above the shield is a bear, and on the sides supporting the shield are a **moose** and a deer. Below the shield is the official motto *Ut Incepit Fidelis Sic Permanet* (Loyal it began, loyal it remains). Queen Victoria granted the shield by royal warrant on May 25, 1868, while the banner, supporters, and motto were granted by King Edward VII on February 27, 1909.

The provincial flag, called the Red Ensign, consists of the Union Jack in the top left corner, again representing Ontario's ties to Britain, and the coat of arms to the right. It received royal approval on April 14, 1965, and was proclaimed on May 21 of that year. The proportions are two by length and one by width.

The trillium is the official flower of Ontario. The official gem of Ontario is amethyst, a deep purple semi-precious stone found mostly along the north shore of Lake Superior. Amethyst is found in only six other countries in the world. The largest concentration of stones in the province was found at Panorama mine, east of **Thunder Bay,** in 1955. The common loon became Ontario's official bird on June 23, 1994, while the official tree is the eastern white pine. White pine was an important resource for building ships and houses during Ontario's pioneer days and continues to be valuable to the province today.

# 1000 Islands

For nearly 400 years, voyageurs, soldiers, settlers, and more recently, tourists, have been awed by the beauty of the 1000 Islands (also referred to as the Thousand Islands). This collection of small islands is scattered between **Kingston** and Brockville, at the mouth of the **St. Lawrence River** where the waters of the **Great Lakes** begin their 1,600-kilometre journey to the Atlantic Ocean.

The 1000 Islands, which are actually made up of between 1,687 and 1,800 islands, are a byproduct of the ice age, sculpted along with the Great Lakes Basin beginning about one million years ago. They form part of the ancient **Canadian Shield.**

In 1615, French explorer Samuel de Champlain wrote in his diary, "The whole country is very beautiful and attractive." In 1792, Elizabeth Simcoe, wife of John Graves Simcoe, first governor of Upper Canada, wrote: "After passing Grenadier Island we came to the 1,000 Islands. The different sizes and shapes of these innumerable isles have a very pretty appearance."

First settled by the Iroquois, the 1000 Islands were on the route of the French *coureurs du bois* in pursuit of the **fur trade.** During the Seven Years War between England and France from 1756 to 1763, both nations constructed small fortresses throughout the islands, leaving behind legends of sunken and buried treasures.

The islands played a role in the American Revolution as well. **United Empire Loyalists** displaced from the eastern seaboard settled here and assisted the English during the **War of 1812.** When the war ended on Christmas Eve in 1814, Americans and Canadians signed the Treaty of Ghent, which forbade warships to enter the St. Lawrence, a provision still in force today.

In 1825, the British surveyed the islands and divided them into three groups or chains: the Admiralty Group, the Fleet Group, and the Navy Group. Each island of considerable size was named after a British admiral, battle, or ship. Names such as Forsythe, Melville, Tidds, Camelot, and Downie recall a bygone era.

Today, all but 25 of the 1000 Islands are privately owned. Of these, 21 are the property of the Canadian government, operated as park islands, and four belong to the American government. There are cottages on most of the islands, ranging from tiny seasonal cabins to sprawling year-round family homes built by American millionaires. About half of the islands are on the Canadian side of the border.

The 1000 Islands is a summer playground offering **camping,** swimming, boating, and hiking. Anglers pursue large-mouth bass, walleye, northern pike, and muskellunge. The world's largest muskie, weighing 31 kilograms, 426 grams, was caught in the area. In fall, the islands are brilliant with the changing colours of the leaves.

# Thunder Bay

This city on the shores of Lake Superior was born out of the long rivalry between two communities, Fort William and Port Arthur. Thunder Bay officially came into existence in 1970, thanks to an amalgamation of these twin cities.

Fort William, as its name suggests, began as a fort in the 1670s, was rebuilt in 1803 and named for Sir William McGillivray of the fur-trading North West Company three years later. Prince Arthur's Landing, as Port Arthur was originally known, lies to the east of Fort William and was blessed with an excellent harbour. Fort William was designated in 1875 as the Lake Superior terminus of the transcontinental railroad. Not to be outdone, Port Arthur built its own connecting link to the railway three years later, and both towns prospered in the following years.

Prince Arthur's Landing changed its name to Port Arthur in 1882, and became the main station for the newly constructed Canadian Pacific Railroad. In the meantime, however, Fort William was the beneficiary of a growing concentration of grain- and freight-handling facilities, which were a direct result of the new railway. The two port cities combined to become the largest grain storage area in the world. Port Arthur and Fort William also became important distribution centres for the growing lumber and mining industries of **northern Ontario** in the late 19th and early 20th centuries. In 1907, both communities officially became cities and by 1911 their total population was 28,000.

Like most Ontario cities, Fort William and Port Arthur suffered economic depression in the 1930s, but the opening of the Trans-Canada Highway in 1935 and a new airport four years later stimulated economic growth and opened **tourism** possibilities. The arrival of new waves of immigrants after World War II, the opening of the **Great Lakes–St. Lawrence Seaway System** in 1959, and the growth of such industries as pulp and paper, mining, and various manufacturers had the two cities burgeoning by the 1960s. Their combined population hit 90,000 in 1961, and talks began that decade about merging the two "Lakehead" cities. The name Thunder Bay is an English translation of the name for this area given by 17th-century French settlers—*Baie de Tonnerre*.

Thunder Bay's metropolitan population today stands at more than 115,000, and the city boasts two post-secondary institutions, Lakehead University and Confederation College of Applied Arts and Technology. Thunder Bay is the largest city in Ontario's northwest and the centre for health, technology,

**education,** culture, and **manufacturing.** It remains an important harbour on the Great Lakes–St. Lawrence Seaway route and is a popular tourist centre because of its magnificent location among the **forests,** rivers, and mountains. Its most famous landmark is the Sleeping Giant rock formation, which guards the harbour and can be seen from almost anywhere in the city. About 1.4 million visitors generate some $350 million for the local **economy** annually.

Thunder Bay is also the home of the Terry Fox Monument, in honour of the young man from Port Coquitlam, B.C. who was forced to abandon his "Marathon of Hope" cross-Canada run near here in September 1980 because of the recurrence of cancer. Stone tablets on the monument recount the story of Fox's 5,432-kilometre run for cancer research.

# Thunderstorms

Ontario lies in a zone of active weather movement, and although they don't last long, thunderstorms play an important role in the province's weather.

On average, thunderstorms occur on 25 days each year south of Lake Superior and on as many as 35 days in the **London-Windsor** region, which, as Environment Canada weather expert David Phillips says, "offers more of nature's sound and light shows" than any other area in Canada. The frequency of thunderstorms drops rapidly to the north; the shore of Hudson Bay sees such storms on five days or fewer annually.

In many cases, thunderstorms are accompanied by lightning that can cause forest fires. And occasionally, during more severe thunderstorms, hail batters fruit and garden crops. On May 30, 1986, for instance, a hailstorm inflicted $30 to $40 million worth of damage in the Leamington-Windsor area of southwestern Ontario, when hailstones as big as golf balls smashed greenhouses and damaged early crops.

Thunderstorms usually occur in late afternoon or early evening after a string of hot and humid days. Although they have caused flooding and wind damage, the more gentle variety are usually well received because they are often followed by cooler, more comfortable air.

# Tobacco

Ontario tobacco country occupies Canada's southernmost region on the north shore of Lake Erie south and east of **London.** The soil is coarse and sandy there, and the growing season offers reliable, sunny days, mild evenings, and growth-nurturing rainfall for most of the season.

Approximately 97 percent of Canada's tobacco is grown in Ontario, in the counties of Brant, Elgin, and Oxford, and the Regional Municipality of Haldimand-Norfolk, where approximately 20,000 people are directly involved—many on a seasonal basis—in tobacco production, marketing, and processing activities. The industry in the growing region consists of about 1,500 farm families, the Tillsonburg-based Ontario Flue-Cured Tobacco Growers' Marketing Board and its auction system, and two primary leaf processors. Tobacco represents the focal point for many communities, including Delhi, Langton, Simcoe, and Tillsonburg, where businesses are directly linked to the fortunes of the tobacco industry.

The tobacco industry generates a total annual income of about $450 million in Ontario, of which about $315 million stays in southwestern Ontario.

*Tobacco farmer Maurice Crabbe (gesturing) in a field on his tobacco farm near Simcoe in 1960.* (Victor Aziz, National Archives, PA-124814)

The tobacco board controls the production and marketing of all tobacco grown in Ontario. Tobacco processors located in Simcoe and Aylmer ship product to cigarette manufacturers, which make cigarettes and fine-cut tobacco for the roll-your-own variety. About 40 percent of the crop is exported, mainly to the United Kingdom and the United States.

Tobacco is known as a high-value crop because on average growers spend $2,800 per acre on such expenses as labour, pesticides, and fuel, and earn nearly $1,000 per acre after operating expenses, a considerably higher return than from other crops grown in the area. Tobacco farms average about 41 hectares in size, although most utilize only 20 to 30 hectares per season for tobacco.

Seedlings in March are nourished in black earth that has been sterilized by steam, thoroughly cleansing it of weak seeds, parasites, and other undesirables. The young seedlings are then transplanted into carefully prepared fields where they benefit from fertilizing, cultivating, and irrigating until harvest begins in August. The result is a crop of uniform quality.

After being sorted and graded, the tobacco is sold beginning in October at auction exchanges in Delhi and Tillsonburg. Once the tobacco is purchased, processing companies pack the tobacco to the specifications of customers. Storage facilities are also available, where tobacco may be aged before it is forwarded to end users who manufacture it into cigarettes.

In recent years, all has not been well for the tobacco industry. Between 1981 and 1987, it underwent a downturn in response to the falling demand for tobacco products due to the use of contraband tobacco shipped mainly from the United States and sold on First Nations reserves in Canada and a reduction in smoking. Eventually, in 1986 the industry's Tobacco Advisory Committee stabilized the amount of tobacco grown each year in a bid to correct over-production problems.

A 31-percent reduction in crop size saw many growers lose their farms. In the Tillsonburg area, 840 producers went out of business between 1987 and 1991, or 40 percent of all growers in the region, which led to increased unemployment and family stress, reduced property values, and changes in family work patterns as spouses of tobacco producers sought a second job to replace their lost farm income.

Existing growing area was stabilized at about 24,600 hectares in 1986, which means there is about 40 percent less land used for tobacco growing today than in the early 1980s.

# Toronto

Canada's largest city and the capital of Ontario is the **manufacturing,** financial, cultural, and transportation heart of the province.

Although Toronto began to take shape as a municipality just over 200 years ago, there is archaeological evidence suggesting that humans have been active in the area for some 6,000 years. **First Nations peoples** hunted and fished in the region and used the Humber River as a shortcut to **Georgian Bay** and the upper **Great Lakes.** When Europeans arrived in the 17th century, they found people living in semi-permanent villages and farming the land. French explorers began using the same waterway routes and in 1750 established Fort Rouillé on the site of what is now the **Canadian National Exhibition** grounds to protect their interests in the **fur trade.** They abandoned the fort in 1759 and for the next several decades Toronto was under British control.

Toronto, which is believed to come from a Mohawk word meaning "trees standing in the water" (and not "meeting place," as others have speculated), began to thrive in the 1790s (*see* **Fort York**). The Lieutenant Governor of Upper Canada, John Graves Simcoe, had considered making **London** the capital of the province, but settled instead on Toronto, which he renamed York. With a military presence established there, more civilians came to live in York, increasing the need for roads, fortifications, and other buildings. Thanks to Simcoe's initiatives, roads such as Dundas Street, which went westward, and **Yonge Street,** which headed north, were built. In the late 18th and early 19th centuries, **United Empire Loyalists** and other European settlers cleared land and established farms and businesses that helped the town thrive.

York was attacked by the Americans during the **War of 1812,** but survived the onslaught and continued to grow once peace was established again in 1815. By 1834, York's **population** had surpassed 9,000, and it became incorporated as a city, changing its name to Toronto. As the capital, the city was also the centre of political development and intrigue in the province. During the **Rebellion of 1837,** William Lyon Mackenzie led political protesters through the streets of Toronto. The rebellion was short-lived, and most of the rebels were arrested and either executed or expelled from the colony. Nevertheless, the rebellion led to eventual implementation of the Reformers' ideas of responsible government.

Toronto continued to prosper over the next decades, with the construction of such city landmarks as St. Lawrence Hall, what is now the St. Lawrence

Market, and several important churches. As with other Ontario towns and cities of the day, the arrival of the railway was a boon to Toronto and, combined with improvements in roads and its fine natural harbour, the city became the transportation hub of Ontario.

With reliable transportation, Toronto also became a more diversified manufacturing centre in the last half of the 19th century. Records show that the number of manufacturing plants increased dramatically from 530 in 1871 to more than 2,400 by 1891. Such industries as **agriculture** and forest products, meat packing (the **railways** that brought livestock to market here probably resulted in Toronto's nickname of "Hogtown"), office equipment, and spin-off financial services all became well established.

*Old City Hall in Toronto still stands as a reminder of Toronto's rich history.* (Mark Kearney)

The University of Toronto officially came into being in 1850, although it had operated as an Anglican institution for seven years before that as the University of King's College. It would soon become one of the leading educational institutions in Canada.

With a population of more than 200,000 in 1901, Toronto was Canada's second-largest city, behind Montreal. Torontonians were still predominantly of British origin, but other European immigrants had established a presence here, too.

Toronto's downtown changed dramatically on April 19, 1904, when a huge fire that began on Wellington Street near **Bay Street** swept through the core. More than 100 buildings were destroyed in a fire that caused $10 million in damage, but fortunately no one was killed. Toronto began to rebuild in the years

*Built in the 1960s, City Hall in Toronto was a key component in that city's renaissance. (Mark Kearney).*

leading up to World War I, and the city annexed the villages of East Toronto, West Toronto, and North Toronto. It wouldn't be until 1953 that Toronto expanded once more.

Toronto prospered through the war years and into the 1920s. Such landmarks as the Royal York Hotel, the largest hotel in the British Empire at the time, and the Bank of Commerce, the tallest building in the Empire, were built in this period. The Toronto Transportation Commission (now known as the Toronto Transit Commission) was created in 1918, and the city remains one of the few in North America to use streetcars today. Union Station opened in 1927 and continues to be the main rail hub of Canada to this day. During the Depression of the 1930s, one-third of Torontonians were out of a job, but such public works projects as the construction of the Malton (now Lester B. Pearson International) Airport helped alleviate some of the economic stress.

As World War II and the post-war boom revitalized the **economy** in Canada as a whole, Toronto was well positioned to take advantage of the opportunities. Suburban communities such as Don Mills were built to meet housing needs, and the amalgamation of surrounding boroughs and villages under the new Metropolitan government in 1953 made Toronto bigger and economically healthier. Though Toronto was accused of being staid and stuffy for much of its history, things began to change in the 1960s. The architecturally interesting new city hall in 1965 symbolized a fresh outlook for the city, and a renaissance in such downtown neighbourhoods as Yorkville gave Toronto a new feel. Young people and the majority of immigrants to Canada flocked to Toronto in the 1960s and '70s, bringing with them a vitality, energy, and flavour the city had never known before. Toronto's skyline began changing dramatically at this time, especially with the construction of several bank skyscrapers and the **CN Tower,** the world's largest free-standing structure.

A key municipal battle in Toronto's modern history was waged over the Spadina Expressway, first proposed in the late 1940s, that was to run from the downtown northward. When funding for the expressway's construction was set up in the early 1960s, angry citizens who wanted to preserve neighbourhoods and priceless architecture fought the idea for more than 10 years. The proposal was eventually defeated in 1971, and no expressway was built. Instead, an extension of the subway line running north under Spadina was built later. The defeat of the expressway did much to help preserve Toronto's downtown residential neighbourhoods and make the city one of the safest, busiest, and most admired in the world. Although construction boomed in the 1980s, and commuter traffic from the outlying suburbs has increased dramatically, the city has maintained a commitment to neighbourhood preservation.

Today, Toronto is the headquarters of hundreds of Canadian businesses; Bay Street is the hub of Canada's financial sector; the **Toronto Stock Exchange** is the biggest in the country; and in recent years, the city has become something of a "Hollywood North," with a booming television and **film industry.** It is also considered one of the most multicultural and ethnically diverse cities in the world. Toronto is home to a vast array of shops, restaurants, and world-renowned **museums** such as the **Royal Ontario Museum** and **Ontario Science Centre,** galleries—including the **Art Gallery of Ontario**—theatres, and four major professional sports franchises.

In 1997, Toronto's political structure was once again altered, this time by the provincial government. Although more than 75 percent of Torontonians opposed the idea, the city's metropolitan structure, which had separate governments in each of its boroughs, was changed to what has become known as the "megacity," with one central municipal government serving the needs of more than three million people.

# Toronto Argonauts

A group of oarsmen interested in playing rugby and looking for an alternate way of staying fit formed the Toronto Argonaut football club in 1873. They played their first game against the University of Toronto team. The Argonauts played sporadically in their first year, but won the Ontario Rugby Football Union championship in 1883. The words rugby and football were used in these years to describe the same sport, but it started to become distinct from the English game of rugby in the 1880s. The Canadian game changed over the years with such innovations as set formations and forward passing.

In 1907, the Argonauts helped form the Interprovincial Rugby Football Union, and in 1911 they played in their first Grey Cup, losing 14–7 to the University of Toronto. Fortunes changed in 1914, however, as the Argonauts scored two touchdowns to win their first of fourteen Grey Cups, in a 14–2 victory over U. of T.

The Argonauts would win the Grey Cup again in 1921, defeating the Edmonton Eskimos 23–0 in the first-ever east-west championship. But it would be another dozen years before the Argos won their next Grey Cup, a 4–3 victory over the Sarnia Imperials. Four years later and led by the Stukus brothers— Annis, Bill, and Frank—they won back-to-back Grey Cups in 1937–38.

The post–World War II years were glory ones for the Argonauts. Led by the "Gold Dust Twins," quarterback Joe Krol and running back Royal Copeland, the Argos won Grey Cups three years in a row in 1945, 1946, and 1947. In 1950, they won again, 13–0, over the Winnipeg Blue Bombers in the infamous "Mud Bowl," so named because of the many puddles at Toronto's Varsity Stadium. The Argos won the Grey Cup again in 1952, but fans would have to suffer through a three-decade drought before the Argos came back on top again.

In 1957, a syndicate that included Toronto *Telegram* publisher John Bassett bought the Argos. The team moved from Varsity Stadium in 1959 and began playing its home games at **Canadian National Exhibition** Stadium. The Argos had a few successful teams in the 1960s, with such stars as Dick Shatto and Bill Symons. Under flamboyant coach Leo Cahill, the Argos finally made it back to the Grey Cup in 1971. However, a late fumble by Leon McQuay sealed a 14–11 victory for the Calgary Stampeders. The 1970s were not winning years for the team, although ironically they set attendance records throughout that decade, averaging almost 47,000 fans per game in 1977.

Carling O'Keefe Breweries purchased the team in 1979 and, in a dramatic turnaround, the club made it to the Grey Cup in 1982, losing to Edmonton 32–16. The drought, however, was over in 1983 as the Argos won the Grey Cup 18–17 over the B.C. Lions. In 1989, the team began playing its home games in the **SkyDome.** The Argonauts went through further ownership changes in the late 1980s and '90s, the most hyped being the 1991 purchase by American businessman Bruce McNall, hockey star Wayne Gretzky, and actor John Candy, who brought glitz, glamour, and money to the CFL team. They won the Grey Cup in 1991, a 42–3 victory over the Winnipeg Blue Bombers, which included an 87-yard kickoff return by their star Raghib "Rocket" Ismail.

The Argos suffered some bad seasons and low attendance in the mid-1990s, but with such stars as Doug Flutie and Mike "Pinball" Clemons they won the Grey Cup two years in a row, defeating the Edmonton Eskimos 43–37 in 1996, and in 1997 beating the Saskatchewan Roughriders 47–23. The 1997 championship team is considered by many to be not only the best team in Argonaut history but possibly the greatest team ever in the Canadian Football League. The Argonauts got a new owner in December 1999, when American businessman Sherwood Schwartz purchased the team.

# Toronto Blue Jays

When the Toronto Blue Jays won consecutive World Series titles in 1992 and 1993, fans were rewarded with championships that had been more than 15 years in the making. On March 26, 1976, the American League had awarded **Toronto** a major league baseball franchise, and by August "Blue Jays" had been chosen as the team moniker from over 4,000 proposed names.

More than 44,000 fans braved snow and cold temperatures when the Blue Jays debuted at the **Canadian National Exhibition** Stadium on April 7, 1977. The team won that first game 9–5 over the Chicago White Sox, but finished their first season in last place with 54 wins and 105 losses. The Jays drew millions of fans during the early years of their franchise history, even though it would be 1983 before they finished a season with more wins than losses. One highlight was Alfredo Griffin winning the American League Rookie of the Year award in 1979.

The 1980s was a good decade for the Blue Jays. The team featured many exciting players, including George Bell, the American League's Most Valuable

Player in 1987; pitcher Dave Stieb; talented hitter and base stealer Tony Fernandez; and excellent fielder Jesse Barfield. In 1985, the team won its first division title and made it to the playoffs, losing four games to three to the Kansas City Royals. That winning season earned Bobby Cox the American League Manager of the Year award. Two years later, in one of the most dramatic pennant races in baseball history, the Blue Jays just missed making the playoffs despite having the second-best record in the major leagues.

In June 1989, the team moved its home games to the new **SkyDome** stadium and that year captured its second division title. The Jays came up short of appearing in the World Series, however, losing to the Oakland Athletics in the playoffs. The following year was another strong one for the franchise as Jays' fans established a new single season attendance record of 3,885,284. A highlight for the team in 1990 was Stieb's no-hitter against the Cleveland Indians.

In 1991, the club became the first in major league history to draw more than four million fans to its home games and captured another division title. In the off season, John Labatt Ltd. purchased the portion of the club previously owned by Imperial Trust and, as a result, controlled 90 percent of the franchise. By the following year, champagne flowed as the Blue Jays defeated the Oakland Athletics in the playoffs to get into their first-ever World Series championship.

Despite losing the opening game, the team won its first World Series by defeating the Atlanta Braves four games to two. Fans had even more to cheer about in 1993 when a dramatic ninth-inning home run by Joe Carter against the Philadelphia Phillies gave the Blue Jays their second World Series title, the first time since the New York Yankees in 1977–78 that a team had won back-to-back World Series championships.

Since then, the Blue Jays' record and attendance have dwindled somewhat, and there have been several managerial and player changes. The team, owned as of 1999 by Interbrew S.A. of Belgium, has enjoyed some recent highlights, such as pitcher Pat Hentgen winning the American League Cy Young Award in 1996 and Roger Clemens winning two Cy Young Awards in 1997 and 1998.

## Toronto Eaton Centre

Although known primarily as one of the premier shopping centres in the country, the Toronto Eaton Centre is also considered the city's biggest tourist attraction, with close to one million visitors each week.

The Eaton Centre is a four-level shopping mall built in the style of the Galleria of Milan, Italy, with a domed glass ceiling that runs its full length. The centre sits on a six-hectare site in the heart of downtown **Toronto,** and features more than 280 shops and services, three office towers, and an attached 450-room hotel. When it opened in February 1977 at a cost of $300 million, the Eaton Centre represented a new thrust in downtown redevelopment in Canada and changed the face of both **Yonge Street** and retailing in Toronto.

The idea for the centre was hatched in the early 1960s, when plans to replace the Eaton's flagship store in Toronto were first proposed. City politicians and residents initially opposed the major downtown development plan because the original concept called for the demolition of a nearby church and part of Toronto's old city hall. Several other plans were discussed before the first of the three-phase project, developed by the Cadillac Fairview Corporation, went ahead, taking some five years to complete. A second phase was completed in August 1979, while a major $42 million facelift, which included some new stores and new street access, began in 1999.

A prominent feature of the downtown retail/office complex is artist Michael Snow's *Flight Stop,* a large sculpture of Canada geese suspended above shoppers in the centre's south end. The centre is also home to a 17-cinema Cineplex.

Now owned by Cadillac Fairview and the Toronto Dominion Bank, the Toronto Eaton Centre was continuing to thrive despite announcements in the summer of 1999 that Eaton's had filed for bankruptcy. The Eaton's store is owned by Sears but still called Eaton's.

## Toronto Maple Leafs

If there is a sports institution in Ontario, it has to be the Toronto Maple Leafs. For more than seven decades, the fabled franchise has helped ease hockey fans through long Canadian winters, winning 11 Stanley Cups and producing some of hockey's all-time greatest players.

The Maple Leafs were born on February 14, 1927, when Conn Smythe took over the team previously known as the Toronto St. Patricks. The team played in the old Mutual Street arena until **Maple Leaf Gardens** was built in downtown **Toronto** in 1931. The Maple Leafs won their first Stanley Cup during the team's first season in the Gardens, led by such players as Joe Primeau, Busher Jackson, Charlie Conacher, Hap Day, and King Clancy. The Leafs continued their regular season success in the 1930s but did not win another Cup until 1942.

Leafs coach Dick Irvin left for the Montreal Canadiens in 1940 after winning one Stanley Cup and guiding the club to seven Cup finals in his nine years as Toronto's bench boss. Hap Day took over, and the Leafs won the Cup in dramatic fashion in 1942 when they lost the first three games of the finals to the Detroit Red Wings, but stormed back to win the next four. It was the first and only time a team has rallied from a 3–0 deficit in a Stanley Cup final.

World War II depleted the Leaf roster as many of the players went overseas, and as a result future captain and star Ted "Teeder" Kennedy got his first chance to play in 1943. Led by goalie Frank "Ulcers" McCool, who set an NHL record with three consecutive shutouts in the 1945 playoffs, the Leafs won the 1945 Cup.

In 1946, Conn Smythe became president of Maple Leaf Gardens Ltd. and 30 percent owner of the team. He would remain president until his resignation in 1961. The Leafs won three consecutive Stanley Cups in 1947, 1948, and 1949, and in the 1950s new arrivals such as George Armstrong and Tim Horton would lead the team to future glory. The Leafs experienced triumph and tragedy in 1951. Bill Barilko's overtime goal in game five of the finals versus the Canadiens won the Leafs the Cup, but Barilko died in a plane crash later that summer. The Leafs didn't make it to the Cup finals again until 1959.

Conn Smythe's son, Stafford, was given control of the team in 1957, and he employed six assistants, including John Bassett and Harold Ballard. The Leafs' coach at the time, Punch Imlach, signed veteran goalkeeper Johnny Bower, who would be an essential part of the Leafs' four Stanley Cups over the next 12 seasons. Other Leaf stars of the 1950s and '60s were "Red" Kelly, Dave Keon, who won Rookie of the Year honours in 1961, Eddie Shack, and Frank Mahovlich, who in 1958 also won Rookie of the Year honours. With defencemen such as Bobby Baun, Carl Brewer, Horton, and Allan Stanley added to the mix, the Leafs dominated the first half of the 1960s. They won three consecutive Cups between 1962 and 1964 and another in 1967.

A long dry spell began after their most successful decade, which saw few winning seasons and no Stanley Cups up to and including 1999. Several Leaf players, including Keon, Paul Henderson, Bernie Parent, and Norm Ullman, left the team for the new World Hockey Association (WHA) in the early 1970s.

New stars such as Lanny McDonald and Darryl Sittler, who would score six goals and earn four assists in one game in 1976, reignited the hopes of Leafs fans in the 1970s, but the team never made it to the Stanley Cup finals during this decade. The 1980s were a difficult time for the Leafs and their fans, and most of the blame was placed on the shoulders of controversial owner Harold Ballard. Imlach was brought back to try to rekindle past successes, but the Leafs went through a string of coaches with little success. Some bright spots during this time, however, were Rick Vaive's three consecutive 50-goal seasons and the arrival of forward Wendel Clark in 1985.

The Leafs' fortunes began to change in 1991 when Cliff Fletcher was hired as chief operating officer, president, and general manager. The playoffs of 1993 and 1994 saw the Leafs reach the final four teams. Mats Sundin emerged as the team's star in the late '90s, and in 1997, he was named the 16th captain in franchise history. A new Toronto Maple Leafs era began that same year in May when Ken Dryden was named president of the club. He hired Pat Quinn, a veteran coach and former Leafs player, as his coach.

In the 1998–99 season, a year that saw the club leave the Gardens for the new Air Canada Centre, the Leafs did better than most had predicted, finishing second in the NHL's northeast division with 97 points. They advanced to the final four before losing to the Buffalo Sabres in the eastern conference finals. In the summer of 1999, Quinn added the role of general manager to his coaching duties.

# Toronto Raptors

When the National Basketball Association (NBA) officially approved the Toronto Raptors as the league's newest franchise in November 1993, it marked a return, rather than the beginning, of major professional basketball to **Toronto.**

Although the arrival of the Raptors began a new era for the sport in the city, Toronto once had a professional team known as the Huskies in 1946. The Huskies were one of 11 teams in the Basketball Association of America, a forerunner of the NBA that included such teams as the New York Knicks and the Boston Celtics, which remain in the sport today. The Huskies, however, only lasted one season, and with the exception of the old Buffalo Braves franchise that played some of its "home" games in Toronto in the 1970s, the city was without a major basketball team until the Raptors.

The Raptors' history began in April 1993, when a group of businessmen, including former Ontario Premier David Peterson, applied to the NBA for a franchise. Once the franchise was approved, John Bitove was named the first team president, and in May 1994, former NBA great Isiah Thomas was named the team's vice-president.

The Raptors played their first regular season home game on November 3, 1995, at the **SkyDome** and defeated the New Jersey Nets 94–79. Alvin Robertson scored the team's first points. Despite the presence of rookie sensation Damon Stoudamire, the Raptors finished low in the standings their first year, winning 21 games and losing 61. The team drafted college star Marcus Camby for its second season, but he would be traded in 1998–99.

In the meantime, Allan Slaight became the team's majority owner in November 1996. Thomas's attempt to increase his percentage of ownership failed to pan out and he left the franchise in November 1997.

Another milestone took place for the team on February 21, 1999 when the Raptors moved into their new home, the Air Canada Centre, and defeated the Vancouver Grizzlies 102-87. They re-signed some of their key players that year, and for the first time in its short history, the Raptors qualified for the playoffs in the 1999-2000 season. Thanks to stellar play by Vince Carter, the Rookie of the Year winner the previous year, the team won more than 40 games en route to post-season play.

Now owned by Maple Leaf Sports and Entertainment Ltd., the Raptors are looking forward optimistically.

# Toronto Stock Exchange

A stock exchange is an association of brokers and dealers formed to enable shares in companies to be bought and sold. The Toronto Stock Exchange (TSE), located in the heart of downtown **Toronto,** is Canada's busiest and most prestigious stock market.

As the centre for the issue and trading of Canadian equities and related investment products, the TSE plays a vital role in the Canadian **economy** and has inspired the entrepreneurial instincts of generations of Canadians. It is seen as a gateway into Canada for global investors who seek to diversify their holdings.

With more than 1,400 listed companies offering more than 1,700 issues, the TSE provides investors with a diverse range of stocks, proprietary derivatives, indexes, and market information. The S&P (Standard & Poor's)/TSE60 Index, launched in December 1998, provides Canadian companies with increased exposure in international markets.

The fully automated TSE is the third-largest stock exchange in North America and the seventh largest in the world. It is Canada's premier market for equities and equities-based derivatives, accounting for more than 90 percent of all equity trading in Canada. In 1998, more than 26 billion shares were traded, worth more than $490 billion—about $2 billion a day in share transactions. That's a far cry from its early years, when trading on some days amounted to as few as two or three transactions valued at a few hundred dollars at most. In those days, there were about a dozen TSE members, and trading was limited to 18 securities.

The TSE was founded in 1852 by a group of Toronto businessmen who formed an association of brokers to create a market in industrial securities. Incorporated in 1878, the TSE is owned by 99 member investment firms and is governed by a 15-member board of governors. Leading experts from the securities industry, investment community, and listed companies volunteer as committee members and help the TSE develop policies that enhance trading efficiency and protect investors.

Junior companies seeking to raise capital and investors interested in growth stocks can utilize the Canadian Dealing Network, Canada's largest over-the-counter market and a subsidiary of the TSE, which enables trading in securities not listed on a recognized stock exchange. Trading volume through this network has grown enormously and, in the late 1990s, totalled more than two billion shares a year.

In 1977, the TSE launched its Computer Assisted Trading System (CATS), the world's first, which set a new standard for other exchanges to follow. Trades that previously took 30 seconds could now be completed with the push of a button. A further upgrade came in April 1997 when the TSE's 145-year-old trading floor open-outcry trading practice was replaced by TOREXTM, a completely electronic trading system that ranks among the most advanced in the world.

In June 1999, TSE members voted to demutualize the exchange, which changed it from a nonprofit capital corporation to a shareholder-based, for-profit corporation, enabling the exchange to respond more quickly and efficiently to the future needs of the capital market.

To help ensure that investors' interests are protected, the TSE has strict regulations that listed companies and member firms must observe. A team of specialists dedicated to market surveillance looks for any trading activity that might be a breach of regulations. The Ontario Securities Commission also regulates the markets and protects the interests of investors.

# Toronto Zoo

Although the Riverdale Zoo had existed in **Toronto** since 1887, it never attracted the national and international attention of its replacement, the Toronto Zoo, which opened in 1974. The zoo's opening followed the founding of the Zoological Society of Toronto in 1966. A 287-hectare site in the Rouge River Valley in the city's east end was chosen, and Metro Toronto council allocated $22 million for the project. Work on the zoo began in 1970 and was completed four years later.

The Toronto Zoo is one of only a few in the world to group animals according to where they're found in the world. The zoo's six regions are: Africa, Australasia, Eurasia, the Americas, IndoMalaya, and Canada. As much as possible, the animals are in environments similar to their natural habitat. The zoo was also one of the first to allow the animals to roam freely within large enclosed areas.

Some 5,000 animals live at the zoo, representing more than 450 species. Included in these numbers are several rare and endangered species, such as the western lowland gorilla, the wood bison, the Puerto Rican crested toad, and the snow leopard. Toronto Zoo is the only one in Canada, and one of just six in the world, with a successful cheetah breeding program. In 1998, the zoo opened a new African Savanna, which reproduces the landscape features of that continent and focusses on **education** programs and conservation of African species.

More than 30 million people have visited the zoo in its first 25 years.

# Tourism

Tourism is a critical part of Ontario's **economy,** benefitting from an array of world-class attractions. It is ranked as the province's ninth-largest economic sector, ahead of **agriculture,** mining, and forestry in terms of its contribution to Ontario's gross domestic product. In fact, Ontario has Canada's largest tourism industry, accounting for 37 percent of national tourism revenues and drawing 44 percent of all visitors who come to Canada.

The industry represents more than 88,000 mainly small and medium-sized businesses in the following sectors: food and beverage, accommodation and amusement, transportation and travel services, and car- and tourism-related retail. And it is not just outsiders who spend money at the province's various tourist attractions: on average in Ontario, trips within the province account for 7.5 percent of all household expenditures.

In total, tourism is responsible for $14.1 billion worth of annual expenditures in Ontario and is the province's sixth-largest export industry, bringing in $6.1 billion in foreign exchange. It also generates about $6 billion in tax revenue for federal, provincial, and municipal levels of government.

More than 242,000 people are directly employed in the industry, with an additional 170,000 indirect jobs. These combined figures represent nearly 8 percent of Ontario's total employment.

The province's tourism sector has been divided into 12 regions, each of which boasts attractions that lure visitors from around the globe. Among Ontario's many tourist sites are **Niagara Falls, Paramount Canada's Wonderland,** the **CN Tower,** the **Stratford** and **Shaw Festivals,** the **1000 Islands, Agawa Canyon, Science North, Manitoulin Island,** and the **Parliament Buildings,** as well as the shopping areas, **casinos,** and national and **provincial parks,** galleries, **museums,** beaches, lakes, and waterways across the province.

## Trilliums

The trillium was selected as Ontario's provincial flower in 1937, during the tenure of Premier Mitch Hepburn. Specifically, Ontario's trillium is the *Trillium grandiflorum,* or white trillium, a member of the lily family. This species turns pink with age. The three other species of trillium that grow in the province are the red, the painted, and the nodding.

Trilliums are delicate three-petalled perennial flowers that grow in profusion in the province's deciduous **forests** and woodlands in late April and early May. Over the years, many have been transplanted into private gardens because of their beauty and the flower's longevity. As a means of protection, it is illegal to pick trilliums in all Ontario provincial parks and in some Ontario municipalities.

## TVOntario

Since 1970, TVOntario, originally established as the Ontario Educational Communications Authority, has been broadcasting educational programming to Ontarians of all ages. The mandate of the **Toronto**-based broadcaster is to provide viewers, through its English- and French-language networks, with programs and services that respond to specific learning needs.

Funded primarily by the provincial government as well as by viewers, corporate donors, and through program sales, TVOntario has produced award-winning shows that have been seen around the world. The organization has developed an expertise in the design, development, and application of technology to learning, and in recent years has refocussed its vision on lifelong learning. A new division of TVOntario, the Ontario Centre for Advanced Technology in Learning (OCATL), was established as a way to take full advantage of existing technologies.

TVOntario reaches more than three million viewers each week. Its audience share in Ontario is higher than such networks as YTV, Newsworld, PBS, CNN, or TSN. Its French-language counterpart, TFO, has more than 350,000 viewers per week. TFO plays a key role in helping Franco-Ontarian educators serve the needs of their primary and secondary school students, as well as the more than 13,000 students enrolled in French-language programs in four community colleges and six university campuses.

Approximately 70 percent of the broadcast schedules of TVO and TFO are devoted to educational programming for children at home, students and teachers in the classrooms, and parents and adults seeking distance learning opportunities. The other 30 percent of TVOntario's schedules provides non-commercial prime time programming that focusses on science, culture, documentary, and current affairs shows, as well as a range of international programs. Among the more popular shows broadcast on TVOntario are the public affairs program *Studio 2* and *Saturday Night at the Movies*.

In the 1990s, TVOntario began developing multimedia resources in response to the evolution of technology, the needs of students, teachers, and parents, and the mandate of government. The network has branched into new technologies, such as laser discs, CD-ROMs, satellite teleconferences, electronic conferencing, virtual classrooms, databases, the Internet, and the World Wide Web.

# 24 Sussex Drive

Arguably one of Canada's most famous addresses, 24 Sussex Drive has been the home of Canada's prime ministers since 1951. Louis St. Laurent was the first PM to call the place home.

The house was built between 1866 and 1868 for Joseph Currier, a lumber baron and member of the first Dominion Parliament. Originally a Gothic revival villa, it was dubbed with the tongue-twisting name *Gorffwysfa* (spelled Gorphwysfa in some books), which is Welsh for "abode of peace" or "haven of rest." In 1902, the property was sold to William Cameron Edwards, another lumber manufacturer. Between 1943 and 1946 the government expropriated the home from its then owner Gordon C. Edwards.

The question of a permanent residence for the prime ministers of Canada had not been an issue before 1945 because most had private homes in **Ottawa.** But when St. Laurent took office in 1946, his home was in Quebec City and it was difficult to find suitable premises for his family. So, following $550,000 worth of renovations that rendered the original house unrecognizable, St. Laurent moved into 24 Sussex in 1951.

The 34-room residence overlooks the Ottawa River and the Gatineau Hills in Quebec from a 2.15-hectare parcel of land, which lies about five minutes by car from Parliament Hill. Also on the property are a chauffeur's residence, an indoor swimming pool, and guard houses constructed for the Royal Canadian Mounted Police by Public Works Canada. The home has a federal heritage designation, which will protect it from the wrecker's ball.

# Underground Railroad

In the early 19th century, a movement known as the Underground Railroad helped enslaved black people escape from the southern United States to freedom in the north, and occasionally to western territories, Mexico, and the Caribbean. Neither a railroad nor underground, the Underground Railroad was a network of routes and houses where the slaves could travel, hide, and receive assistance from people willing to risk their own safety to help them make a new life.

Slaves passed information about how to escape by word of mouth and through songs. Those who helped them along the way (they were known as "conductors") included white and black abolitionists, other slaves, Native Americans, and members of such religious groups as the Quakers and Methodists. Main terminuses in Canada included southwestern Ontario's Essex and Kent counties and the Niagara Region's communities, such as Fort Erie and St. Catharines.

After the American Revolution, many **United Empire Loyalists** moved to Upper Canada and brought their slaves with them. In 1793, a bill was passed to prevent the further introduction of slaves into Upper Canada, making the province a haven for many blacks. More than 40,000 slaves, using the North Star as their guide, fled to Canada in the years before the American Civil War. The first permanent black settlement was in Sandwich, near **Windsor,** followed by other sites, such as the Elgin Settlement in what is now North Buxton.

One of the most famous settlements began in the 1840s near present-day Dresden. It was here that the Reverend Josiah Henson and others purchased 82 hectares to establish the British American Institute, one of the first schools in Canada to emphasize vocational training. The former slaves who lived and studied here built farms, sawmills, and other local industries. Some of the residents returned to the U.S. after emancipation for slaves was proclaimed in 1863, but others remained to establish a significant black community in this part of Ontario.

Henson, a former slave from Maryland who escaped to Canada with his family in 1830, is best known as the man whose life story inspired Harriet Beecher Stowe to write her classic novel *Uncle Tom's Cabin.* The cabin where Henson and his family lived during the latter part of his life is now a historic site near Dresden.

The site, which went through a four-year redevelopment in the 1990s, also includes five other historical structures, a new interpretive centre, and Henson's gravesite. Other significant sites of African-Canadian heritage in this region include the North American Black Historical Museum and Cultural Centre in Amherstburg, the John Freeman Walls Historic Site in Maidstone, and the Buxton Historic Site and Museum in North Buxton.

# Unique Claims to Fame

Many Ontario communities possess unique attributes, landmarks, and characteristics that give them a special identity or help them promote **tourism.**

One of **Sudbury's** claims to fame is the Big Nickel, the world's largest nickel, measuring more than 9 metres high and 61 centimetres thick. It was issued in 1951 and, ironically, is made of stainless steel. The Northern Ontario Mining Museum in Cobalt has the world's largest display of native silver ore.

The Wawa Goose, a nine-metre steel Canada goose at the entrance to Wawa, is one of the most famous pieces of highway art in North America. *Wawa*, which means "wild goose" in Ojibwa, is named for the thousands of Canada geese that congregate on Lake Wawa. Visitors to Kenora will be greeted by Husky the Muskie, a 12-metre-high statue in honour of the muskellunge, one of the mightiest fighting **fish** in the world.

Brighton, in southern Ontario, is home to the world's largest apple. The Big Apple stands more than 9 metres high, is about 11 metres in diameter, could hold 653,800 apples, and is composed of 42 tonnes of foam and fibreglass over a metal frame.

The Chapleau Game Preserve and Wildlife Sanctuary in northern Ontario, comprising 800,000 hectares, is the largest game preserve in the world, and the only shooting done here is with cameras. Creatures that can be viewed include **birds** of prey, otters, mink, fox, wolves, **moose,** and black bears.

A bear of a different kind is the pride of White River. This northwestern Ontario community is the birthplace of the real Winnie the Pooh. A Winnipeg soldier adopted a bear cub during World War I and took it with him to England. He later donated the bear to the London Zoo, where it became the inspiration for A.A. Milne's famous stories.

**Ottawa** is well known as Canada's capital, but every February at Winterlude, the city's annual winter festival, the Rideau Canal turns into the world's longest skating rink, almost eight kilometres long. The biggest Scottish festival in North America takes place in Fergus in the second week of August. For more than 50 years, the festival has featured highland dancing, pipe bands, Celtic music, and a range of athletic events, such as the caber toss.

**Toronto** can, of course, boast of the **CN Tower,** the world's tallest free-standing structure, but Ontario's capital is also considered the most ethnically diverse city in the world. Some 70 international cultures thrive side by side.

Toronto is also home to the world's largest fireworks display at the Symphony of Fire held each July.

## United Empire Loyalists

Although most of what is now Ontario was officially under British control as of 1763, it would be several years before a large wave of British people began moving to the region. It was the American Revolution, which began in 1775, that would cause settlers in early Canada to choose whether to ally themselves with the Americans or to support the monarchy.

Those loyal to the British cause began trickling north into present-day Ontario from the United States while the war was still being waged. Led by people such as Sir John Johnson and John Butler, Loyalists came north and fought against the Americans during the war, then settled in the British colony when the Revolution ended. The northeastern part of North America was now divided between British and Americans, and in 1783, the Treaty of Versailles created a new boundary line along the upper **St. Lawrence River** and through the **Great Lakes,** leaving the western portion of the colony wholly in British hands.

*A group of Loyalists makes camp for the night during a trip up the St. Lawrence River.*
(National Archives, C-073449)

United Empire Loyalists, as they came to be known, began moving from the United States in greater numbers after the war. Most settled in the area of New Brunswick and Nova Scotia, but a significant number came farther west. They supported the Crown and opposed republicanism, and while most were British, there were Irish, Dutch, French, and Germans among them. The Loyalists were a broad cross-section of people that included wealthy merchants and land owners as well as shopkeepers, farmers, artisans, labourers, and soldiers. Approximately 7,000 moved to present-day Ontario, which at that time was still largely wilderness with a few scattered settlements. The Loyalists who had already settled in Canada during the war did not want to return to their homes in America, primarily because of their belief that the new government there would not respect their rights, debt claims, and land ownership.

A royal decree in 1783 called for Loyalists to be given land—about 40 hectares to the head of a family and another 20 hectares for each family member. Sir Frederick Haldimand, the governor of Quebec during the Revolution, decided that the thousands of Loyalists who needed land could best be served by forming new communities in the "upper country" along the St. Lawrence River and Lake Ontario. Other land for Loyalists was surveyed north of Lake Erie between Lake Ontario and Michigan. Haldimand's decision to encourage settlement of these areas laid the foundation for an English-speaking colony alongside the French-speaking region. Loyalist land grants were increased in 1787, giving more land to the heads of families, as well as for each son on reaching 18 years of age and for each Loyalist daughter when she married. As of 1789, those who had fought for the empire were also allowed to add the letters "U.E." after their names as a title.

During this time, Ontario was still part of the Quebec colony, but with the growing influx of Loyalists and their desire for some kind of representative government that would not be overwhelmingly French, the prospect of dividing the territory was raised. The Constitutional Act, or Canada Act, went into effect in December 1791, creating the colonies of Upper Canada (Ontario) and Lower Canada (Quebec).

The presence of the Loyalists and their descendants in Ontario throughout the late 18th and early 19th centuries helped maintain the strong ties between the province and Great Britain. By the mid-1800s, societies and organizations had sprung up to honour the contributions Loyalists had made in Ontario. The Upper Canada Historical Society was formed in 1861, followed by the United

Empire Loyalist Association in 1896. Ontario's motto, "Loyal it began, loyal it remains," reflects the important role the Loyalists played in Ontario's development. The Loyalists were the first non-Native people in large numbers to put down roots in the province, and they brought with them British traditions of law and politics that remain today.

# Unusual Place Names

Like other parts of Canada, the names of Ontario's communities are often rich in history and tradition. Many names originate with the terms **First Nations peoples** used for the areas they lived in or that were nearby. Ontario itself may mean "sparkling **water**," "beautiful lake," or "a large body of water."

Abitibi, which was located at about the midpoint between the trading posts on Hudson Bay and the Ottawa River, is said to come from a Native word meaning "halfway water." Other examples are **Toronto,** which most sources say means "trees standing in the water," and Penetanguishene, which is translated into "place of white falling (or rolling) sands."

Ontario, long a British colony, also has many communities named for towns and cities in Great Britain. Some good examples are Scarborough, **London,** Perth, and **Windsor.** The little town of Madoc, in Hasting's County near Peterborough, may sound like a Native name, but isn't. Madoc was the name of a Welsh prince who, legend has it, discovered America in 1170.

But Ontario is also home to several unusual place names, and areas with names that are either unique to the province or that have interesting origins. Perhaps the most whimsical name in Ontario is Punkydoodle's Corners, a small community that lies in the Waterloo Region between Kitchener and Stratford. There are several theories for how the name came about. One suggests that it is based on an early settler's confused rendering of the song "Yankee Doodle." Another theory says that the farmers of German descent in the area resented a lazy farmer who grew only pumpkins, and that led to the name.

The community of Ajax, near Toronto, was named in honour of a British cruiser, the HMS *Ajax,* that fought a German battleship off the coast of South America in 1939. Ajax rose to prominence during World War II as the site of a munitions factory.

The name for Sarnia, in southwestern Ontario, was suggested by Sir John Colborne, who said the area reminded him of the island of Guernsey, where he used to live. Historians believe that Sarnia was the ancient Roman name for the island. Kenora, in northwestern Ontario, was originally called Rat Portage but was renamed in 1905. Its name is derived from the first two letters of three communities in the area, **Ke**ewatin, **No**rman, and **Ra**t Portage.

Two other **northern Ontario** communities have interesting names with a history. Foleyet, west of Timmins, was accidentally named in 1912. The story goes that the Canadian Northern Railway president, Sir Donald Mann, wanted to name the station in the area after the contractor Timothy Foley. When told there was already a station with that name, he replied, "I'll name that place Foley yet." The name stuck. The town of Swastika had nothing to do with Hitler or the Nazis. It had been named several years earlier, after a good luck charm, but the provincial government tried to get the townspeople to change the name to Winston (in honour of Winston Churchill) during World War II. The townsfolk resisted, and the name Swastika remains.

Finally, the sombre-sounding name of Gravenhurst, in Ontario's **cottage country,** was adopted in 1862 after a fictional name that had appeared in American author Washington Irving's novel *Bracebridge Hall.*

# Upper Canada Village

When construction of the St. Lawrence Power Project and Seaway permanently raised the level of the **St. Lawrence River** in the 1950s, several eastern Ontario villages between Iroquois and Cornwall became Ontario's version of Atlantis. In order to preserve the sunken heritage of the area, to make proper educational use of historically significant buildings from those villages, and to commemorate the rich heritage of the rest of eastern Ontario, Upper Canada Village was built at Morrisburg on the banks of the St. Lawrence.

In June 1961, when the village opened, several buildings and other artifacts had been moved to the site, and a significant 19th-century collection was created. Over the years, Upper Canada Village has continued to acquire buildings and other items throughout eastern Ontario and has developed its own restoration and reproduction programs.

A walk through the village is a stroll back in time to experience life in a bustling 1860s community. Visitors will find constant activity, from the spinning of wool in a log home, to the grinding of wheat into flour in a steam-powered

mill. Tradespeople demonstrate their skills by forging iron, shaping and solder-
ing tinware, and shoeing horses. Throughout the village costumed interpreters
work busily in homes, livestock barns, shops, and on the streets.

In the one-room schoolhouse, visitors can join in on a lesson in the three R's;
at Cook's Tavern and Livery, Mrs. Cook, the tavern keeper, offers accommodation, food, and beverages. She also rents horses and carriages, as was done 130
years ago. And at the physician's house, an interpreter will discuss the role of the
doctor in the community and the latest advances in medicine, in an era when
people relied on homeopaths and midwives. Upper Canada Village attracts
180,000 visitors a year.

# War of 1812

On June 18, 1812, United States President James Madison declared war on Great
Britain and set the stage for what would be one of the most important conflicts
in the development of Ontario and Canada.

The War of 1812 had two main causes. One was a battle over maritime
rights, created by Britain's ongoing conflict with French emperor Napoleon. The
British Navy, which essentially controlled lakes Champlain, Erie, and Ontario,
had been stopping ships, including many from the U.S. that were entering ports
under Napoleon's control, and searching them for contraband goods and desert-
ers. In the Americans' view, the searches were illegal and interfered with their
profitable seagoing trade. They believed they could control the waterways if they
could take possession of the British-held lands north of the **St. Lawrence River**
and the **Great Lakes.** Nevertheless, Americans were divided on the idea of wag-
ing such a war, and this division would plague them throughout the two-and-a-
half-year conflict.

A snapshot look at Upper Canada, as Ontario was then called, prior to the war shows that its citizens would not likely have been able to resist invasion by the Americans. The non-Native population was only about 100,000, there were few trained soldiers, and the colony had few roads and not enough resources to support an army without the help of Great Britain. The U.S., on the other hand, possessed relatively well-developed transportation links, a larger population, rich farms, and established factories.

But the war was about more than territorial rights on the waterways. The eastern **First Nations peoples,** led by Tecumseh of the Shawnee nation, had joined together in an attempt to create their own nation to the south and west of Lake Erie. The British supported this idea because it would provide a buffer zone for Upper Canada, while the Americans feared such an alliance because they believed it would encourage First Nations tribes to wage warfare on settlers who were already moving into that territory. After Americans attacked Tecumseh's home base beside the Tippecanoe River in Indiana in 1811, many of the Native tribes allied themselves with British North America. They hoped that if they assisted the British, they would be able to create a nation north of the Great Lakes.

Although the first large battle took place in the summer of 1812, the British did not formally declare war on the U.S. until January 1813. The governor of Upper and Lower Canada, Sir George Prevost, believed the best plan for preserving the colonies was to defend against any attacks without venturing onto American soil. He thought that attacks on Americans in their own country would only increase their support for the war cause. The War of 1812 was characterized by short skirmishes between relatively small armies and navies.

In July 1812, Americans led by Brigadier General William Hull crossed the Detroit River near present-day **Windsor.** But successful attacks by Canadians and Native allies in northern Michigan and to the south in Brownstown, as well as the arrival of General Sir Isaac Brock in Amherstburg, caused the Americans to retreat less than a month later. Despite Prevost's concerns, Brock and Tecumseh followed Hull across the border to Detroit. The British troops fired some cannon shells at the Americans, and Hull soon surrendered.

Following this, several battles took place in the province, the most famous one arguably being the Battle of Queenston Heights, on October 13, 1812. British troops led by Brock and aided by First Nations allies defeated the Americans here, but Brock was killed.

In the spring of 1813, American troops sailed across Lake Ontario to York (now **Toronto**), met little resistance, and occupied Fort York for six days. They then burned some of its buildings and left. The Americans would return to attack the fort again in July of the same year, but its defences held. Another small but important victory over the Americans took place at Beaver Dams near Queenston in June 1813. It was here that heroine Laura Secord made history. She overheard American officers planning an attack and walked 30 kilometres through woods, over rocks, and through streams to warn the British commander. A force largely composed of Mohawks attacked the Americans, who eventually surrendered to British Lieutenant James Fitzgibbon.

Among the key naval clashes was the Battle of Lake Erie in September 1813, which the Americans won. This allowed them to control that Great Lake, and from there they pursued the retreating British-Native force to Moraviantown in the southwest. The Americans won decisively here in a battle that is noted for resulting in the death of Tecumseh. Despite these victories, the Americans could not gain control of Lake Ontario or the St. Lawrence Valley. A small clash at Chateauguay on October 25, 1813, became important to the growing Canadian sense of nationalism because the battle was won entirely by Canadian soldiers.

By 1814 the war was essentially at a stalemate, and with more British troops arriving by the middle of the year, the Americans began realizing that their dream of conquest was fading. They were able to successfully invade the Niagara peninsula in the summer of 1814, but the Battle of Lundy's Lane, where losses were heavy on both sides, marked the turning point toward the end of the war.

Later in the summer, British troops invaded Washington, D.C. and burned the president's house. When it was later rebuilt and the walls were covered with whitewash to cover the burn marks, it took on the name the White House. The British retreated, and on December 24, 1814, both sides signed the Treaty of Ghent, officially ending the war. It would take two months for the news to reach the U.S., however, and in January 1815, the Americans defeated the British at the Battle of New Orleans. While both sides claimed victory in the War of 1812, each returned what land they had conquered.

The First Nations people did not see their dream of an independent Native nation become reality. Instead, the agreement between Britain and the U.S. meant that much of their former lands were now being settled by Americans. The Native nations of Upper Canada were in possession of widely scattered territories, already under threat by the growing European population.

The government encouraged people whose loyalty could be counted on to settle in the Canadian colonies as a way of preserving the territories that had been successfully defended in the war. With the arrival of peace in 1815, hundreds of thousands of people from the British Isles would emigrate and settle in Canada over the next 30 years.

# Wasaga Beach

The longest freshwater beach in the world lies on the southern shores of **Georgian Bay** in the town of Wasaga Beach. The town has 14 kilometres of white sandy beach as well as inland sand dunes, attracting 1.5 million visitors each summer.

The beach was created by retreating glaciers during the last ice age more than 10,000 years ago, and the dunes were then formed by prevailing northwest winds that shifted the sands. The parabolic or U-shaped dunes are the only ones known in Ontario and are thus classified as a Natural Environment Zone where vehicles are prohibited. A variety of native plants and grasses stabilize the sands. The beach also has historic importance because it served as an airstrip in 1934 for the first flight from mainland Canada to England.

Although locals have been enjoying the beach for almost a century, it wasn't until the 1940s that Wasaga Beach became a popular tourist spot. Bikinis, junk food venues, and souvenir stands eventually became common sights. Wasaga Beach Provincial Park, which lies within the town, contains 143 hectares of beach and picnic areas, as well as access to nearby hiking trails.

# Water

Ontario has plenty of water. To be precise, the province lays claim to 12 percent of the surface freshwater found in Canada. Ontario also has a significant but undetermined amount of freshwater under the ground, known as groundwater.

The ready availability of water has long been key to the province's economic and social prosperity. Lakes and rivers provided transportation routes for **First Nations peoples,** and later for explorers and traders to move such goods as furs and logs out of remote areas. In more recent times, Ontario's extensive network of waterways has allowed for the development of large hydroelectric projects on the Niagara River, Ottawa River, and **St. Lawrence River,** which produce relatively cheap power for manufacturers and home-owners. Water is used extensively by farmers, municipalities, and industries, and the **Great Lakes–St. Lawrence Seaway System** provides one of the world's finest water-based commercial transportation systems.

Lakes, rivers, and **canals** are also the source of a wide variety of water-related recreational activities, such as fishing, cottage living, boating, and swimming, which have helped make **tourism** Ontario's number-nine industry. Even Ontario's name is connected to water, rooted in an Iroquoian word with various translations, including "shining water," "sparkling water," and "beautiful lake."

Studies have identified more than 250,000 lakes and rivers in the province, but there are at least another million which are too small to be identified. Lakes that have been mapped total an area of about 177,000 square kilometres. When combined with rivers and streams, about 20 percent of Ontario is covered by water, 43 percent of which is provided by the **Great Lakes.** Four of the Great Lakes—Superior, Huron, Erie, and Ontario—lie partly in Ontario. Other large bodies of water are Simcoe, Nipigon, Nipissing, St. Clair, Lake of the Woods, Lac Seul, and Rainy Lake.

The St. Lawrence and Ottawa rivers are the most significant rivers, forming the province's boundaries in the southeastern corner. Other sizeable rivers are the St. Clair River and Detroit River, which border southwestern Ontario, and in

*Ontario's lakes attract visitors from around the world who take part in a variety of water-related activities including canoeing, fishing, water-skiing, and boating.*
(© 2000 Ontario Tourism)

**northern Ontario** the Severn, Winisk, Atawapiskat, Albany, Missinaibi, and Moose, which empty into Hudson Bay and James Bay.

Ontario's network of rivers drains about two-thirds of the province north to **James Bay** and Hudson Bay, or into Manitoba. The remainder drains into the Great Lakes–St. Lawrence River system and, eventually, into the Atlantic Ocean.

Water use is defined in two ways: withdrawal, which means water that is taken from rivers and lakes and mostly returned; and consumption, which means that water is not returned to the source, either because it evaporates during a **manufacturing** process such as steel-making, or is incorporated into products such as foods and juices.

About 95 percent of all water withdrawn from lakes and streams is used by water-powered hydro-generating facilities. Of the remaining 5 percent, 82 percent is used for cooling purposes at nuclear and fossil-fuel hydroelectric stations, 10.6 percent for manufacturing, 6 percent by municipalities, 1 percent by the **agriculture** sector, and 0.4 percent by the **mining industry.** On the consumption side, about 24 percent is used by hydroelectric facilities, 21 percent by the manufacturing sector, 27 percent by municipalities, 25 percent in agriculture, and 2.4 percent in mining.

In Ontario's urban areas, the average individual uses about 350 litres of water every day for domestic needs such as bathing, cooking, and lawn watering. That's one of the highest per capita rates of water usage in the world.

Although Ontario has a seemingly endless supply of water, the resource was threatened beginning in the 1960s by acid rain and other industrial and municipal pollutants, many originating in the more populous and highly industrialized United States. But with the implementation of stiff environmental regulations and clean-up efforts by industry, farmers, communities, and governments, many of these threats have lessened: in late 1999, for instance, the Ontario and federal governments reported that the Great Lakes are cleaner than they've been in 50 years.

More recently, concerns have been raised in Ontario and other provinces over the potential of depleting supplies of fresh water as a result of the export of water to other countries. Ontario has passed a regulation that prohibits bulk removal of water from the province's three major drainage basins. This regulation reinforced Ontario's commitment in 1985 to work with Quebec and eight U.S. Great Lakes states to control the diversion and consumption of water.

# West Montrose Covered Bridge

As Ontario's only remaining bridge with a roof, the West Montrose Covered Bridge has been officially recognized as a historic site. Built in 1881 by the Bear brothers, the structure, also known as the "Kissing Bridge" because its enclosed design encourages a feeling of intimacy and romance, crosses the Grand River north of **Kitchener-Waterloo.**

Roofs were built over five bridges in Ontario, as well as elsewhere in Canada and the U.S., because they provided protection from weather for the large timbers and trusses used in construction. It's also said that horses will travel over flowing **water** more easily if a bridge has walls and a roof. Built mostly of white pine, the West Montrose bridge is slightly more than 63 metres long and 5 metres wide, with approximately 4 metres of headroom.

Today, with the continued presence of many **Mennonites** in the area, horses and buggies still cross the West Montrose bridge. The bridge was completely restored in 1955 with a laminated deck of two-by-fours and new centre pier bearings. Its most recent repairs took place in 1999 to ensure that the bridge will last well into the new century.

# Wiarton Willie

Every February 2nd since 1956, Canada's furry forecaster, Wiarton Willie, has been coming out of hibernation to predict the length of winter. Groundhog Day ceremonies in the town of Wiarton in Grey County centre around its albino groundhog mascot.

Although Groundhog Day predates Wiarton Willie, legend has it that if he sees his shadow on February 2nd there will be six more weeks of winter; if there is no shadow, Ontarians can expect an early spring. The people of Wiarton claim that Willie, who lives in a fenced-in area south of town the rest of the year, has been accurate 90 percent of the time. The annual Groundhog Festival is sponsored by the Wiarton and District Lions Club and attracts almost 10,000 visitors each year to the town who want to be on hand for Willie's predictions, and to participate in a variety of other activities held over several days.

Local lore says that Wiarton Willie's mystique is enhanced by his white colour and because he was born on the Bruce Peninsula precisely on the 45th parallel—the midway point between the Equator and the North Pole.

Several albino groundhogs have played the part of Wiarton Willie over the years. Just days before the Groundhog Day celebrations in 1999, that particular Wiarton Willie died at the age of 22, and two new albino animals have been brought in to replace him. One of them, nicknamed "Wee Willie," officially took over as the new Wiarton Willie on February 2, 2000. Groundhogs generally live 10 to 15 years.

# Windsor

Although it sits in the shadow of the much larger Detroit, Michigan, across the Detroit River, Windsor proudly points out that it lies *south* of that American city. The first Europeans arrived in Windsor in 1640, and French settlers began to move there in the early 1700s. More settlers moved to the area during the 1760s after the British conquered the French in the Seven Years War, and this part of Ontario now claims to be the oldest continuously inhabited European settlement in the province.

The British set up a jail and courthouse in the area by the late 18th century, but a fire in 1799 gutted the structure. Its replacement was destroyed by Americans in the **War of 1812.** Following the war, a townsite was laid out at the foot of what is now Woodward Avenue, and in 1836, settlers chose the name Windsor after its counterpart town in England.

From its earliest days, Windsor was coveted by French, British, and Americans because of its strategic location on the Detroit River. Despite that, Windsor did not develop greatly until 1854, when it was chosen as a western terminus for the railway being built in Upper Canada. Its ferry service to Detroit, which allowed trains to connect with the Michigan Central Railway on the American side of the river, also made Windsor a key link in the railway system being built across the continent. Passengers, and even trains, were transported by ferry, but several years later a railway tunnel was constructed under the river to make transportation more efficient.

In 1855, a Detroit businessman, Hiram Walker, needed to relocate his distillery from Michigan because of American temperance laws. His move across the river to Canada would prove to be an important milestone in Windsor's economic history. In 1858, he opened a distillery there, and other industries began to grow around it. Assumption College, which eventually became the University of Windsor, was founded in 1857. A year later, Windsor officially became a town, and by 1881 the **population** had grown to 7,000.

Windsor officially became a city in 1892. By the 1920s, it began to follow Detroit's lead in becoming an automobile manufacturing centre. The proximity of Windsor to Detroit was a boon to the city, and automobiles have been the lifeblood of Windsor's **economy** ever since.

An important border city, Windsor is joined to the U.S. by the Ambassador Bridge, which was built in 1929 and is the world's longest international suspension bridge, and the Windsor-Detroit tunnel, which was completed the following year. Like many Ontario cities in the years after World War II, Windsor enjoyed a boom and an influx of European immigrants looking to start a new life in Canada.

Windsor's harbour serves commercial fishing interests, and its location along the **Great Lakes** route to the Atlantic Ocean has continued to boost industries throughout the city. With a current population of about 200,000, Windsor took another leap forward economically in the 1990s with the construction of the province's first casino (*see* **Casinos**).

# Wineries

A combination of ideal soil, moderating effects of the **Great Lakes** on the weather, and a latitudinal location similar to other great wine-making regions of the world has made southern Ontario home to several world-class wineries.

The three main wine regions in Ontario are the Niagara Peninsula, which has by far the largest concentration of wineries, Lake Erie North Shore, and **Pelee Island,** which has the longest growing season of any of Canada's wine regions. In addition to the more than 30 wineries in these areas, some eight other wineries are located in and around **Toronto.** All of Ontario's wine regions are located between 41° and 44° North latitude, which is similar to such areas as Provence in France, the Chianti Classico region of Italy, and Spain's Rioja region. The only types of grapes now used in the province for making table wine are *Vitis vinifera* and *Vitis vinifera* hybrids, the classic grapes of Europe.

With about 5,800 hectares of vineyards, Ontario produces 80 percent of Canada's homegrown wine. Although the province has a long history of grape-growing, Ontarians for many years turned their noses up and their palates away from drinking Ontario wines. However, such programs as the Vintners Quality Alliance (VQA), which was introduced in 1989 and allows for better quality control from vineyard to wine glass, have made Ontario wines nationally and internationally praised and sought after.

Wines that carry the VQA label must be tested and graded by a panel of experts. They can receive either a provincial designation, which allows them to use the word "Ontario" on the label, or the superior Geographic Designation, which allows them to merit the DVA (Designated Viticultural Area) label. For both designations, 100 percent Ontario-grown grapes must be used.

Although Ontario has a range of award-winning products, including table wines, sparkling wines, and dessert wines, it is icewine that opened the door to international praise for the province's wineries. Produced in Canada since 1973, icewine is made by leaving grapes on the vine well into winter. The freezing and thawing of the grapes dehydrates the fruit and concentrates sugars and acids that intensify flavour. The grapes are picked ideally when the temperature is between $-10°$ and $-13°$ Celsius, while the fruit is still frozen. In 1991, an Ontario icewine received France's highest award possible, the Grand Prix d'Honneur at Bordeaux's Vinexpo. Ontario has since become the world's largest producer of icewine.

## Yonge Street

More than 200 years after the Queen's Rangers began clearing the 20-metre-wide route that would become Yonge Street, the busy north-south thoroughfare is a far cry from the vision of Lieutenant-Governor John Graves Simcoe, the founder of what is now **Toronto.**

When work began in May of 1794, Simcoe saw Yonge as the model for a network of important military roads, which would also include Dundas Street and Kingston Road. One of Simcoe's first projects after establishing the town he named York as the capital of Upper Canada, Yonge was to be a northward route that would open the way to Lake Simcoe and on to the Upper Lakes, enabling new residents of the young community to press outward to the surrounding countryside. He named the road for his close friend Sir George Yonge, British Secretary of State for War at that time.

Originally, the 55-kilometre-long street between York and Lake Simcoe was often in appalling condition, studded with stumps, fallen trees, swamp, and sections rendered nearly impassable by mud. Today, the street stretches from the Lake Ontario waterfront to Rainy River in northwestern Ontario, where it ends at the

*A streetcar travels north on Yonge Street near Wellington Street in 1924.* (John Boyd Collection, National Archives, PA-86462)

Ontario-Minnesota border. For much of the 20th century, Yonge has been a busy and, in some areas, seedy roadway which has attracted people who simply wanted to be where the action was in downtown Toronto.

In December 1837, William Lyon Mackenzie, a member of the legislative assembly, felt the government of Upper Canada was not responsive enough to the people. So he gathered supporters at Montgomery's Tavern on Yonge Street and launched the **Rebellion of 1837** in a bid to provoke government reform. His plan for a surprise attack on the city failed because the group was not well organized.

In 1902, a large crowd spilled into the intersection of Yonge and Queen, just a few blocks from Lake Ontario, to commemorate the end of the Boer War. People also celebrated on Yonge after both World Wars ended, and they have flocked onto the pavement to celebrate two World Series wins by the **Toronto Blue Jays** in the early 1990s.

Stretching 1,896 kilometres, Yonge is the world's longest street. But it has etched its way into the annals of Canadian history for more than its length. It began as a corduroy road made from logs laid side by side, but soon proved to be too uncomfortable for horses and human travellers. In 1833, it became the first road in British North America to be paved and by 1850 was surfaced all the way to Holland Landing. In 1835, Toronto city council approved the construction of a main sewer line on King Street with feeder lines on five cross streets, including Yonge Street. In 1841, gas lighting arrived. Tolls helped maintain the road between 1830 and 1890, and for a brief period in the 1850s, Yonge Street was privately owned.

In 1849, Toronto's first horse-drawn omnibus opened on King and Yonge streets with a fare of sixpence, and 12 years later Alexander Easton opened the first horse-drawn street railway in Toronto. Electric streetcars made their debut on Yonge in 1894. Their success helped the street prosper and eventually led to Canada's first subway being opened in 1954 between Union Station and Eglinton Avenue.

With the dawn of the 1900s, the street became the premier shopping street in Toronto. The first public demonstration of television in Canada took place at Eaton's on Yonge Street in August 1933. In the summer of 1971, the city turned three blocks into a pedestrian mall for three days, an experiment that was repeated in 1972 and 1973, but discontinued after 1974.

The street was redefined in 1976 with the opening of the **Toronto Eaton Centre,** which soon became the city's most visited attraction. The re-opening of the Elgin Winter Garden and Pantages theatres created a new theatre district around the venerable Massey Hall, and the **Hockey Hall of Fame** in the restored Bank of Montreal and BCE Place created a lively complex near the bottom of the street. In North York, a huge commercial complex, the Ford Performing Arts Centre, and a string of excellent restaurants and shops injected new life into Yonge Street north of **Highway 401**.

Yonge Street also has its raunchy side. At times massage parlours and strip joints have been as common as fast-food outlets on the street's downtown stretches. It continues to attract panhandlers, hustlers, hookers, and young people who cruise the strip on weekends looking for love and showing off their sporty cars.

After leaving Toronto, where the signage changes to Highway 11 and further north to Highway 17, then back to Highway 11, Yonge passes through a variety of different landscapes and a string of growing communities, including Newmarket, Barrie, Orillia, Gravenhurst, Bracebridge, Huntsville, Burk's Falls,

North Bay, Temagami, New Liskeard, Cochrane, Kapuskasing, **Thunder Bay,** and Atikokan. It finally comes to an end at Rainy River on the Canada–U.S. border. For its last few blocks, it is called Attwood Avenue West. The final building is the Canada Customs office at the Baudette–Rainy River International Bridge.

# Zebra Mussels

Since their discovery in Lake St. Clair in 1988, zebra mussels have been creating problems for boaters, cottagers, and municipalities in Ontario. These small freshwater mollusks, with their distinctive striped shell, have spread throughout much of the southern half of the province and have attached themselves to intake pipes of municipal **water** treatment plants, cottage water supplies, power plants, and other industries. According to the Ministry of Natural Resources, the mussels have reduced water flow by more than 50 percent in some cases.

The zebra mussels are believed to have arrived in Ontario in the ballast water of ships travelling from Europe, where they have created similar problems. Female mussels can produce as many as one million eggs a year, and the larvae are too small to be seen by the naked eye. The mussels secrete fibres that allow them to attach to any underwater surface, including pipes, docks, rocks, boat hulls, boat motors, and buoys. Under certain conditions, they can build into large colonies, and as many as several hundred thousand mussels per square metre have been reported in Lake Erie.

The mussels have disrupted the water-based ecosystems of Ontario because they eat large amounts of plankton, which reduces the food supply of different species of **fish.** Removing the mussels has proved costly and difficult. Some ducks and fish feed on the mussels, but they have had little effect on overall numbers. The mussels have also filtered the water in Ontario lakes and streams and made it clearer water. This clarity affects certain members of the fish community, most notably the walleye, which is light sensitive and has sought out deeper waters and changed its feeding behaviour as a result.

By attaching themselves to boats, mussels have spread through Ontario's inland waterways. The Ministry of Natural Resources has encouraged boaters to be extremely diligent in keeping their hulls clean and free of water when not in use to help prevent the mussels from spreading further. Cottagers have also been encouraged to look for evidence of mussels and to consider buying filtering devices that control the spread of these mollusks.

# About the Authors

Mark Kearney has been a freelance journalist and writing instructor since 1989 after working in media relations for the provincial government for six years and as a *London Free Press* reporter before that. He has written some 2,000 articles for more than 60 publications in Canada and the U.S., including *Toronto Life, The Toronto Star, The Financial Times,* and *Stitches.* Mark grew up in Pickering, Ontario, and lives in London, Ontario, with his wife Catherine. He is a graduate of the University of Western Ontario.

Photo: Catherine Blake

Randy Ray has been a freelance writer since 1989 after working for the *London Free Press* for thirteen years, including three years as the newspaper's Parliament Hill correspondent. His articles have appeared in more than 60 publications, including the *Ottawa Citizen, The Globe and Mail, Profit Magazine,* and the *Canadian Farmers' Almanac.* Randy is a native of Toronto, has three children, and lives in Ottawa with his wife Janis. He is a graduate of the University of Toronto and Ryerson Polytechnic University.

Photo: Janis Ray

Mark and Randy are the co-authors of three best-selling books, *The Great Canadian Book of Lists, The Great Canadian Trivia Book,* and *The Great Canadian Trivia Book 2.* They also co-authored *Canadian Music Fast Facts: Profiles of Canada's Pop Music Pioneers* and were contributing authors to *Shakin' All Over: The Rock 'N Roll Years in Canada.* Their website address is www.triviaguys.com.